LORD CREWE
The Likeness of a Liberal

LORD CREWE IN THE EMBASSY IN PARIS, 1922

LORD CREWE

1858 : 1945

The
Likeness of a Liberal

JAMES
POPE-HENNESSY

LONDON
CONSTABLE & CO LTD

LONDON
PUBLISHED BY
Constable and Company Ltd
10–12 ORANGE STREET W.C.2

•

INDIA
Orient Longmans Ltd
BOMBAY   CALCUTTA   MADRAS

•

CANADA
Longmans, Green and Company
TORONTO

•

SOUTH AND EAST AFRICA
Longmans, Green and Company Ltd
CAPETOWN   NAIROBI

•

AUSTRALIA
Walter Standish and Sons
SYDNEY

First published 1955

Made and printed in Great Britain by William Clowes & Sons, Limited, London and Beccles

Contents

List of Illustrations

vii

Foreword

W E have, many of us on our shelves, Lives of the Eminent, in one, two or three volumes. Every detail leading up to each crisis or important event is carefully noted and commented on, and the result is worthy, but very often only suitable for experts or research.

That, I understand, is not the purpose of this little volume. It is meant to be read by anybody interested in the life of a man who served five Sovereigns; who, in his time, occupied most of the chief offices of State—amongst others Secretary of State for the Colonies when South Africa was granted self-government (a fact that I, myself, heard General Smuts recall, only three years before his death, with enthusiastic gratitude)—and who as Lord President of the Council, when he had charge of the passing of the Education Bill through the House of Lords, led fifty peers against the Conservative hordes in a dramatic fight. While he was Secretary of State for India the capital was moved to Delhi from Calcutta, and it was on his taking over the India Office that Lord Minto remarked: 'I do not wish Charlie Hardinge *any* harm, but I should like him to have six months of Morley before the advent of Crewe.'

He was a member of the 1906 Government, which has now slipped unobtrusively into its rightful place in history. In this great Government of progress and reform no individual belonging to it could be unimportant, least of all one who has been unanimously declared one of its wisest, if not the wisest, counsellor.

It is written 'the more uniform a man's step, voice, manner of conversation, handwriting—the more uniform his actions and character. Vociferation and calmness of character rarely meet in the same person.' The above description might well suit the personality of Robert Crewe, except that it does not

ix

explain the motive and incentive of power which inspired the zeal for Liberal causes; the happy sense of enjoyment, the love of a joke, a good story, and an intense optimism which carried him through the worst of crises. He was, I should add, completely devoid of affectation of any kind. When I asked when and where he had written his well-known poem *A Grave in Flanders*—expecting to hear of some dramatic moment—he replied, after a moment's thought: 'Oh, I think in the dining-car, coming up from Crewe.'

It is true he had several disadvantages for public appeal: an almost classic profile, which did not lend itself to great facial expression; in speech, a quiet, pleasant voice, but with at times, in public, prolonged moments—almost minutes—of hesitation while he fastidiously chose the correct word, and this prevented him from ever being a very impressive speaker. His speeches when read were invariably good, but the dramatic moment was never attempted. He was a good and imaginative administrator, but his chief attributes were his judgement and moral courage and that unusual quality—common sense. These were his most positive qualities. He had unfailing charming manners, but which at times seemed rather formal and aloof.

I have heard it said that the son had all the success for which the father longed. This is, to a certain extent, true, but Lord Houghton was noted for his indiscretion which, in those times, made him an impossible candidate for office. His son, perhaps for that reason, carried discretion, if that were possible, almost to excess. His axiom was that one must never divulge a secret, and even when it became public property, better never admit you had ever known it.

Lord Houghton would rather see anybody than be alone. That was not so with his son. Both had certain qualities in common: a leaning to extravagance; an appreciation of pageantry; a passion for books and writers; and intense generosity. I do not think either were ever appealed to for any worthy cause without response—a response, very often beyond their means—and this is surely a rare quality. In Lord Houghton this quality was well known, notably in the case of the poet David Gray. In his son, the case is unknown—that of a young midshipman accused of violating the law; who after years of persistent litigation was cleared, after great sums had been spent, far beyond his (Crewe's) means.

Lord Houghton was a collector of pictures, books, carpets and everything he came across; a benefactor, as it has turned out, to his descendants. His son, with more sense of responsibility, also had these tastes. Lord Houghton, it is said, had not the success of his son: it is known that he did not obtain office, but letters beginning 'Dear Poet' and 'Dear Maître' no doubt gave him great pleasure.

His son on the other hand had, as he himself said, no public appeal at all, but he was appreciated by the wise, for he had the essential qualities in a pre-eminent degree. His opinion and advice were asked on every sort of occasion and, sometimes, through myself; to such an extent that I occasionally wondered, when this happened, if I were linked to the Oracle of Delphi.

He enjoyed golf, hunting, shooting—but what he really loved was racing (Lord Palmerston once remarked that racing was inferior in excitement to politics. I wonder!); and there again, as my brother tells me, even in the entirely different sphere of the Jockey Club, nobody's views were more respected, and no one's advice was more continually sought. He bred the famous sire Polymelus, (by Cyllene out of Maid Marion), which, when urged by my father and myself to sell (as we had financial difficulties and the horse had not so far shown its true form), he sold. If he had kept it, Polymelus would have been a gold mine, but he never uttered a word of reproach. My brother (twice winner of the Derby himself, and owner of a famous stud), has been asked by Mr. Pope-Hennessy to contribute a note on racing to this book.

James Pope-Hennessy has written the life of Richard Monckton Milnes, and now writes that of his son with the same taste and discrimination. I have every reason to be grateful to him for presenting such a faithful portrait of my husband.

Lord Samuel in his *Memoirs* writes: 'Lord Crewe held an unique position in the Cabinet. This was not on account of any pre-eminence in Parliament, or in the country, or in the counsels of the Party, but through an almost uncanny soundness of judgement. In any difficult situation, where pros and cons were nicely balanced, it was Crewe, more than any other colleague, that the Prime Minister was accustomed to consult. He was always ready indeed to help any of us with our problems. His great experience made him an invaluable counsellor; he had held a minor Government post as far back as 1886; had been Lord Lieutenant of Ireland in 1892; and had held several great offices since then. We could be sure that any opinion he offered would be as clear-cut as the conditions allowed, and bear the stamp of that wisdom which was his outstanding quality'.

The word 'uncanny' brings to my mind a curious, persistent phenomenon in his life. He was always pursued by fire. The first at Crewe Hall, which was devastated by fire; the second at the home of his youth, Fryston, where some part of the library was lost; the third at Crewe House, where there were one major and two minor fires; and, lastly, at Argyll House, where I woke to see my ceiling with a scarlet line of fire creeping over it.

The third fire at Crewe House was indeed dramatic, and merits a description in greater detail. It broke out almost simultaneously with the birth of my son—I think about midnight. It raged, and for a time there was a fear that the trees in front of the house would catch fire, and that would have made it difficult to leave or save the house. I was always told that fourteen fire-engines were employed. Happily, all was subdued, and in the early hours of the morning, my child and I were taken in an ambulance to my father's house, number 38 Berkeley Square. The strain on my husband was great, and it was due no doubt to this and other anxieties that, a short time after, he was brought back unconscious from the Pricking of Sheriffs' Dinner at Claridge's by John Burns, and for a time my father's house became a sort of hospital.

I have described his father, but there remains his mother— perhaps the greatest devotion of his life. He spoke of her as having the most delightful character he had ever known. She loved the country, flowers, books, and had an excellent and profound education, though she lived long before the days of the School Certificates and girl graduates; and, as Lord

Houghton said, when his son won the Shakespeare prize, she had taught him all the Shakespeare he knew. Her death, at the comparatively early age of fifty-nine, when her son was only sixteen, completely overwhelmed him. Fetched from Harrow back to Fryston by the news, he lay absolutely prostrate for three days.

During his time at Harrow he won the Prize Poem *Gustavus Adolphus*. On this occasion Lord Houghton wrote to Lady Holland to the effect that he had no idea his son could write a line of poetry, and it was indeed a case of *Strangers Yet*.[1]

But the son's childhood until his mother's death was uniformly happy. In the comfortable, almost luxurious, home at Fryston, where his quiet, sympathetic mother, who was not without a sense of humour, was amused to observe her son, aged about five, and one of his sisters, completely under the influence of cowslip wine (which they had been helping to make), stagger into the dining-room, and merely urged them with a smile: 'to go and have a rest.'

His sisters must not be forgotten. He once addressed a poem to them, and they adored him. They represented to him all his earlier life at home. His youngest sister was nearest to him in age, and later wrote several forgotten books. I have found the reviews, which show that, though no doubt good of their kind, the critics represented them as negligible, though Thomas Hardy collaborated in one novel. His sisters did their best to help him with the entertainments which were given in Dublin while he was Viceroy of Ireland. He was then a widower. The tragedy of the deaths of his wife and son, Richard,[2] had occurred some years before.

It was years after the Viceroyalty in Ireland that we met at a dinner-party at the Asquiths, though I had known him at a distance as a child. We talked at dinner and the rest of the evening, and Margot Asquith said afterwards that she immediately prophesied our marriage. We became engaged at the coming-out ball of his daughter Annabel, who was eight months younger than myself and our marriage was strongly opposed by my grandmother (the Duchess of Cleveland). She thought the difference in age and three

1 Poem written by Lord Houghton.
2 Richard Charles Rodes Milnes, b. 1882, d. 1890.

dimly realising that it was a lifebuoy held out to us; and in the warm civilised atmosphere of one of the most brilliant capitals in the world, so rich in wit and culture, he regained a certain interest in life, having to deal with serious world problems, though I doubt if he was ever the same again.

It was agreed that I should write this personal account, so I have written thus of him, who was the centre of my life for so many years, in the detached manner that I think he would have wished and which conforms to my own taste. It is impossible to describe great happiness, or the bitterness of parting—neither is it desirable.

We do not know for what purpose life is given us, but his, I think, was one of complete fulfilment, so I have had written on his tomb: 'For God giveth to a man that is good in his sight, wisdom and knowledge and joy,' but the line on the monument of little Temperance Crewe, in the church at Stene, seems equally applicable to him:

'A constant lover of the best.'

April, 1955   MARGARET CREWE

Author's Note

Except where otherwise stated, this study of the life and achievements of Lord Crewe is based upon material drawn from the great quantity of his private and official papers, now kept at West Horsley Place, Leatherhead, Surrey.

Her Majesty the Queen has graciously permitted me to quote from the letters to Lord Crewe of Queen Victoria and of King George V, as well as from the letters which Lord Knollys and Lord Stamfordham wrote to Lord Crewe in their official capacity as successive Private Secretaries to the Sovereign. I have also to acknowledge similar permission from Lady Curzon of Kedleston and from Lady Violet Bonham-Carter to publish passages from the letters to Lord Crewe of Lord Curzon and of Mr. Asquith respectively, as well as to thank Lord Rosebery for contributing a note on Lord Crewe's interest in racing. I have in addition received valuable advice from Lord Stanmore, from Mr. Walter Roch, and from Mr. Charles Rankin of the Lord Chancellor's Office.

April 1955   J.P-H.

Chapter One

ROBERT OFFLEY ASHBURTON MILNES was born in London on 12 January 1858. He was the third child and only son of Richard Monckton Milnes, M.P., later Lord Houghton, and of his wife Annabel, the younger daughter of John, second Lord Crewe, of Crewe Hall, Cheshire. Both the parents had entered middle age when their son was born.

Known to posterity as the first biographer of Keats, Lord Houghton in his lifetime enjoyed a number of additional reputations. A familiar figure in the worlds of London Society and of English letters, he was known about in Paris and had been heard of in Berlin. His erudition was considerable and was curiously allied to a voracious passion for a life of ceaseless social and fashionable movement, and to a taste for verbal paradox which practically amounted to a vice. Generous and inquisitive, he was also somewhat vain and, in later life, irritable, for he had a clear knowledge, as gnawing as the ache of a bad tooth, that he was as great a failure in public life as he was a success in more personal and intimate spheres. Lord Houghton liked to blame his own persistent ineffectiveness in the House of Commons on his father's careless attitude to him in his youth, and he was accordingly determined that any son of his must be encouraged to succeed where he himself had not. All this combined to make Houghton an impatient and ambitious parent in an age when power and privilege were still regarded, in Whig as well as Tory circles, as the birthright of the few.

Born at 16 Upper Brook Street, a small Mayfair house then memorable for his father's bizarre but cultivated hospitality, Robert Milnes was christened at a neighbouring church in the middle of March. This ceremony was followed by a cheerful breakfast-party at which, besides Milnes and

Monckton relatives and the more restricted connections of the child's mother, a group of Lord Houghton's oldest friends, such as the millionaire banker Ashburton and the journalist Venables, also assisted. Mid-Victorian families were not only larger than those of the present day, they had a keener sense of kinship. Numerically the Yorkshire cousins who flocked to London for the christening made a formidable band. Alien to Houghton by their tastes and their interests, it almost seems as though before retiring once again to their draughty country-houses—or in the case of the maiden aunts to their stucco villas at Tiverton and at Torquay—these collaterals of the Northern squirearchy had endowed the new baby with their own traditional affection for the English countryside and its wholesome but not agitating pursuits.

Lord Houghton himself had never even tried to fit into the slots of Yorkshire life. He was an anomaly to most of his relations, a sport one did not think to find on Yorkshire soil. His native originality had been fostered by a home education (he had never been to school) and by eight formative years spent merrily in Germany and Italy, where he had acquired agreeable cosmopolitan ideas and foreign manners. Houghton could not even shoot and had no use whatever for the quiet rural interests of his neighbours round Fryston Hall. He knew nothing about turnips, nor how to deal with an excessive apple crop, nor how many sheep should be kept on the land in each season, nor how to combat gardeners who liked crowding the fruit-trees. His son, on the contrary, learned all about such things as he grew up, and succeeded in combining a long career as statesman and ambassador, book-collector and classicist, with all the normal occupations of an English land-owner, a taste for hunting and shooting and an eager passion for the Turf. In these hereditary pastimes, as well as in the political judgement for which he was always known, we may detect some resemblance between Robert Milnes, the subject of this study, and his paternal grandfather, 'a wise and honourable man' who had refused the Chancellorship of the Exchequer in Perceval's Cabinet at the early age of twenty-six. This grandfather, Robert Pemberton Milnes, died in the year of his grandson's and namesake's birth.

Another reason for the choice of the first name Robert for

the new baby was that it had been borne many centuries back by two medieval members of the Cheshire family of Crewe. The second name, Offley, related more directly to the boy's mother's connections. Richard Monckton Milnes had married Annabel Crewe, an acquaintance since youthful Roman days, in the year of the Great Exhibition, 1851, when he was forty-two and she was thirty-seven. It was a solid marriage of affection and produced three children—Amicia, born in 1853; Florence, called after Miss Nightingale and born during the Crimean War; Robert, born in 1858. Annabel, the daughter of the second Lord Crewe of Crewe—a title given by George III to an ancient and influential Cheshire family which, unlike the Milnes family, could trace its direct line back into the twelfth century—had one brother, Hungerford, third Lord Crewe, a bachelor living at Crewe Hall, and a devoted sister, Henriett, a Roman Catholic convert who had spent many years with their father in the north of France. Hungerford Crewe was a shy and religious neurotic, a short-tempered man whom his family often found awkward but whose eccentricities his Cheshire and Staffordshire tenants regarded with a modest local pride. Fond of his sister Annabel, he attended the christening breakfast as a matter of course. Inevitably he was the object of much speculative curiosity on the part of the more practical members of his brother-in-law's family.

It was judged exceedingly unlikely—although always just on the cards—that Hungerford, Lord Crewe would ever marry. If he died childless his married sister's only son would automatically become heir to the large estates, the highly comfortable fortune and the celebrated Jacobean mansion of the Crewes. Annabel Milnes had herself been an heiress, and after his father's death her husband also inherited some land and money. But, like his son after him, Lord Houghton was not of an economical turn of mind. He was generous and hospitable, as well as very self-indulgent and a great collector of books. Asked by friends at his club whether his son would inherit the Crewe estates he would make flippant rejoinders, but it was clear to him and to everyone else that the addition of the Crewe possessions to the Milnes' more modest properties would one day place the child just christened in a position of consequence. In 1858 such calculations could be made with a mathematical

3

precision; land, particularly coal-fields, meant money and money meant power. If a peerage were added to these, it would be better still, and should the child by any chance show any symptoms of intelligence, its future was assured: for as Houghton himself had once remarked: 'we never calculate among the democratic influences, as we should do, the effect of the stupidity and helplessness of our present aristocracy.'

The English world of 1858, when the baby was born, was not a very different one from that of 1894, when he did in fact inherit his uncle's properties, being created in the next year Earl of Crewe. But when in 1905 Robert Milnes first achieved the responsible position for which his father would have wished, it was in a society in which ability was just beginning to count for as much in government as names or riches. We often think of the Edwardian period in terms of vulgar ostentation and of the small group of idle and sybaritic persons who clustered round the King. We forget that it was in fact an active period of those great Liberal reforms which laid the foundations of modern England. In all of these the boy christened in March 1858 played a leading and constructive part.

The child's second name, Offley, was chosen to commemorate the aunt who had adopted Annabel Crewe and had brought her up, first at her house in Staffordshire, later in Rome. It was to her aunt, Mrs. Cunliffe Offley, that Annabel Milnes owed many of her rural and literary tastes, her love of flowers and gardens, her affection for the works of Cobbett, her know-ledge of Italian and French. All these she handed on to her son. She also handed on to him the pleasant appearance and agreeable manners for which she was universally admired. The boy grew up to be tall and good-looking, of a very different physique from that of his father, who was squat and short, with a countenance described by Disraeli as being like a face cut out of an orange. The third name, Ashburton, was after his Baring godfather.

When, a young man of twenty-seven, the future Lord ghton had taken up life in London, after years spent w_ering with his parents about the continent, he had known very few people, and had had to make his own friends, his own reputation and his own way. This he had achieved in the

4

face of disapproval in some quarters and ridicule in others : his determination to be accepted by the Hollands, for instance, led to the nickname of 'Cool-of-the-Evening' and 'In-I-go Jones.' But he was not deterred, and now, in 1858, Monckton Milnes was one of the most popular and ubiquitous of Londoners. There was no one he did not know, and he delighted in jumbling up his guests at the famous breakfast-parties to which people eagerly came, never knowing next to whom they might find themselves seated at the great round table in Upper Brook Street. In this sense Houghton's son and his two daughters Amicia and Florence started life with advantages which their father had never had. From the nursery state onwards they were accustomed to see everyone of interest amongst their parents' contemporaries : poets, politicians, men of letters, actors, painters, languid members of the fashionable world, foreign visitors of every nationality, explorers like Sir Richard Burton or clever clergymen like Frederick Maurice. In some instances familiarity even bred contempt, and not all Lord Houghton's children appreciated the catholicity of 'Papa's' taste in friends : 'Swinburne (in a very excited state) came in in the evening,' wrote Florence Milnes to her brother in 1875 : 'He is madder than ever, to my astonishment he *flopped* down on one knee in front of me, & announced that my hair had grown darker. This was rather embarrassing, and he is also so deaf now, which does not make it easier to talk to him.'

Lord Houghton's three children, upon whose attentions he relied after the death of his wife Annabel in 1874, were much attached to him, but as he aged he became to them increasingly a subject for concern. An old man, 'the Poet-Nobleman' (so they jocularly called him) was as restless as he had been as a young one, when his wife would refer to him as 'the Genius of Locomotiveness.' Figuratively speaking, he kept his son and two daughters at the end of the telegraph wire, expecting one of them to be ready to leave wherever they might be at any moment to join him at The Grange or at Dunrobin, or to accompany him to some banquet at Guildhall. Tormented by gout, Lord Houghton had been for many years obliged to undergo long 'cures' at foreign spas, but in the intervals between these sojourns he still managed to move about the earth as swiftly as in his extreme youth—indeed he now moved far more expeditiously, since good rail communication had made travel easier than in the old days of the Doncaster stage-coach to Ferrybridge or of vetturino-travel through the Veneto. His children would learn suddenly by telegram that their father was laid up with pneumonia at Loch Luichart or had had a spasm of angina on the Acropolis. It did not make things any better that he took them so light-heartedly: 'I am now sorry I did not carry out my Roman plan at all risks,' he wrote after his family had persuaded him to return straight home from Athens. 'At the worst Keats would have laid very pleasantly between his friend and his biographer, with a wreath of fresh Athenian violets over his head.' 'Have you a lift?' he enquired of a friend who wished Lord Houghton to join him at an hotel in Cannes; 'for if I run upstairs I may find the Elysian fields at the top.' A great lover of good food he had once predicted in a famous witticism that his 'exit would be the result of too many entrées'; and when he did at length die, in 1885 at Vichy, it was of a sudden heart attack after a rich meal and a bottle of champagne.

Although Lord Houghton remained lively and anecdotal until his dying day, it must early have become plain to his children, and especially to his growing son, that while many people loved their father, others thought him odd and unpredictable and in some instances regarded him with positive repugnance. Age is not invariably attractive, and some of Lord Houghton's coarser mannerisms became notoriously exaggerated with the years. But in his children's eyes he was primarily a humorous and loving parent. On leaving a dinner-party at the St. James's Club in Montreal, the old man slipped and hurt himself by rolling down some steps. It was the evening before a planned excursion to some water-falls, and the sixteen-year-old Robert Milnes noted in his diary that despite insomnia and pain 'the first thing' his father thought of in the morning 'was *my* missing the rapids—just like him.'

Chapter Two

'OTHING escapes his large, calm eye, and so he is always amused wherever he is,' wrote Robert Milnes' mother when her son was four years old. She added that while Robert had 'not so fanciful a nature' as his sisters, he was 'endowed with greater powers of observation than either of these.' In another letter she refers to his 'persevering turn and unselfish temper.' It is evident that the equable character and capacity for thoughtful judgement which distinguished the boy in after life declared themselves early.

Robert Milnes passed an uneventful and pleasant childhood, partly in London, where he would be taken to walk in what he termed 'Stupid Hyde Park' or to laugh at the newly-imported penguins in the Zoological Gardens, partly at his father's bleak West Riding house, Fryston Hall, famous for its owner's genial parties and comprehensive library. Robert and his sisters also passed some weeks annually at Crewe Hall, where their unpredictable uncle would suddenly ask his nieces and nephew to stay and as suddenly suggest that they should leave. In a paper on Crewe Hall which he wrote late in his life, Robert Milnes describes the house as he knew it in childhood, dwelling particularly on the great Gallery where:

as children we used to have splendid games on winter afternoons, the distance from the Oak Parlour, where the rather dread presence of my uncle was assumed to be, was sufficient to dull all the noise we could combine to make. Games of 'bears' with leather hassocks as missiles are fresh in my memory and my mother enjoyed them as much as we did. . . . My uncle was by no means a playfellow, but was always kind to us, though with a certain terror on his side which he entirely threw off when the next generation came into being. He never caressed us in his life, or greeted us beyond placing a trembling hand into ours . . . nor did he ever make us a present of any kind, until, later on, when I was at Harrow, my mother made him give me the gold watch-chain which I now always wear. . . . But I am pretty sure that he never gave either my sisters or myself a gift of coin.

With the assistance of the architect Edward Blore, 'Uncle Crewe' had spent much money renovating, or, as we may now think, ruining, Crewe Hall; and when the newly reconstructed building was destroyed by fire in 1866 his family felt that the blow might further affect his reason. Robert Milnes, aged eight, and his mother were in the house at the time, and assisted in getting the pictures and furniture out on to the snow-covered lawns where, braving the January night, old Lord Crewe settled himself at a writing table under the stars and drafted a telegram to his architect describing the disaster and asking him to undertake to build Crewe up again. 'Well, Annabel,' he remarked to his shivering sister, 'you have always said Crewe was a cold house, but you can't call it that now.' The great fire at Crewe was the first of an uncanny chain of similar disasters which dogged Robert Milnes throughout his life.

In the autumn of 1868, at ten years old, Robert was deposited in a private school, Winton House, a villa surrounded by cold shrubberies on the outskirts of the city of Winchester. 'Robert is quite a *specimen boy* as to good looks & bright happiness, but we cannot get him really *to care* for boyish games, the secret of which I believe to be that he likes no pursuit in which he does not feel himself *capable of excelling*,' wrote the headmaster's wife to Robert's mother. It is likely that this distaste for recreation, which remained with him throughout life (it was once said that Crewe's only idea of relaxation was to take up another kind of work), may be attributed to an essential lack of youthfulness in his make-up, already noticeable when he was a boy, and which his later experiences of intimate personal tragedy naturally enough did nothing to diminish. 'You are old for your age,' a Harrow friend wrote to him when they were both sixteen. Nor was this surprising. The adored only son of parents who were no longer young when he was born —and who had themselves aged quickly, owing to indifferent health—Robert Milnes was in addition the focal point for the

ROBERT MILNES AS A BOY
from a painting by Chapman at West Horsley Place

doting admiration of his father's three old aunts, spinster ladies living in Torquay, and of the rather more nervous and transitory attentions of his old uncle Lord Crewe. When he was at school his parents were already at the age of other boys' grandparents. Moreover in his father Robert had a formidable rival for the enjoyment of the pleasures normal to his own age: 'His Lordship is going to the boat-race on somebody's steamer; it is rather a quaint idea that he should be going and I not!' he wrote during his early Cambridge days. The only entirely youthful characteristic, and one which he retained through life, was an amiable recklessness about money, first manifested in constant letters asking his mother for two or three extra shillings when he was at Harrow, and which by the time he went up to Cambridge had reached what his father considered excessive proportions.

It was while he was at Harrow, in February 1874, and when he was sixteen, that there fell a blow from which he never recovered—the unexpected death, after a short illness of some days, of his mother. One of the greatest attachments and influences of his whole life, Lady Houghton had taught the boy her own tastes, and though for almost all her son's lifetime she had been a nervous invalid she had none the less retained the natural charm of her character. Much of her time had been passed in that absorbing concern of mid-Victorian ladies called 'keeping up the strength'; but her children worshipped her.

On returning to Harrow after this tragedy Milnes suffered from a four-months' malady, but won the Shakespeare Gold Medal for his knowledge of Shakespeare, taught him by his mother; and he later won the school poetry prize with a long piece on Gustavus Adolphus in blank verse. In the winter of 1874 he went up to Cambridge, entering Trinity like his father before him, but unlike his father he found a Trinity devoid of really exciting or interesting personalities. Some of his Harrow friends were there, others were not. He was soon absorbed in working, spending money, acting in amateur theatricals and describing everything in the current jargon of the very young of those distant days—'It is simply *damned* slow'—'rather slow'—'awfully jolly'—'glue yourself together soon after your accident.' While still up at Trinity he was elected to Boodle's Club.

9

From August to October 1875, Milnes toured Canada and the United States with his father, keeping an unimpassioned little record of these journeys in a pocket-diary. Robert Milnes' appearance about this time may be gleaned from a speech by Bayard Taylor, delivered at the Lotos Club dinner in New York, in which he referred to the fact that the appearance of Lord Houghton's son had startled him: 'A young English giant, tall as myself, though scarcely more than seventeen years of age, broad-shouldered, vigorous, and with an expression on his frank brow and in his dark eyes which, to my mind, confuted the theory of certain ethnologists that genius is not transmitted from father to son.'

They set off in the steamer s.s. *Sarmatian* from Liverpool in August 1875, stopping at Ireland to pick up the usual load of emigrants bound for the U.S.A. The most interesting among the passengers was 'Mr. Butler, author of *Erewhon*, who is very amusing and clever though infidel,' but, although he played whist with Samuel Butler, the young man was far more interested in the Eustace Smiths (parents of his friend W. H. Smith), and in a Canadian family named Macpherson, the youngest of whose two daughters, the dark-eyed Isobel, caught his fancy: he saw them afterwards in Toronto, and when they parted she gave him two larger than carte-de-visite photographs of herself, he gave her a smaller one of himself together with the inevitable volume of his father's verse. Later he sent her a comic serenade, to be sung to the tune of *The Danube River*:

> Do you recall that August night
>   Upon the wide Atlantic?
> When both the moon and you were bright
>   And I got quite romantic?
> I've often watched the moon's pale flame
>   But never, Miss Macpherson,
> Has she to me been quite the same
>   With any other person,
> No doubt the moon was not to blame
>   But still she seemed a worse 'un!

The usual ship's concert was held, during which Lord Houghton read out to the passengers quantities of his own verse.

Landing in Canada in mid-August, they spent ten days visiting Quebec, Montreal and Toronto. The journey was marred almost at the outset by Lord Houghton's accident, which left him with perpetual neuralgia for the remainder of the journey. 'It has damped all my pleasure, and a week of medicine in New York has only made it worse'; it also damped his son's, who was obliged to help Dey, the Fryston house-steward who was travelling with them, look after the ailing old man. Later they went on to Buffalo, Chicago, St. Louis, New York and Washington. In St. Louis they dined with the Civil War hero, General Sherman, an evening which Robert records in his diary:

Went home to dress and got to General Sherman's about 6.30. The party were the General and Miss Sherman who is not handsome, the married daughter Mrs. Fitch and her husband who was in the navy, General McCook on the staff, who lost a father and *six* brothers in the war, and whose only surviving brother came to England with General Grant's son last year, Mr. Garrison and his daughter Emma who is fair and very handsome. I sat between her and Miss Sherman and had a very pleasant time. After dinner we sat and talked in the General's room; he talked of the war which, as his son-in-law said, he very rarely did, giving us an account of Macpherson's death and the March to the Sea. He is a dear old boy, the sort of man one would be proud to serve under and die for, tall with a close-cut beard and moustache, and a short soldierly almost nervous manner of speaking. He gave Father a handsome map and me some photos writing our names upon each. General McCook is very good-looking and soldierly, quite youngish. . . . I shall never forget the evening, Sherman is the man of all others that I wanted to see, & feel most admiration for. We left about 9.30.

From St. Louis they railed on to Cincinnati, where they made friends with families named Pendleton, Skenk and Probasco.

They reached Washington at nine on a Fall evening, after passing Harper's Ferry and other places of historic interest. In Washington they stayed at the Arlington, and were taken next morning by an attaché to the newly built British Legation, where they met the Minister, Sir. E. Thornton:

He has a pleasant and diplomatic manner, speaking precisely, and saying unimportant things in a low and mysterious voice. He has just got into his new legation, a handsome brick building with good rooms. We walked with him to the Secretary of State's office in a very handsome building, part of the new offices, built of the usual white marble. After ascending in the 'Elevator' we were introduced to the Hon. Hamilton Fish, who is a rather coarse-looking man with a strong mouth and jaw and the same sort of mysterious manner as Sir E. The latter confided to us that Fish is a great humbug for all his hearty manner, and that you couldn't believe a word he said! We discovered from him that the President was not here, as reported in the papers, so I fear I shan't see that distinguished and intoxicated ruler.

From Washington they went to Baltimore, to Philadelphia and finally to New York, to which they crossed the Jersey Ferry in the rain and settled in at the luxurious Brevoort House Hotel, where 'Uncle Sam' Ward hastened to welcome them. As assiduous as Sam Ward was William Henry Hurlbert, editor of the *New York World*, a friend of Landor and an old acquaintance of Robert Milnes' father. The wine at the Brevoort House was found to be excellent, and Lord Houghton gave a number of dinner-parties, mostly including Ward and Hurlbert:

Was ever a party so pleasant [wrote his son of one of these entertainments]. Father was better, Hurlbert as brilliant as usual, Uncle Sam quite wonderful in wit and knowledge and Evarts brimming over with cleverness and wisdom. I discovered that Sam Ward is a brother of Julia Ward Howe; a capital story is told of her, that when Charles Sumner was elected Senator, he was to have dined with her, but he said that his 'new burden of office obliged him to relinquish his social relations.' 'Lor! Mr. Sumner,' she replied, 'God Almighty hasn't got to that yet!' Our dinner was excellent of its kind with the same capital wine as yesterday.

The American trip provided many other humorous anecdotes which the youth duly recorded. They also met Bret Harte—'most agreeable and entertaining, full of fun and anecdote.' Later Robert and 'Uncle Sam' travelled up to Boston together, where they stayed in the house of Ward's friend Wright on Chester Street, visited some acquaintances:

. . . and then on to our destination, the shrine of Mr. Longfellow! He lives about four miles out at Cambridge, where is also Harvard University. The drive is pretty, giving a good double view of the bay and town. Longfellow lives in a delightful old house, with low, wainscoted rooms, and charming furniture. Words fail me to describe what a dear old bird he is, so kind & genial, with his beautiful old face & long white hair & beard. He gave us a capital lunch and pleasant conversation, his three daughters and a niece were there. L. said he was sure it was a mistake to revise or correct a second edition, far better to reproduce entirely. He also asked much about Browning, Swinburne, etc., etc. We left him with great regret, and drove through the town, the part that was 'burnt out' was especially fine, streets wide and houses high.

From Boston the young man returned to New York to rejoin his father, and then sailed for England, to resume his studies at Trinity, leaving Lord Houghton a prey to transatlantic osteopaths in the Brevoort House.

This was Robert Milnes' only visit to the United States of America in the course of a life of eighty-seven years. He brought back with him a short travel diary, an attitude of amused tolerance for the Americans, a list of the hotels in which they had stayed, a self-compiled glossary of 'Americanisms' and two recipes for making 'John Collins' and a whisky-rum-and-angostura-bitters cocktail.

Chapter Three

THE career of Robert Milnes at Trinity College, Cambridge, sped along expected and conventional lines. He took up the pursuits, the interests and the pastimes usual to a youth of his age and status—membership of the University Pitt Club, play-acting at the A.D.C., eating and drinking more expensively than he could afford. 'This expense makes it doubtful whether it is advisable that you should return to Cambridge unless you can reduce your cost of living,' wrote his father in a carping parental mood. 'I wish there had been something to pay for Private Tutorship that might have left a future advantage. . . . I do not know what your London bills amount to, but it is clear that we, as a family, are living beyond our means—which must be arrested—or we shall be.' Milnes did, of course, return to Trinity and completed his full time there, taking a B.A. degree, which he described to a friend as 'a quaint performance,' in 1879.

Already, while still up at Trinity, Milnes had begun to lead the life of country-house visits and London dinner-parties, which continued, interrupted only by sorrow or ill-health, until the date of his second marriage in 1899 and his serious entry into Liberal politics. The tone of his letters during this early period is light and gossipy, for unlike his father he seems not to have had any overpowering literary or political interests in his youth. A random phrase such as: 'Is it true that Lord de Ramsey is going to marry Rita Beaumont?' might be taken as the theme-song of his letters at this time. The atmosphere of these late-Victorian country-houses was jolly and, to modern eyes, distinctly strenuous. 'They did make a row in this generally orderly house,' wrote Robert's younger sister, describing for his benefit a New Year's rag at Taymouth, 'ran the lifts up and down, broke the windows, baited old Alastair

14

Murray nearly mad, sugared the top of his bald head and generally raised him finely.' 'We made a great row two evenings ago,' the same carefree girl wrote from Laidlawstiel, Galashiels, on another occasion, 'on going to bed, in the passages—Lord Melgund bounced out upon us in a cocked hat and cloak and mask and Amy nearly went into hysterics and fled down into the hall where she encountered Lord Minto and Sir H. Smith, who naturally were a little surprised to see her.' Some elderly persons like the widowed Lady John Russell thought the Milnes girls 'fast,' but in fact this was the tempo of the new young generation, who were setting the pace for the Edwardian age. Moreover, the grim era of the practical joke had dawned across the country-houses of England. It formed a sharp and, to older people, unwelcome contrast to the pleasing, restrained manners of mid-Victorian country life.

In London Robert Milnes led the ordinary existence of other young men of his age and standing—going to the theatre, going to balls during the Season, frequenting his two clubs, Boodle's and Brooks's. Although he did not usually keep a journal, and never wrote a book of memoirs, he liked in old age to jot down for the benefit of others short recollections of London in his youth. One of these gives an interesting picture of Brooks's Club as it was when Robert Milnes first joined it, shortly after coming down from Cambridge:

It was a very small and old-fashioned club [he wrote] with practically nothing except the beautiful Adam rooms, and of course no bed-rooms.

I think there is a short scene in it in one of Trollope's novels, perhaps 'Phineas Redux', but no description of the house.

We dined upstairs in the room overlooking Park Place, and the large front room, formerly devoted to gambling, was much used as a sitting-room in the evening. So far as I can recollect, there were none but Circulating Library books, except for a very few in the smaller front room, including the General Stud book. I have not seen the Club Betting Book lately, and do not know if wagers are still made, but in those days there were a good many, mostly on political, but sometimes on social events, and often for considerable sums. No smoking, except in the billiard room, which was behind the

3   15

morning room, and in the small room on the right-hand in which visitors could be interviewed.

A notable figure was Williams, the Steward, an old-fashioned personage who was the friend of all the members, and I think is described by Lord Edmond FitzMaurice in one of his books. All the servants wore knee-breeches, and our fine silver plate was greatly in evidence, even if one dined alone. The solemn splendour of the surroundings caused somebody to observe that to dine at Brooks's was like dining at a Duke's house with the Duke lying dead upstairs! There were oil-lamps, of course, but the favourite light was that of real bees-wax candles with their soft diffused illumination. The note-paper was solid and creamy and that for private correspondence was gilt-edged, and when the time came for 'Brooks's' to be inscribed, it was said that an old member complained that if that sort of thing was going to begin the old character of the Club would be altogether lost. All the furniture was old-fashioned, but the leather chairs were deep and comfortable.

I recall a dramatic moment on May 6th, 1882, when we were lingering on in the dining-room after a pleasant meeting of the Fox Club, and Bill Kensington, our popular Whip, rushed into the room saying, 'They have murdered Freddy Cavendish!' I drove down to 10 Downing Street with another member to hear the story from Edward Hamilton, who told us that Mr. Gladstone had just gone across to Carlton House Terrace to break the news to Lady Frederick.

Four years later there was a crisis in the Club of which accounts have appeared elsewhere. Mr. Gladstone's conversion to Home Rule was splitting the Party, and two youngsters who afterwards became Cabinet Ministers were involved. The first was Lewis Harcourt, the son of a brilliant father who had many enemies, and when he came up for election his chances were smothered by a crowd of black-balls, the handiwork of enraged Unionists. This was obviously a case for reprisals, & the victim was to be Willie Palmer (Lord Wolmer) whose father, Lord Selborne after being Liberal Lord Chancellor, had broken away on the question of Home Rule. It looked as though nobody would be elected except an occasional whist-player who detested politics. Lord Granville intervened. When the next ballot day came he stood up on a chair & made a speech. I was not there at the moment, but when I came in was told what had happened. Lord Granville was our leader in the Lords, and probably the most distinguished & popular member of Brooks's. But even he dreaded such a departure from tradition. 'Will they stand it?' he said to another old member. They not only stood it, but with his matchless powers of persuasion he induced them to drop the vendetta altogether, and subsequent elections proceeded in the ordinary course.

During Robert's second year at Cambridge he had visited Ireland with his father. On their leisurely way homeward via Dublin they received a telegram informing them that Fryston Hall had been virtually destroyed by a fire which had burned out all the big front rooms and damaged much of Lord Houghton's precious library. In spite of fire-insurance, the reconstruction of the house proved an additional strain on Lord Houghton's impoverished finances. When, at the age of eight, Robert had watched his mother directing the salvage of the family pictures during the great midnight conflagration which damaged Crewe Hall, he had cried out, 'Oh! what a good thing that it isn't Fryston!' It now was Fryston, a house which had sheltered his happy childhood and was filled with recollections of his mother. While flitting from country-house to country-house Robert was pursued by anxious letters from his father, increasingly illegible owing to gout in the hands, describing the progress of the rebuilding of Fryston and the extremities—such as the sale of the carriage-horses—to which the old man was at times driven by lack of ready coin. All the same, Lord Houghton somehow managed to go on hiring houses in Mayfair for the Season—the lease of his own house in Upper Brook Street having fallen in some years before his wife's death: Clifford Street, Berkeley Square, Wilton Crescent, Bruton Street, are all addresses at which the family lived in one year or another. Yet, despite all their father's earnest efforts, the Milnes sisters seemed to remain resolute spinsters and in point of fact the London houses were taken quite as much for their father's benefit as for their own. A stooping old man in a black skull cap, Lord Houghton still entertained at his *omnium gatherum* parties, and was still to be seen everywhere in London, too often leaning with bibulous geniality upon the arm of his tall, elegant young son, who must have silently suffered much embarrassment as he guided his parent's unsteady steps out through some drawing-room door.

On 12 January 1879 Robert Milnes came of age, an event celebrated at Fryston by a tenants' ball. Milnes' future was not yet decided, although the possibility that one of the two Members for Pontefract might soon resign naturally encouraged him to think in terms of a political career. Neither Milnes' own letters nor the accounts of him in his youth suggest an impetuous or emotional character; yet, suddenly, at the age of twenty-one, with no job and no prospects, he insisted on taking a step which startled even his father: he announced his engagement, in June 1879, and married just one year later. His twenty-one-year-old bride was Sibyl Marcia, a daughter of a North-country baronet, Sir Frederick Graham of Netherby, and by her mother a grandchild of the old Duchess of Somerset, sister to Caroline Norton and Lady Dufferin, and Queen of Beauty at the Eglinton Tournament in Lord Houghton's remotest youth. 'The Graham girls are as nice as they are lovely,' was the general verdict upon the four Graham sisters, who, while highly decorative, were not in the worldly sense well endowed, although one of them became Duchess of Montrose. 'Just like a little Sir Joshua,' was someone's description of Sibyl Graham.

The extreme youth of the couple struck many people as well as Lord Houghton, whom it not unnaturally displeased. 'Count Bathyany told me last night that in some paper they say you are going back to school,' wrote Robert's sister Florence. 'It was the most child-like wedding I ever saw,' Lord Houghton told a friend. 'There was a profusion of presents—over two hundred. The tenants sent some beautiful plate and jewellery.' Miss Florence Nightingale, whom in his youth and early middle-age Lord Houghton had persistently tried to marry, and who had remained one of his most fond and faithful friends, wrote of the event:

My dear Friend—I *will* give you joy, I *do* give you joy, and I condole with you too as you desire on your boy's marriage. Such promise—not only promise—such proof of so much being in him, it seems a pity that he should not have served his apprenticeship to hard work, which not alone but generally forms the best foundation for the future edifice if there is plenty of stuff. For that he will do something great for his country— and what times are these?—we do not allow ourselves to doubt for one moment. On the other hand there is something very

THE HON. MRS. ROBERT MILNES in 1880

inspiring in the faithful love, the early and the late, when two always say 'we.' . . . I think one has known such instances of two in one through a long life together, God in both and both in one: but then the wife must help the husband in work, not prevent him.

The real explanation for this youthful love-match—that it did much to repair the emotional wreckage left by the sudden death of Robert Milnes' mother—was overlooked by relatives and friends alike.

A married man of twenty-two, it was now absolutely vital for Milnes to find some ways of earning a living and fitting himself for a career. Both his father's ideas and his own inclined towards a life of public service, and the best way of preparing for this was to become Private Secretary to some Cabinet Minister. In the sensible belief that it is always most effective to begin at the top, Lord Houghton approached his old friend Gladstone to find out whether Robert could not be inserted into the Prime Minister's secretariat. Gladstone replied that while he had no doubt that Robert Milnes would make 'a most eligible Private Secretary,' there was at that time no practical vacancy in Downing Street, since the four secretaries already there were 'equal to the demands.' When Milnes' father sailed for Egypt to visit his elder daughter, who had lately married Sir Gerald Fitzgerald, an official in the foreign service there, the young man was still without employment, and still living with his wife at her grandmother's house in Park Lane. In March of 1882, on his way home from Cairo, Lord Houghton became ill in an Athens hotel, an attack followed in a few day's time by an apoplectic stroke which temporarily paralysed his left side. Accompanied by Lord Houghton's old sister, Harriet, Lady Galway, Robert Milnes hastened out to Greece, only to be met by his father with sour reproaches over the cost of their journey. Milnes brought his father back to London at Easter time, not long before the younger sister's marriage to an impecunious soldier, Arthur Henniker-Major. None of his children's marriages pleased the old worldling: 'I used to say I cared only for one thing in my children's marriages—*Money*.' he wrote during disappointing settlement negotiations with the Henniker family: 'I am well paid off for my desires.'

But however tetchy he could sometimes be in old age, Lord Houghton never lost his sense of the humorous for long. 'I quite understand all your wife's feelings,' he wrote after the birth of his first grandchild, Annabel, in 1881, 'having just read in *Pot Bouilli* a most elaborate detail of all the phenomena and sensations of child-bearing, showing that . . . Madame Z. must co-operate with him in his books. Perhaps he thinks that as all French literature turns on the various machinery of propagation it is right there should be some account of the result.'

In April 1883 Milnes entered on his first experience of official life, as one of the Assistant Private Secretaries to Lord Granville, the bland and courteous Foreign Secretary, an unexcited Whig of the old school, who himself exemplified the classic description of the Whig party as composed of 'Liberals opposed to further progress in democracy.' Under Lord Granville's rule the Foreign Office remained as aristocratic as it had always been—'the last choice preserve of administration practised as a sport.' At first the new Private Secretary saw little of his chief. 'Lord Granville has been laid up with lumbago, so has not been able to come down often,' Milnes wrote to his father soon after his entry into the Foreign Office, in a letter in which he added that he was 'getting into the way of the work,' which he would, he thought, 'find interesting': 'the other secretaries Sanderson, Henry Hervey and Carew have received me in a most friendly way.' He declared the Foreign Office work to be 'not arduous except by fits and starts'; but by the end of the year the problems of Egypt and the Sudan, with which Lord Granville had been languidly and somewhat cynically toying for months, came to a sudden crisis. In January 1884 Gladstone's Government decided to send General Gordon to advise on the evacuation of Khartoum—a decision due partly to what Lord Granville called 'having hardly ever had anything but bad alternatives to choose from' and partly to the Government's weakness in the face of press campaigns such as that of the *Pall Mall Gazette*. The results of this step—the fall of Khartoum and the murder of Gordon in February 1885—are well known; they raised a tumult of anger throughout England against the Government and against Gladstonianism.

These events provided Milnes, at the age of twenty-six, with his first glimpse of politics and diplomacy from the inside. Already capable of judging a situation without party prejudice, and with a cool head and a calm eye, he privately disagreed with Granville's handling of the Sudanese crisis while realising · the reasons for it. Replying some fifty years later to a question on the subject sent to him by an old friend, Lord Crewe agreed that Rosebery and 'almost everybody . . . who was not behind the scenes and able to realise the astounding difficulties' of the Government's position then believed that they had shown 'culpable indecision about Egypt.' He recalled that in June 1884 Acton had written of the withdrawal from the Sudan as England's 'giving up an undertaking in which we have disappointed the expectation of the world, in which we have shown infirmity of purpose, want of forethought, a rather spasmodic and inconclusive energy, occasional weakness and poverty of resource':

So far [Crewe continued] as this was true, it was undoubtedly due to the incompatible views of several members of the Government, but also to the fact that Mr. G.'s mind did not work as other people's did. It must have made him, as Head of the Government, quite different from any other Prime Minister who ever held office in England. Setting the Sudan aside, people are apt to forget now that the evacuation of Egypt proper was then the policy accepted by all parties. . . .

Now as to Gordon. I was an Assistant Private Secretary at · the Foreign Office, and therefore followed everything that happened. I never saw him myself, but I recollect a long conversation with his brother Sir Henry when I happened to be left in charge of the room, about methods of communicating with him, of course long before his situation became critical. I distinctly remember always doubting the policy of sending him, and afterwards I was convinced that it was Wolseley who was really responsible for influencing the minds of the four Ministers, who, as we know, took it on themselves to ask him to go. Not very long after the disaster I asked Lord Hartington whether he had understood that in the event of its being impossible to withdraw all the Sudan garrisons, Gordon himself would come down the river from Khartoum with such elements of its garrison as might be in danger of the Mahdi's vengeance, it being understood that the bulk of all the garrisons would submit to the Mahdi and be in no risk of their lives.

Hartington said that it was quite correct that in such circumstances Gordon himself would return to Egypt.

It seems to be generally admitted, even by the most adverse critics of the Government, that Gordon completely misapprehended the extent of his own influence in the Sudan, and no doubt his self-confidence must have greatly encouraged those who sent him. I happened to be at Zanzibar at the beginning of 1890, when von Wassmann brought to the Agency Emin Pasha, a strange unwarlike little figure, in a white drill uniform, girt with a cavalry sword nearly as big as himself. I asked him whether in Darfur, or in any other Province of the Sudan, there had remained a legend of Gordon as a powerful figure. Emin said No, that he had heard little or nothing of Gordon, but that the memory of Sir Samuel Baker had survived throughout the Sudan. I had known Baker very well in the old days, and was not at all surprised at this.

Another personal reminiscence is that at the time I felt sure they were wrong in not sending Zobeir Pasha, and I see that Mr. G. himself was strongly in favour of it. But I can understand why it was not done. Not merely the Exeter Hall sentiment would have been excited to frenzy, but the Conservative opposition would have jumped at the chance of attacking the Government in company with a number of other people whose principles they hated. It would have been a marked instance of what you describe as the unscrupulous opposition which afterwards, however much it may have admired Gordon and believed him to be sacrificed, valued him even more as a piece on the political chessboard.

I think it must also be admitted that the situation was one for which Lord Granville's particular gifts and merits—which, like Rosebery, I should be the last one to underrate—were not well fitted.

The reasonableness, the lack of vehemence and the unemphatic tone of these reflections are those of Lord Crewe's later life; but the judicious conclusions and careful assessment of fact and motive were typical of him in youth as well as age.

Instructive though his period at the Foreign Office proved, Robert Milnes had no intention of making diplomacy his career. In 1884 he and another young man, Arthur Acland, became rival candidates for the Liberal nomination for the newly formed Barnsley Division of the West Riding: 'The choice fell on me,' Milnes wrote, 'owing no doubt to my local connection with the constituency, and Mr. Acland moved to the Rotherham Division next door.' Milnes never fought this election; for on 11 August, 1885, his father died suddenly of a heart-attack at Vichy, at the age of seventy-six.

Lord Houghton's death changed Robert Milnes' prospects and position radically. He not only became a land-owner but, of greater political importance, a young peer vowed to the sacred creed of Gladstonian Liberalism—at a moment when the majority of Whig peers were withdrawing their support from Gladstone owing to his attitude to Irish Land and Home Rule. Liberal peers would soon be thin upon the ground, and in this sense his succession to a peerage was of far more potential value to young Milnes' career than could ever have been a seat in the House of Commons—where his dry and hesitant way of speaking and his lack of *brio* would have precluded political success.

At first it was only of his loss that he thought, writing to one of his sisters:

I cannot at all grasp it yet, or believe that we shall never see him again here: he had seemed so much better lately, and had evidently felt so, that it is in one way a more dreadful shock than it would have been a year or two ago. Like you I can't help thinking how much more would have been said, and how much more one would have been with him, if one had only known, but I suppose it is so always.

Lord Houghton had been blessed with an excessive quantity of intimate and affectionate friends, and the survivors among these released a positive avalanche of letters upon his bereaved children. The most apposite was that from one of his oldest and most faithful cronies, Mrs. Procter, the widow of 'Barry Cornwall':

The death of your father carries off many recollections of old days—I knew him when he had just left College—He was to me the best company I had. He knew so much. He had seen so much. The World never did him justice. To be famous one must only do one thing. Like Lubbock and his Ants, or Clarkson and the Slave Trade. There is a story of Farinelli, a great singer 100 years ago—a friend heard him play on the violin and said, how wonderfully you play. Hush, said Farinelli, never mention it—the World will not permit you to do two things well.

After his father's funeral in the little marshy churchyard of Ferry Fryston in the West Riding, Robert Milnes took up the title of Lord Houghton—a name too much connected, as Rosebery remarked in a later context, with the character and the achievements of one man.

For the remaining months of 1885 Houghton and his wife busied themselves settling into Fryston with their family, which now comprised three girls, two of them twins, and a boy, christened Richard after the late Lord Houghton, and like him called 'Dickie' or 'Dick.' Fryston Hall was a rambling, undistinguished-looking house with Ionic pillars and pediment, and it stood on a bleak hummock in the midst of a park of fine trees near the market-town of Pontefract in the West Riding. It was also near the coalmines and the Great North Road. Inside, it was a comfortable, old-fashioned country-house, the chief interest of which was its library, which Robert thus analysed for a German professor who was compiling a work upon the private libraries of Europe:

The library at Fryston Hall, Yorkshire, numbers about 24,000 volumes, and was mainly collected by the late Lord Houghton, the father of the present owner, who continues to add to it. There are about 3,500 volumes in French, 1,000 in German and 1,000 in Italian. The principal strength of the library is in English literature, especially poetry and political history. Other special collections are concerned with Oriental subjects, and with the French Revolution. There is also a considerable collection of first editions of English books, and of books which have belonged to persons distinguished in literature or in history, many of them with autograph signatures and notes. The library also contains a large collection of autograph letters relating to the Civil War in England, to the French Revolution, to British Literature and to the Literature of Foreign Countries, as well as a nearly complete set of the works of William Blake, including many of the original drawings.

Not unnaturally this list omits to mention the large and famous collection of pornographic and sadic literature and manuscripts which old Lord Houghton had lovingly assembled, and which had so much influenced Swinburne and other young men to whom these treasures were exhibited. This portion of the library Lord Houghton's heir made haste to sell.

Now definitely out of the running for a House of Commons seat, Houghton could only stand and watch the course of the famous election of the autumn and winter of 1885, which resulted in the victory of the Gladstonian Liberals, supported by the Irish members. Gladstone's declared intentions over Irish Home Rule alienated many of his patrician followers, and inclined his enemies to attribute his anxiety to return to power to 'the senile passion of an old man.' 'To get into power I really believe that he would not only give up Ireland but Mrs. Gladstone and Herbert,' Labouchere is reported to have said of the aged leader's attitude to this election. Parliament met in January, Lord Salisbury resigned, and on 1 February, much against her will, the Queen sent for Gladstone. Several influential members of Gladstone's last Cabinet refused to join this one, and though Lord Granville continued to support him, the Queen would not allow his reappointment to the Foreign Office, which was allotted to Rosebery. Another new figure in the Cabinet was John Morley, an eminent journalist and man of letters, able, high principled, adaptable, interesting in conversation but vain and touchy. Morley was to play a considerable part in Houghton's future political life, but though Houghton once listed him as among the five most agreeable men he had known—the others being his own father, Henry Cowper, Frederick Locker and Rosebery—it is doubtful whether he always found him easy to get on with. Gladstone formed his Third Administration during the early days of February 1886, and on the eighth of that month Houghton was writing to his sister:

One line to say that I received today the offer of the post of one of the Whips in the House of Lords, joined to that of a Lord in Waiting—I think it will be interesting work and a good thing as demanding one's constant presence in the House. But who can say how long it will last?

Houghton was right: the post, which brought him his first direct experience of the inner workings of the Upper House as well as his first contact with the Sovereign and her Court, did not last long, for Gladstone's Home Rule and Irish Land Bills soon brought the Government down. Gladstone resigned and a General Election returned the triumphant Tories to power in October.

Just before Christmas 1886 Houghton had written a letter
to the *Leeds Mercury* replying to a suggestion in that paper that
an agreement on the Irish Land question, as apart from Home
Rule, might be made the basis for a rapprochement between
Gladstone's supporters and the Dissident Liberals whom Gladstone's proposals had driven out of the fold. He sent a copy
of this letter to Gladstone, who replied from Hawarden in the
first week of the New Year:

My dear Houghton—overwhelming postal work—1,300 arri-
vals I believe in three days—compelled me to postpone reply
to your letter of the 30th.
    I think you wrote to the newspaper (it does not often so
happen) with much judgement as well as force. Since that
time the pot has been boiling, not at all to my dissatisfaction.
Almost all the world seems to be pleased with Goschen's
joining on the one side. On the other there seems to be some
further evidence that Chamberlain is sensible of the weakness
of his position.
    We shall soon I suppose know how long we can stay here. If
it be until you visit this part of the world it will give us particular pleasure to have a visit from you and Lady Houghton, but
not a day-visit only.

Since, beyond watching the pot boil, there was little for him
to do politically at that moment, Houghton determined to take
his wife on a visit to India, to which the Dufferins, then Viceroy
and Vicereine, had cordially invited them. The later summer
of 1887 was spent partly in Yorkshire, partly in the country-
houses of friends, and partly in making plans for this journey.
In September of the year Lady Houghton and her children
were staying at Crewe Hall, with 'Uncle Crewe.' The children were convalescing from the bouts of scarlet fever they had
had at Fryston. At Crewe their mother suddenly contracted
the same disease. Within a few days she was dead.
    The youth and gaiety, good looks and popularity of the
Houghtons made this death particularly shocking to their
friends, all of whom sympathised with a young widower left
with four small children to bring up on his own. 'Old
people,' Houghton wrote in a note-book at this period, 'seldom
understand on what occasions, seldomer still in what terms,
they may acceptably condole with the young,' and yet it was

again an old, old lady, again Mrs. Procter, who wrote most sensibly of this loss. She did not like to write to Houghton in person, and so sent his sisters the following lines:

I had a great admiration and love for Lady Houghton—she was so good—so wise, so sympathetic—and so lovely to look at. I see her now (some time before her Marriage) on your brother's arm at the Private View of the Grosvenor Gallery and I can never forget the pretty picture the two made. I have not courage enough to write to your brother. What could I offer him? 'To know her was to love her.' I am sorry he did not go to India—here everyone is grieved for him—Away from home he would have been compelled to take up other people's interests.

Although he did not go to India, nor indeed anywhere out of England, Houghton felt unable to resume at once the daily run of London life. After listening to much advice from his friends and relatives, he decided to resign his position as Assistant Whip in the House of Lords and to undertake a course of serious and even arduous agricultural studies at the Royal Agricultural College, Cirencester. These studies would both serve as a distraction and would also prove useful in the management of his Yorkshire land, as well as of the more important Cheshire and Staffordshire estates he would at some time be inheriting from his uncle. The decision did not come easily. He consulted his fellow-Whip Lord Oxenbridge and, through Oxenbridge, the Leader of the Opposition, his old chief Lord Granville. The latter wrote to him on 17th December in typically judicial and non-committal vein:

I feel some hesitation in advising you. When I was offered the Chairmanship of the North-Western, I consulted Lord Lansdowne who advised me to accept, and Lord Russell who advised me to refuse, unless I gave up politics, on the principle that one must stick to one thing or the other. I followed the latter's opinion—but perhaps not quite for the same reasons.

As regards yourself I should think the plan would be an agreeable one, giving you interest and occupation, without the jar which business in London might cause—& in these times it is certainly desirable that Landowners should know something about land—there being however a question of whether a knowledge of farming is as necessary as that of the business of a land agent, if you could make an argument for really studying the business of that profession.

On the other hand you have now a greater hold of the House of Lords than any of the younger Peers, and though you might come up for show debates and important divisions, it would not give you the same position as constantly taking a share in the business of the House.

The very small number of Gladstonians not only makes the presence of individuals unusually desirable for his party but gives the individual unusual advantages for speaking, and taking up his proper place.

But you are a better judge than any one, and I hope you will not be much biassed by what I have written.

Houghton finally took his decision in January of 1888, informing Oxenbridge of it and asking him to tell Lord Granville:

My dear Houghton [replied Oxenbridge], I should have replied to your letter earlier but have failed to see Lord Granville who is seriously made anxious about Leveson who swallowed a half crown on 26 of last month. The Doctors declare there is no danger but until the coin reappears, the uneasiness of the parents naturally continues. Personally I shall miss your kind assistance very much but subject to the approval of the 'Chief' I should prefer the 2nd Whip being put in commission and not filled up definitely, so that in happier days you might again undertake the duties, if it so pleased you.

Lord Granville himself wrote again on learning of the decision:

Oxenbridge told be this morning of your decision [he wrote from Eaton Square]. I am very glad that after consideration you decided for yourself—& that after a visit to Cirencester. Both Oxenbridge and I came separately to the same conclusion viz that it will be better to say nothing about any change but to let Oxenbridge do the work for the present which he is quite prepared to do.

Leveson is going on well [he added in reference to the Boxing Day mishap] with the great exception that the coin has not yet passed. But the doctors are very confident.

But no sooner had he taken the contemplated step and settled at Cirencester in rooms overlooking the Market Place, with a valet to look after him and a dog-cart in which to drive to and from the College, than he fell ill. It was neither the first nor the last of Houghton's bouts of illness, for, together with her distinctive charm and amiable manners, he had inherited his mother's physical weakness. He was particularly liable to trouble with his lungs.

My dear Lady Hermione [Granville wrote a week later to Houghton's mother-in-law], How good of you, knowing the interest I feel in Houghton, to write to me. I had heard nothing of his illness, and am happy to have at the same time the news of his convalescence. The explanation of his attack is only too probable. I trust he will take the greatest care of himself. I am much obliged to you for your enquiry about Leveson. Barring the suspense he is going on as well as possible.

In February 1888, while on the point of settling at Cirencester on recovery from his illness, Houghton was put up for the Travellers' Club by some of his friends, and, like his father before him, was turned down:

If I might venture to give you a bit of advice [wrote the friend proposing his name], do not ask too many of your political friends to attend! At a Club where politics are never considered I have known occasions when it has been thought that a demonstration of a political nature has been intended that the Candidate has been sacrificed.

I cannot account for it! [wrote the same friend after the black-balling]. Nearly everyone in the room, a large gathering, was known to your friends, but there were two enemies!

In March, in June and again in the late autumn Houghton fell ill, a malady perhaps as much induced by his unhappiness as by anything else. His doctors persuaded him to resign from the course at Cirencester and to travel to Egypt to stay with his elder sister, Amy Fitzgerald. He left for Cairo in November, meeting some of his wife's family there by rendezvous, and returning with three of them through Italy. They spent Easter week in Florence. It was during this journey to Egypt and back that Houghton began to write verse seriously: these poems he collected two years later in a volume of *Stray Verses*, published by John Murray in 1891, and later described by their author as 'the lowly gleaning of two dead years'—the years following his wife Sibyl's death:

> They dare not hope, with gay or tender meaning
>> To stir the springs of laughter or of tears,—
> These gathered rhymes of mine, the lowly gleaning
>> Of two dead years.
> If on your ear one cadence yet may linger
>> Or haunt your memory but one refrain.
> 'He sang,' let Friendship whisper of the singer,
>> 'Not quite in vain.'

Houghton's verses, about which he was himself exceedingly modest, aroused the praise of the Poet Laureate, to whom he had dedicated the volume:

Lord Tennyson of my verses [he jotted in a note-book] : 'I may say of you the description of Diomed in Homer, that you have surpassed your father—in this respect at least.' I might have preferred a different compliment but this seems to me a very high one.

Some of *Stray Verses* deal with specific subjects such as Millet's *Angelus*, Zola's *La Terre*, or Tolstoy's *Anna Karenina*, while others are memories of the Eastern and Italian tour, such as *Easter in Florence*:

> · 'Twas Eastertide of Eighty-Nine,—
>> That time of rest for every nation,
> When weary legislators pine
>> For ten brief days of relaxation:
> Her finest crown Queen Florence wore,
>> Produced her fairest April weather,
> In welcome to the Travellers four
>> Who roamed her storied streets together.
>
> .   .   .   .   .
>
> Beside the Strozzi walls we strolled,
>> And grumbled at Palotti's prices,
> But somehow found ourselves consoled
>> By Doney's *déjeuners* and ices!

We drove along to sound of bells,
　Past villa walls and marble fountains,
To where the white Carthusian cells
　Peer out towards the snow-capped mountains:
On Fiesole's historic crest
　The thrushes sang a Paschal chorus
While, lighted from the lurid west,
　The teeming plain rolled wide before us.
　　　.　　.　　.　　.　　.
Now turn the page, and seek the round
　Of daily pleasures, pains and duties;—
It's good to stand on English ground,—
　A London summer has its beauties.

But the journey had not rid his mind of his seven years of happy marriage and of his wife's death, as the poem *Seven Years* bears witness:

To join the ages they have gone
　Those seven years,—
Receding as the months roll on;
Yet very oft my fancy hears
Your voice,—'twas music to my ears
　　　　　　Those seven years.

How perchance, do they seem to you,
　Those seven years,
Spirit-free in the wider blue?
When time in Eternity disappears,
What if all you have learned but the more endears
　　　　　　Those seven years?

For the time being, at least, Houghton's grief seems to have turned him away from politics and towards literature. In June 1889 he distributed amongst his friends and acquaintances a volume of translations which he had made from the Songs of Béranger, and of which two hundred copies had been privately printed. These are graceful and accomplished verses: 'The translations,' wrote Swinburne, 'seem to me as happily selected as they are graceful in execution.' Robert Browning, a life-long friend of Houghton's father was more enthusiastic:

It is indeed a delight to me to know that, in the words of the old Jewish proverb, 'the apple falls not far from the tree,' and my beloved old friend's son proves a Poet like his father before

him.   Very capital versions are these of the fine old Chansonnier I was privileged more than once to see in the flesh: you
must now leave his arm (there he still is, stumping along, hat
far back on head and stout stick in hand, in the rue de Rivoli)
and speak for yourself, as you surely can.

While from Hawarden Mr. Gladstone sent a firm approval:

I am greatly struck, struck with your admirable spirit of translation (the first requisite of all as I think) and your command
of forcible and delicate phrase. . . . Some of the originals are
as perfect as the Odes of Horace!   But you have given us a
real Béranger in English.

Thomas Hardy thought Houghton's work showed 'long experience in the art of translating, which I did not suspect you to
possess.'   Arthur Balfour declared that anyone who could
write as Houghton did 'would be very ill employed in making
speeches *even* on the right side of the Irish Question.'   Princess
May of Teck said she was taking the little volume with her to
read in leisure at St. Moritz.

Meanwhile a new sorrow fell upon the young widower.   His
only son, Dick, a child of eight years old, became gradually more
and more gravely ill.   The best doctors and nursing could not
help him, and when in the winter of 1889 Houghton was himself once more ordered abroad by his medical adviser and
unwillingly set off for Madeira and Capetown with his brother-
in-law, the Duke of Montrose, he knew that he would not again
see the boy alive.   It was in March 1890, at Capetown, that he
received a telegram announcing his child's death.   'You have
had a sad youth,' wrote his old aunt Harriet Galway, 'with
every prospect bright before you, you have within four years
lost present, past and future.   I feel much for you and I trust
it may please God that you will enjoy many bright days and a
long useful life as your dear Father's heir.'

On his father's death in 1885 Houghton had commissioned
Thomas Wemyss Reid to compile from his papers one of those
massive two-volume 'tomb-biographies,' as Lytton Strachey
called them, which were then considered appropriate.
This book occupied Reid for five years, and emerged in 1890,
to be grudgingly greeted by the press.   Some of Monckton

Milnes' surviving friends were, however, delighted with the volumes, and one thanked the donor in impromptu verse:

> *On receiving a copy of Lord Houghton's life*
>
> The King of Friendship—friendliest with the best!
> Natures like thine recruit a worn-out age,
> Giving to common days a light, leaven and zest
> With salt of wit and precepts of the sage.
> For such men surely there is more than fame
> They have immortal seeds and must outlast
> The sordid seekers of a selfish name
> Or traders on renown of memories past.
> Friend:—Christmas could no worthier gift impart
> Than this life record of a golden heart.

In May 1891 Houghton's own *Stray Verses*, a little volume bound in apple green ornamented with gilded garlands, was published by Sir John Murray. The book was well received both by its author's friends and by the press. Throughout his life Houghton quietly kept up the habit of writing occasional verse, his poem on the Harrow boys killed in the 1914–18 war being rated one of the best war poems in the language.

Back in London after this new bereavement, Houghton worked assiduously in the House of Lords, particularly as member of a notoriously dull committee, that on Railway Rates, for which he had unselfishly volunteered. This was for him, politically, a period of consolidation and of making his mark as a sober-minded but hard-working and promising young Liberal in the Upper House. In August 1892 Gladstone was again returned to power—although it was to power of a diminished and indeed rickety nature. The aged Premier had never been afraid of appointing young men to public position, and his eye lighted naturally upon young Houghton, whom he knew well and with whose father he had been intimate all his life:

The Gladstones were also intimate with my mother's family and were often at Crewe Hall [Lord Crewe wrote in some recollections of Gladstone which he prepared in 1942]. . . . So that my early introduction to the Great Minister was natural, all the more as by 1883 I was one of Lord Granville's private secretaries. . . . The friendship and confidence uniting the two leaders was delightful to witness.

My personal intimacy with the Hawarden circle developed when in 1880 Herbert Gladstone took his father's place as Member for Leeds. We were almost contemporaries, and he was often at Fryston. . . . At Hawarden I saw his elder brother William, a figure of cultured refinement, and Stephen, the admirable rector. Henry was making his mark in India, and we only became intimate years later.

Of course the illustrious host was the one person who mattered, and it was charming to see how Mrs. Gladstone moved her guests about like pawns on a board so that each might get a fair share of his conversation. He liked taking hold of a subject which would interest his hearer, turning it inside out and finishing with it. . . .

On my last visit to Hawarden I went with him for a drive in his little carriage. He had been looking up works on eschatology and spoke of death and eternity as an intending traveller to the East might name the handbooks he had studied. To him, no doubt, the coming journey was as natural and as unalarming. He laughed cheerfully over the possible belief in conditional immortality of the soul, depending on the power of its intrinsic qualities of resistance. 'Confucius,' a Chinese philosopher had said, 'is still lasting on, for he is such a strong man.' I thought that as much could be predicted of my host.

Against this background of easy familiarity and admiration, is it any wonder that Mr. Gladstone, searching the thinning ranks of Liberal peers for a suitable candidate for the Viceroyalty of Ireland, should have selected Houghton? In August 1892 the young man, who was at that moment in Yorkshire, received the following letter from Mr. Gladstone:

My dear Houghton, I have to ask that you will give me leave to submit your name to Her Majesty for the ViceRoyalty of Ireland in connection with the new Administration. And I hope alike on public and on private grounds that it may be agreeable to you to accept the proposal.

Houghton accepted promptly. It was the commencement of his public career.

34

Chapter Four

SINCE Gladstone's policy over Irish land during his first Home Rule administration had alienated almost all the Whig land-owning peers, greatly reducing the number of his supporters in the House of Lords, the Prime Minister's choice of Houghton for the Lord-Lieutenancy of Ireland may seem an obvious one. In fact, owing to the new Lord-Lieutenant's youth (he was thirty-four) and to his lack of any administrative experience, the appointment caused surprise at the time: 'It is odd,' wrote his elder sister, 'that it was never hinted at in the papers.' 'It would have been a great pleasure to your father to have seen such a distinction conferred upon you at so early a stage of your political life,' Lord Dufferin wrote from the British Embassy in Paris, while Arthur Balfour was heard to declare it 'a brilliant appointment.' Several Gladstonian peers, convinced that they had senior claims, were naturally disappointed. In particular Lord and Lady Aberdeen, who had briefly occupied Viceregal Lodge in 1886 with what they themselves felt to have been spectacular success, were much startled at being passed over. Writing to congratulate Houghton, Lady Aberdeen begged him to patronise her Irish Industries in Dublin and enclosed in her letter a bulky shamrock root to bring him luck.

While not exactly a sinecure, the post of Lord-Lieutenant of Ireland was largely a shop-window one. The Chief Secretary, who, as a member of the Cabinet, spent more of his time in London than in Dublin, was the real ruler of the country, and though Mr. Gladstone had once defined the relative powers of the Cabinet and the Queen's Viceroy as 'the Cabinet ·for policy, the Lord-Lieutenant for administration,' this lucid distinction did not always correspond to Dublin Castle facts. 'Mr. Morley,' writes Lord Aberdeen in a revealing passage of his

35

Memoirs dealing with his Viceroyalty of 1886, when John Morley was for the first time Chief Secretary, 'being much absorbed with his share of the preparation of the Home Rule Bill, and other Parliamentary duties, was the more ready to leave matters to be dealt with at our end, and even asked me to administer his rights of patronage.' The Lord-Lieutenant had in practice to rest content with what crumbs of power the Chief Secretary let drop: Morley's tone in his correspondence with Houghton is that of an indulgent but preoccupied and imperious tutor. Moreover, the position of Lord-Lieutenant was in itself paradoxical: representing the Sovereign it was in theory the Lord-Lieutenant's duty to hold himself aloof from and above all Party politics, yet since he was also a member of the Government, his term of office limited by their tenure of power, his every action was scrutinised both by the Irish themselves and by the Parliamentary Opposition in London. 'He is in an anomalous position,' wrote Houghton, 'and no definite rule exists for his guidance. His interference in, or abstention from, politics must vary in amount according to circumstances, and for the amount he is not directly responsible to anybody. My own view is that the less he mixes in Parliamentary business the better.' Whatever the Viceroy did, whatever he did not do, he was sure to be criticised and attacked. 'It was always a mystery,' writes Lord Newton in his biography of Landsowne, 'that anyone could be found voluntarily to accept the Irish Viceroyalty.'

There was, moreover, the matter of expense. Lansdowne himself called the traditions of the office 'horribly extravagant,' and complained that there was too much 'flunkeyism and parade,' the Viceroy keeping up a semi-royal state with levees 'as elaborate as those held at St. James's.' The fact that Houghton was a widower made entertaining especially irksome to him. He found the weeks preceding his official entry into Dublin distinctly hectic. 'I shall be the most harassed man in the 3 Kingdoms for the next month or two,' he told his sister Florence. 'I am uncertain as yet whether I should be congratulated or condoled with.' 'I am now beginning the agonies, which will last for some weeks, of enquiring about household, servants, houses, etc.,' he wrote to her in another letter: 'There is of course a great

36

deal to be got, but as mercifully the Dublin season is still far off, I shall be able to some extent to operate gradually. I dare say you and Arty may be able to think over some possible aides-de-camp; they are 12 in number, and there is no need that they should be political sympathizers. The collection of servants is the most troublesome part.' In those days the Dublin season was much enlivened by the presence of the battalions of the Foot Guards stationed there for duties at the Castle. The Lord-Lieutenant was expected to give many dances besides holding the state levees at which he had to kiss debutantes on the cheek. More agreeable to Houghton than any of this, there were also many race-meetings within easy reach of Dublin, at Baldoyle, Leopardstown and the Curragh—the last being both the Newmarket and the Aldershot of Ireland.

Yet this was a not uninteresting moment at which to go to Ireland as the Liberal representative of Queen Victoria. It was only ten years since the Phoenix Park murders, when the Chief Secretary and his assistant had been killed with long thin knives under the very windows of Viceregal Lodge. This crime had occasioned the sternest repressive measures, so that the Lord-Lieutenancy of the Liberal Lord Spencer remains notorious in Irish annals, while the Salisbury Cabinet which in 1886 succeeded Gladstone's Third Administration also made itself loathed by its Coercion Act, legalising persecutions and brutalities almost unparalleled even in the history of the English occupation of Ireland. The Irish reaction to these measures was an increase in sporadic acts of violence or rebellion—the murder of police officers in lonely outposts, dynamite explosions, the burning of English houses, the boycotting of Unionist shopkeepers and the stubborn refusal of tenants to pay rent or to obey eviction orders. Although the two first Irish measures of Gladstone's Cabinet in 1892 were the repeal of the 1887 Crimes Act and the appointment of a Special Commission to enquire into the whole matter of evicted tenants, the Irish regarded this progressive Administration without enthusiasm, nor was there any valid cause for them to jubilate over the cancellation of the unjust and foreign laws. Although Parnell, personally discredited, was now dead, his followers swarmed in Dublin. They remained unmoved by the spectacle of the aged and noble-minded Gladstone grinding the Liberal Party

37

to powder in his determination to do by Ireland what he deemed to be right.

Meanwhile the inhabitants of the Castle led an existence for which a modern parallel might be sought in day-to-day life in contemporary Nairobi. In 1886 the Aberdeens had been astonished to find that when they set out to walk the few hundred yards which separated the Castle from Christ Church Cathedral—where they wished to attend afternoon service—they were preceded by a brace of armed policemen, two armed detectives and two A.D.C.s, a similar contingent bringing up the rear. Inside the Lodge and the Castle the alien court, with its English aides-de-camp and English equerries, its grooms of the chamber walking backwards, kept up its pomp in vast saloons ornamented by English royal portraits and crowded with pot-palms, occasional tables and settees. Here the Viceroy, wearing the Irish diamond insignia, reputed to be worth £20,000, round his neck, would preside in the throne room as the representative of his Sovereign. 'Lord Houghton is a fine show figure,' wrote a Tory girl who was enjoying a Dublin season in 1894. 'He is not popular here because of his reputed stiffness, but I believe if he is properly treated that, though not satisfactory, he could be made tolerable.' In some ways this stiffness, very evident in all the official photographs taken of him in Dublin at this time, was what was wanted. No amount of carefree charm would be likely to placate or mollify the natives of this occupied territory, and a fine show-piece like Lord Houghton, who was tall and handsome, could ride a horse to perfection, sit erect in a state carriage, 'kiss a regiment of women' on presentation nights, and make a good bow, was a suitable and decorative symbol of English rule. Although visitors like Princess Henry of Pless found the 'bachelor Viceroy . . . gallant and delightful and a perfect host,' he was in fact aloof in conversation and thus a difficult target even for Dublin criticism and gossip. Often commented upon throughout Houghton's career, this aloofness was perhaps developed in his extreme youth as a reaction from his father's eager and, at times, unseemly curiosity. Like the exquisite, old-fashioned manners for which he is still remembered, this aloofness also masked a very fundamental attitude towards individuals he did not know intimately—indifference:

38

I have always drawn a very clear line betweeen friends and acquaintances [he wrote many years later in a private letter] and do not trouble myself much about the characters or proceedings of the latter—within liberal limits. I don't go as far as my father did in positively *liking* the company of shady people. But I do feel that uniform respectability may become tiresome; and so may uniform agreement, so that I don't mind the acquaintance of people who may make unfair and venomous attacks, though I don't want to see much of them.

After going down to Osborne House in August to kiss hands and to be sworn of the old Queen's Privy Council, Houghton crossed to Dublin, took the oath and made his state entry into his capital, an ostentatious but not usually genial occasion. One of the Lord-Lieutenant's duties was to write personal reports to the Queen, and these, together with her terse replies and her messages sent through her Private Secretary, Sir Henry Ponsonby, form the most enlightening part of the mass of Houghton's Irish papers.

The Lord-Lieutenant's entry on Monday 3rd instant [Houghton wrote in his first semi-official despatch to the Queen, dated 6 October 1892], took place in fine weather and passed off without any special incident. The reception in the streets of Dublin was of a friendly and cordial, though not of an enthusiastic, character, accompanied by all the respect due to Your Majesty's Representative, without any of the features of a political demonstration. In fact, the good-humoured enjoyment of a pageant which is so characteristic of an Irish crowd proved too strong for the sentiment encouraged by the leaders of the Parnellite section—who are very strong in Dublin—that any recognition whatever of the Government is undesirable at the present time.

After discoursing further on the current condition of Ireland, Houghton went on to venture some favourable comment upon his Chief Secretary:

The Lord-Lieutenant cannot refrain from expressing to your Majesty his opinion that the Chief Secretary, whose assiduity and devotion to his work have been continuous, is determined to act in a spirit of moderation and justice to all parties.

His next report, explaining to the Queen that he had thought fit to reject out of hand those addresses of welcome which contained contentious or disloyal matter, ended with a reference to the 'serious condition' of Sir Bernard Burke the genealogist, one of whose sons, then aide-de-camp in waiting at Dublin Castle, had told the Lord-Lieutenant that his father was lying in a semi-conscious condition after paralysis. Always interested in serious illness Queen Victoria replied with alacrity:

The Queen thanks the Lord-Lieutenant of Ireland for his two letters and is glad to learn that the state of the Country is favourable and that the number of agrarian Outrages has not increased. The Queen fears that the weather has been un-favourable for farmers throughout the United Kingdom, but is happy to be informed that there is little fear of actual distress.

Sir Bernard Burke's works are so well known that she can well understand how much his loss will be felt.

The Lord-Lieutenant also wrote to the Queen upon the 'sinister' state of affairs in County Clare, then the worst area of the whole island for outrages, and upon the release of those imprisoned under the Balfour régime. He likewise touched early on a matter which was causing him both anxiety and surprise. Prone by temperament and by training to conceal all emotion, the young Englishman found the violence of Irish feelings, and their frank and ready manifestation, hard to understand. As a Gladstonian Liberal, he discovered that he himself and his entertainments would be boycotted both by the Unionist and the Anglo-Irish elements of Dublin society:

The Dublin season has now concluded [he wrote to the Queen on 17 March 1893], it has been marked as the Lord-Lieutenant stated to Sir Henry Ponsonby by the almost complete absence from the Castle of the landed gentry, and the partial absence of the Unionists. This, though, as the Lord Lieutenant thinks, much to be regretted, is not altogether surprising in the heated condition of party feeling.

He had already written more fully on the same puzzling subject to Sir Henry Ponsonby, pointing out that the Lord Chief Justice of Ireland had deliberately absented himself from the viceregal court and had tried to persuade all other judges to do the same:

I confess I do not understand the position taken up by these gentlemen [he wrote of the landed gentry], some of whom have told me in private that they would like to come, and think they ought to come, but that they are afraid of their followers.

Consequently with less excuse they follow the bad example set by the Nationalist party, many of whom, but for the same poor reason, would certainly pay their respects to H.M.'s representative.

Of course I make no complaint of any unwillingness to accept invitations to my parties—even the state entertainments. Those who do not wish to accept the hospitality of a political opponent must use their own discretion. Such a sentiment is happily almost outside one's English experience, but it clearly is one which people are entitled to hold. I can only say that I do not hold it myself and that I should myself be very glad to see them.

But these ladies and gentlemen could quite well have attended the Levee and the Drawing Room, and stayed away from the Dinners and Balls if their principles impelled them to do so.

I understand that those of them who are in the habit of going to London now say that it is sufficient to attend a Levee or Drawing Room there. But this is surely not the case. The ceremonies are held in Ireland for Irish people, who are expected to attend them, and attendance in London does not affect the obligation. In fact if these gentlemen's argument is sound its converse must be sound as well and one must assume they attended Lord Londonderry's and Lord Zetland's Levees not out of respect to H.M., as would be supposed, but as an act of attention to a political ally.

What I have stated as to the Levees and the absence of the landowners applies also generally to the attendance at the Drawing Room yesterday. About 580 people attended as against about 680 at Lord Zetland's last Drawing Room last year.

Ponsonby showed this letter to the Queen, whose comments are an example at once of her long experience, of her governmental technique and of her strong prejudice against her present Cabinet:

I gave your letter to the Queen [wrote Ponsonby from Osborne in February 1893], and have only just got it back with rather a mixed expression of opinion on your observations. I think Her Majesty entirely agrees with you in thinking it uncivil that the Irish Gentry should abstain from going to your Court when you are officially representing the Queen, but then she added you were a Member of Her Government and consequently a political representative, and attendance at your levees used to be considered in Ireland as a mark of support to the measures of the Government. . . . Still you appear to have had a large assemblage. I hear most pleasant accounts of the brilliance and liveliness of your entertainments and I told the Queen that they did not seem to have been affected by the non-attendance of the Unionists.

Of course it is nothing new that the opponents of the Lord-Lieutenant's policy will not go to his Court—tho' I think they are wrong. I believe Lord Normanby's levee was the smallest ever seen.

One of the Lord-Lieutenant's minor duties each Christmas-time was to order the preparation in the kitchens of Dublin Castle of a great woodcock pie sent annually to the Queen. The birds were scarce in the winter of 1892, and there was at first some anxiety that the pie would be too small; but Ponsonby wrote to say how successful it had proved, and also to answer, in an oblique manner, Houghton's queries as to what and when he was expected to write to Her Majesty: 'Does she like,' he had asked the Private Secretary, 'to receive a sort of *chronique de la quinzaine*, or *du mois*, dealing of course primarily with government matters, but also with points of general interest?' It was not an easy question to answer, for even those closest to the Queen found her often non-committal and sometimes downright enigmatic:

I gave the Queen a large letter of yours the other day [wrote Ponsonby]. She did not say anything to me about its contents—but perhaps I ought to repeat that she observed next day that she was always glad to hear from you when there was anything to report but that she trusted you did not feel bound to write periodically unless you wished to do so. This was not given as a message—but I think it as well to repeat it as it bears on your question the other day.

Writing confidential letters to the Queen about Ireland was not an easy task for Houghton, for there were many aspects of the Irish problem which Victoria steadfastly declined to contemplate. 'Irish topics have to be carefully chosen, and, so to speak, peptonized for H.M.'s consumption,' Houghton wrote in May 1895 to Rosebery, who had by then become Prime Minister:

It is surprising [the Lord-Lieutenant continued in the same letter], by the way, how outspoken the most 'loyal' Irish are on the neglect of the country by the Royal Family. There is a really deep-seated bitterness about it. When I was last at Windsor I mentioned the flourishing condition, and immense size, of the Wellingtonia which she planted during her last visit, 53 years ago; but this has been my only hint of the general sentiment. I forget if I told you of the correspondence which passed in 1893, when the Prince of Wales was anxious for the Duke and Duchess of York to come over, and was confident that he could induce The Queen to agree. However, after various appeals she told Ponsonby in so many words that no member of The Royal Family should visit Ireland so long as a Home Rule Government was in office, so the matter dropped and I suppose will not be revived while I am here.

Houghton soon found that what the Queen liked best were tit-bits of sensational information, such as the release after serving a twelve-month sentence for manslaughter of a Mrs. Montagu, who had accidentally killed one of her children by her 'strange theories of discipline.' 'The Lord-Lieutenant confesses,' he wrote to the Queen on this occasion, 'that for once he could not help wishing that the prerogative of mercy was comple-mented by the power of prolonging a sentence, it always seemed to him that twelve months was a surprisingly lenient sentence for such a crime.' He had been asked, he remarked, to shorten the sentence, and had

previously been surprised at receiving a memorial in favour of the prisoner's release, signed by the Roman Catholic Bishop and some of the clergy, on the curious grounds that she ought to be included in the family circle at Christmas, and that her husband was within two lives of the Dukedom of Manchester.

This was the kind of news that immediately stirred the Queen's interest:

The Queen was much interested [she wrote in a later reply to his report on his tour of the South] in what the Ld.-Lieutenant wrote in one of his former letters about that *horrid* Mrs. Montagu and trusts that the poor Children will be protected from their

43

dreadful Mother who does not seem to possess even the *natural maternal instincts*.

The new Lord-Lieutenant's first Dublin Christmas was made lively by a characteristic outrage, right under the Castle walls. 'The next day was Christmas,' John Morley wrote in his 1892 journal, 'and brought a painful interruption to the mood of the season. A dynamite explosion had come off at eleven the night before, close under the wall of the Castle. A constable was blown to pieces. There was an ugly *strages*, and large patches of red-black gore upon the ground—a hateful vision':

What a daring dynamite explosion! [wrote Sir Henry Ponsonby almost gleefully from Osborne]. To blow up the Detectives in full light of Electricity close to the Castle is certainly a defiant proceeding against all authority.

The dynamite desperadoes were hard to deal with or to circumvent:

And the wretched stuff is so cheap, and so easy to handle [the Lord-Lieutenant complained to Ponsonby]. In this case perhaps 1 *lb.* certainly not more than 2 *lbs.* were used—value perhaps 5/-. Yet the street was swept clear, and Jekyll heard the explosion distinctly at the Private Secretary's Lodge—a good 3 miles away.

In May of '93 another dynamite explosion occurred, shattering the windows of the Law Courts but involving no loss of life. And it was not only lawlessness, terrorism and murder with which the staid English administration at the Castle and its representatives throughout Ireland had constantly to deal, for this unpredictable and mysterious country held secrets and surprises against which it was impossible to be forewarned. Such was, for instance, the outbreak of witch-burning in Clonmel in 1894:

The Queen [she wrote from the Grand Hotel de Cimiez at Nice], has been dreadfully shocked at the account in the papers of the murder of a poor young Woman in Ireland who was *burnt* as a Witch!! She is anxious to know if the facts as given are true. If so she trusts that the murderers will be punished *with the utmost severity*. The Queen would be glad to hear from the Lord Lieutenant, will he write to her on the subject.

She was much grieved at the untimely death of the beautiful and charming Duchess of Leinster.

In reply to these enquiries the Lord-Lieutenant regretted:

to say that the statements in the newspapers as to the terrible crime committed near Clonmel in Co. Tipperary are in the main true. The young woman, aged only 27, was put to death with horrifying circumstances of cruelty, by the act or in the presence of her husband and father, and 6 or 7 other persons. The story, as reported by the police, reads like a chapter from the history of the Middle Ages. Many ancient superstitions relating to faeries, changelings, etc., are still current in Ireland, as indeed in some other parts of the United Kingdom, but that such beliefs should be acted on with so dreadful a result was a surprise to the Lord Lieutenant, as to others much better acquainted with the Irish peasantry. In this case the unhappy victim was supposed, at any rate by some of those concerned, to have been carried off by the faeries, while a spirit took possession of her mortal frame. It was supposed that this could be expelled by fire, and hence the burning to which the poor woman was subjected. Afterwards the whole party assembled for several nights at an ancient rath or camp, prepared to see her riding on a white horse, in the belief that if the reins were cut with a black-handled knife, she would return to them in her proper form.

The sad tale of the heavy Liberal defeat of 1895, which banished the disrupted party into what the late Lord Simon used to call 'the cold shades of Opposition' for a decade, is too well known for repetition here. In March 1894, after much internal friction in his Cabinet over the new naval estimates, to which he was himself obstinately opposed, Gladstone offered his resignation to the Queen. She accepted it with eagerness and, consulting no one, summoned Rosebery to take up the Premiership. Sensitive, anxious, hating criticism and afraid of failure, the new Prime Minister kept his jealous and bickering Cabinet together for a little over a year. Rosebery did not feel as whole-heartedly convinced on the Home Rule question as Gladstone had felt, for his chief interest was the reform of the House of Lords—a body which had in fact been largely responsible for the constant setbacks of Gladstone's Irish policy. In June 1895 the Government was defeated, Rosebery resigned with relief, and, during, the following election, the disintegration of the Liberal Party became public and obvious —Rosebery putting forward House of Lords reform as the main issue before the country, while Harcourt supported local option and Morley continued to emphasise Irish Home Rule. The Unionists were returned with a fat majority. The question of Irish Home Rule and Irish Land was thrust into limbo. In Dublin Houghton prepared to hand over to his Unionist successor, Lord Cadogan. On John Morley's urgent recommendation Rosebery had earlier asked the Queen to confer an earldom on Houghton, who, since his old uncle had died in January 1894, leaving him the succession to Crewe Hall and the great Crewe estates, naturally enough chose the family name and was henceforward known as the Earl of Crewe.

After his retirement from his official position Crewe put together some frank thoughts on the future of Ireland, which appeared under the title *The Outlook for Ireland* in *The North American Review* for September 1895. The article recapitulated its writer's staunch and unshakeable belief in the logic and the inevitability of Irish Home Rule. In its concluding paragraph Crewe wrote resolutely:

We believe that the great Unionist triumph neither involves any abatement of Ireland's claims, nor an abandonment of her constitutional position. 'Unfinished questions,' it has been said, 'have no pity for the repose of nations.' Not very long ago it seemed likely that the Home Rule ship might make the harbour for which she was steering, but she was swept by the gale far out into the open sea. To retrace her course she must beat painfully against the wind; but she will reach home at last.

The publication in an American periodical of so bold an article on the Irish problem by a recent Lord-Lieutenant was greeted with attention in the English and Irish press. Leading Unionist papers attacked Crewe violently; one of them, under the heading *Crewedities*, declared the article to be as inconclusive as it was ignorant, made up of nothing but 'superficial speculations.' This paper alleged that Crewe had spent three years in Dublin trying to entertain guests who would not come to his dinners and receptions, visiting Irish industries and touring the country in smiling comfort. Much though this newspaper abhorred John Morley's Irish policy, to denigrate Crewe it was forced grudgingly to admit that Morley had done all the work: 'Lord Houghton's lot in comparison with his was as the humming bird's contrasted with the earth worm's.' Liberal papers, on the other hand, found the article capital, and welcomed its declaration of faith in a cause which, just then, seemed about as forlorn as that of the Jacobites:

Lord Crewe is a man still young whose great capacity is as yet but dimly realised in this country. . . . The son of a poet and a poet himself he had long sympathised with that side of the national story which men of his class, as a rule, seem absolutely unable to understand. His robust and genuine Liberalism reinforced his poetic sympathy with the unfortunate, and made him from the first a convinced and ardent supporter of Home Rule.

Another paper drew attention to the 'unswerving loyalty and complete absence of self-seeking' which Crewe had brought to his thankless task.

Crewe's three years in Dublin had indeed been a discouraging period, for all the work which he and Morley had put into that span of time seemed, by 1895, to have been so much work thrown away. Although in the end he had learned to laugh at the boycotting of his court in Dublin (he would say it 'did not include a conspiracy to deprive the Lord-Lieutenant of the necessaries of life. It would scarcely be possible to include under that head the company of the excellent people who stayed away'), it was dispiriting to find that most of the Irishmen for whose cause he was sincerely working were in fact as sullenly hostile to the Government as the Unionists themselves. He made a note of one of Morley's comments on the Irish nation: 'Ireland would not be a difficult country to govern—were it not that all the people are intractable, and all the problems insoluble.'

'I am engrossed in the melancholy business of packing up and saying good-bye to this place, always rather a depressing affair,' Crewe wrote at the end of June 1895 to a woman friend, 'and it is raining like mad, so the outlook is not cheerful for the moment.' But, in fact, Crewe left Ireland without much regret. When he had first assumed office in the spring of 1892 he

5   47

had written to John Morley, quoting a phrase of Edmund Burke's, that on the whole he rather looked forward to 'the solemn plausibilities' of his new position. Yet three years of the elaborate official state of the viceregal court must have been wearing and tedious to a man of his retiring habits and quiet mind—for, as a later friend of Crewe's remarked, one of the most memorable things about him was the intense pleasure he derived from the simplest pastimes and the most modest pursuits.

Chapter Five

ODAY the headquarters of a chemical manufacturing concern, the great smoke-darkened, red-brick pile of Crewe Hall stands in an exposed position at one end of a long avenue on the outskirts of the industrial town and important railway junction of Crewe. The present house, as Crewe inherited it in 1894, was no longer the same 'pure and perfect specimen of Jacobean architecture' which it had been in his grandfather's day, when it was customary to compare Crewe Hall to Blickling in Norfolk. Built between the years 1615 and 1636 by a Speaker of the House of Commons, Sir Randulph Crewe, the house had undergone some renovation in the eighteenth century—when, amongst other additions, Georgian stabling was tacked on to its west side—and very extensive 'repairs' had been carried out by Hungerford, Lord Crewe, when he came into the house and estates on his father's death at Bois-l'Évêque in 1837.

'In the main,' Crewe wrote of his Uncle Hungerford's 'repairs,' in a memorandum on Crewe Hall which he drew up in the decade before the First World War, 'they must have been carried out with better taste than might have been expected from the period, not so far removed from the dreadful domestic Gothic of Horace Walpole, and impregnated with the superior, but overdecorated, ecclesiastical Gothic of the younger Pugin.' Crewe continues that, aided by Edward Blore and William Nesfield the elder, his uncle 'brought the house and its surroundings into the state which they presented up to 1866, and which they retain to me in the distinct though narrowly limited recollections of a child of eight. The entrance hall was low, there being two mezzanine bedrooms above it, named the Buff and the Blue room from the old Whig colours.'

49

In the later eighteenth century, Crewe Hall had achieved a certain fame as the scene of the cultivated Whig hospitalities of Frances Greville, daughter of Fulke Greville and wife of John, first Baron Crewe.   This beautiful and brilliant woman was much painted by Reynolds, and it was to her that Sheridan dedicated *The School for Scandal*.   Fox, Burke and Canning were among her intimate friends.   In her day Grillion was one of the French cooks employed at Crewe Hall, while the housekeeper, clearly remembered as a remarkable story-teller by Annabel Houghton, was a certain Mrs. Dickens. Lady Houghton was convinced that Mrs. Dickens was the grandmother of the novelist, but, as Crewe writes in his note on the house, 'more probably she was his great-aunt, since I remember my mother's story of her saying "many's the cuffs I've given that idle fellow John," little realising that it was Mr. Micawber that she had chastised.   The correction may have been maternal, but the tone is surely that of a collateral.'

In 1866, not long after Hungerford Crewe's repairs had been completed, Crewe Hall was burned out one winter's night. Discouraged to learn that all his precious work had been destroyed, old Edward Blore refused to undertake to build the Hall up again.   After some hesitation, Lord Crewe chose Edward Barry, the popular and successful architect of the Charing Cross Hotel.   Barry agreed to reproduce the old Hall, but, egged on by his employer, he was unable to resist enriching the whole design with a wealth of mid-Victorian detail: stone was everywhere replaced by alabaster and by marble, leaded pànes gave way to stained-glass windows showing armorial bearings, the gasoliers were made of elaborate wrought iron, and complicated designs were carried out in plasterwork. The woodwork and plasterwork of the Carved Parlour, which had been 'one of the most beautiful Jacobean rooms anywhere, both in proportion and in decoration,' was intended to be an exact copy of that which had been burned, but the heads along the cornice were made 'less grotesque' and the plasterwork itself 'more conventional'; Crewe considered that this famous room, like the others, 'suffered accordingly in effect.' Another of his uncle's innovations was 'an avenue of Wellingtonias parallel with the lime avenue along the drive to the Golden Gates.'   Crewe notes that most of these trees, planted in imitation of a similar rank at Bowood, 'fortunately died, which saved me from the onus of removing them.'

In 1679 the Crewe family, for many generations 'among the wealthiest class of country gentry,' had doubled their estates by a judiciously arranged marriage between a Crewe of Crewe and an Offley of nearby Madeley in Staffordshire. This marriage united two large landed estates in the same part of the world, and accordingly, in 1894, Crewe also inherited Madeley Manor, an agreeable house in which his mother had passed her youth. Although he did not live at Madeley, Crewe always remained fond of the old house. After his final return from Ireland in 1895 he lived chiefly at Crewe, with short periods at his Yorkshire house, Fryston Hall, where he stayed for Doncaster Race Meetings and, from time to time, entertained shooting parties. For one of these, in September 1896, the Prince of Wales, in whose small set Crewe in these years moved freely, was at Fryston, and while there he was alleged to have shot some iron railings, wounding five beaters in the face when the pellets rebounded off the fence. Commenting on this incident, which was subsequently officially denied on Rosebery's advice, the *Saint James's Gazette* reported in the fatuous tone of the moment that the beaters 'speak of being shot by the Heir Apparent to the English throne with a considerable degree of pleasure, and retain the small pellets taken from various parts of their persons as relics of the incident.' After his second marriage in 1899, Crewe only stayed once more at his father's old house, which he afterwards let. Some years later, Fryston Hall was sold and demolished. Lord Houghton's library was moved across country to Crewe, where his son made a great book-room, and where he once replied to a young guest, who commented on the extraordinary number of books in the house, that he never read a book he did not buy, nor bought a book he did not read. In London he occupied the Mayfair house he had inherited from his uncle, number 23 Hill Street, Berkeley Square.

Apart from the time taken up by the responsibilities of his possessions, and by racing and shooting, Crewe spent the last years of the century and of the old Queen's reign consolidating his position within the dishevelled Liberal Party. In spite of the disastrous defections of 1886 (which Crewe termed 'the

51

fiercest disruption of Liberalism since the French Revolution'),
the Liberals had tottered on through one more period of uncertain power—1892 to 1895—in conditions of contention and
unrest which (as we have seen in connection with Ireland)
finally blossomed during Rosebery's Premiership into open dis-
cord among the Party's leaders. On a hot evening in June,
1895, the Government was defeated in the House of Commons
on a minor division over Army Estimates. 'In haste to fling
down the reins of office' Rosebery resigned; and towards dusk on
the sultry Sunday of that week-end—a day memorable to many
people in Mayfair for the eerie effect of the Muezzin's call to
prayer which echoed out across Hyde Park from the Garden of
Dorchester House, where the Shahzada and his attendant priest
were staying—it became known that Lord Salisbury was for the
third time Prime Minister.

The General Election which followed gave the Conservatives a substantial majority. For the first time Liberal Unionists—Goschen, Sir Henry James, the Duke of Devonshire, Lord
Lansdowne and Joseph Chamberlain—entered a Conservative
Cabinet. Although these dissident Liberals claimed that their
only disagreement with the official Liberal Party was over
Irish Home Rule, Crewe shrewdly perceived that there were
other and more personal motives. 'The break-up of 1886,'
Crewe wrote half a century later, 'was not due only to mistrust
of the Home Rule Policy': he realised that the Philosophical
Radicalism voiced by John Morley during his fifteen years'
editorship of the *Fortnightly Review*, and appealing strongly to a
large section of the younger Liberals of that day, had proved
more and more suspect and detestable to 'the heirs of old-
fashioned Whiggery'—the great landowners such as the Duke
of Devonshire or Lord Lansdowne, as well as to more enlightened men like Goschen. Crewe was one of the only great
landowners in England to stand firmly by the real Liberal
Party, earning with them the welcome epithet, 'radical.'

'Liberalism has flourished when the wind is bleak,' Crewe
once declared, but even he had to admit that the outlook for
Liberalism after 1895 was cold indeed.

After the Liberal defeat of 1895 [he wrote in a reminiscent
article, *The Eclipse of Liberalism*, for the seventy-fifth issue of the

Fortnightly Review in 1940], the gloom was deepened by dissensions amongst Gladstone's successors. Morley was for hammering on with Home Rule; Harcourt for tackling the drink question; Rosebery, with greater prescience, for curbing the House of Lords. The South African War developed fresh divergencies of a more serious kind, for they involved moral principles, not mere preferences or parliamentary expedients. Then once more, *quod minime reris*, the enemy saved the situation. The sudden though not unforeseen conversion of Joseph Chamberlain to the Protectionist creed, added to dislike of the almost Prussian attitude of Balfour's Government towards the racial problem in South Africa, with memories of the Chinese Labour fiasco, drove the Liberal Party into confident reunion and obliterated all recollections of personal squabbles.'

The year 1903 proved the turning-point, for Chamberlain's open campaign for Protection—which Crewe aptly referred to in later years as 'the explosion of the Tariff Reform land-mine in 1903'—and the vacillating attitude of Balfour, who had succeeded his uncle, Salisbury, as Prime Minister the previous year, gravely disturbed the Liberal Unionist members of the Cabinet. With the exception of the Duke of Devonshire, who kept on in office for three more weeks, these ex-Liberals resigned in a body in September 1903. They began to busy themselves with the activities of the Unionist Free Trade Club, an organisa-. tion to oppose Protection which grew out of their Free Food League, formed in July of that year. But the position of the Liberal Unionists, who had now treated the Conservatives in 1903 as they had treated the true Liberals of 1886, was neither strong nor enviable. In 1886 the Conservative Party had urgently needed their support—although as Crewe many times remarked in conversation no Tory ever really trusted a Liberal Unionist. After 1903 the Liberal Opposition had closed and rallied its ranks. Liberals were increasingly conscious of popular sympathies throughout the country. Certain that the nation was behind them they could cheerfully dispense with any help from Devonshire, Goschen and their clique, aid which in any case could only imply some drag on the fine new Liberal programme. The electoral victory of 1906 showed how right the true Liberal leaders were in their assumption that both Tories and Liberal Unionists had lost the confidence of the country.

The position of Crewe during the ten years 1895 to 1905 when his party was out of office was that of Morley, Campbell-Bannerman and their followers—that is to say the radical element of the Liberal Party—rather than that of the Liberal Imperialists who were led by Asquith, Grey and Haldane, with the blessing and wayward support of Rosebery. In a memorial tribute in the House of Lords in 1945 Lord Salisbury referred to Crewe as a Whig statesman—'perhaps the last of the Whig statesmen.' The term, used no doubt in relation to Crewe's family background and possessions, courteous old-fashioned manners and general style of life, is inexact. On both sides of his family Crewe had Whig traditions, but he himself was far more of a radical than any of his forebears, his own father included. He was, for instance, infinitely more radical than Lord Rosebery.

Crewe's friendship with Rosebery was of long standing. In October 1890 on his way to stay at Dalmeny he was turned away at the station by a note announcing the sudden illness of Lady Rosebery, which ended fatally the next month. Like Crewe, Rosebery was left a widower with a family of young children. Crewe's senior by eleven years, Rosebery, as a young man had been an amused friend of Crewe's father, Lord Houghton. Crewe often stayed with him amidst the Rothschild accumulations at Mentmore, or at the Durdans at Epsom and at Dalmeny looking over the Firth, but he could not lure Rosebery to Fryston, even for Doncaster race week: 'If I go to Doncaster I shall only do so for a day to a pothouse in the town,' Rosebery replied to one of Crewe's invitations. 'The noise, stench and villainy of the town of Doncaster are essentially a part of the entertainment.' Besides politics Rosebery and Crewe had two other interests in common—racing and literature, although Rosebery confessed, when Crewe sent him his *Stray Verses* in 1891, that he 'was no judge of poetry.' 'Perhaps I do not really taste it as I ought,' wrote Rosebery, 'for it always seems to me to express either too little or too much. But I know at any rate what my imperfect palate relishes. . . . To appreciate poetry one must be in the heights rather than in the depths,' he concluded, after a reference to the inadequacy

LADY CREWE in 1900

even of *In Memoriam* to console sorrow, such as he had felt after his wife's death. As Foreign Secretary in Gladstone's last Administration Rosebery had gone to stay with Crewe in Dublin while he was Viceroy. When in 1894 he became Prime Minister he asked Crewe to send him personal letters on Irish affairs: 'I make the suggestion that when you feel disposed, or even if you don't, you should fire off a letter to me for my benefit: not as Lord-Lieutenant to First Lord, but as Irish mouse to town mouse.'

In October 1896 Rosebery had suddenly and unexpectedly announced his resignation from the Leadership of the Liberal Party. In his letter to Mr. Gladstone on the subject he characteristically questioned whether he had in fact 'ever held' this leadership. 'You have handed us over to Harcourt without escape, and you are not ignorant of all which that means,' Ripon wrote to him, and in the eyes of many other Liberals this sudden gesture seemed a species of betrayal. Crewe himself looked on this resignation, its manner, and the great speech explaining his conduct which Rosebery made at the Empire Theatre as illustrating 'some of Rosebery's strength and a touch of his weakness—the strength, the capacity for prompt action at need, and for eloquent defence of that action; the weakness, the failure to make generally clear the motives that inspired the action.' Crewe saw it also in its wider and more sinister context as the 'outward and visible demonstration of the truth long apparent to initiates, that the gulf between the two sections of the Liberal Party, roughly distinguished as Imperialists and Little Englanders, was steadily widening. As always happens in such disputes, the wildest partisan utterances were treated as confessions of faith by either hostile group.' With the South African War these differences inside the Party deepened, and in March 1902 Rosebery announced the formation of his 'Liberal League,' an organisation which Crewe did not support. 'I never joined the Liberal League,' Crewe told Alfred Spender some years later, 'and therefore Rosebery and I very seldom talked party politics.' But meanwhile, in 1899, he had developed a closer tie with Rosebery. He had become his son-in-law.

Congratulating Crewe on his election to the Jockey Club in 1895 Rosebery had described it as affording 'a refuge at Ascot from intriguing dowagers and speculative virgins.' It is indeed apparent that a wealthy and personable young widower with great possessions, rare qualities of distinction and sensibility, and a mental capacity which marked him down for high public office would be a target for many mothers with a daughter to marry. Yet for eleven years after his wife Sibyl's death Crewe remained an unconsoled widower. It was not until he was over forty that he fell in love and wished to marry again.

As a child the subject of a famous Academy picture by Sir John Millais, Lady Peggy Primrose was the second daughter of Lord Rosebery and his wife Hannah, only child and heiress of Baron Mayer de Rothschild. When Lord Crewe asked her to marry him she was eighteen and he was almost forty-one. On her eighteenth birthday, which fell on New Year's Day 1899, he sent Lady Peggy the following verses, which show no sign of the fact that he had let an interval of several years elapse without writing poetry, and which certainly rank as amongst the happiest examples of Crewe's uneven poetic talent:

> Long years ago they laughed and wrote,
>   In lyric strain and lilting measure,
> The famous lines we all misquote,
>   The shafts of wit, the songs of pleasure.
> With here and there a graver note,
>   A glimpse of life's diviner treasure.
>
> Thus beneath merriest skies of blue,
>   Long days without a tear to wet them,
> May all the years so run that you
>   Look back and smile 'Must I regret them?'
> With just a graver hour or two
>   To tell your friends you don't forget them.

When the engagement was officially announced in February 1899, just after the coming-out ball given for Crewe's eldest daughter Annabel at Crewe Hall, it caused surprise owing to the great discrepancy in age. Opposed on these grounds by the bride's grandmother, the old Duchess of Cleveland, the marriage none the less took place in Westminster Abbey on 10 April 1899, the ceremony being performed by Crewe's old friend and mentor Dr. Butler, the Master of Trinity College, Cambridge.

The amazing popularity of Lord Rosebery with the London crowd was never more impressively demonstrated than at the wedding of his younger daughter. Hours before the time fixed for the service, Parliament Square was filled with a dense mass of sightseers, the majority of them wearing real or artificial primroses which street vendors were peddling by the basketful. Boys climbed the trees and lamp-posts near the Abbey. Traffic came to a standstill; 'It was quite apparent,' ran one press report, 'that the police authorities were totally unprepared for so large an assemblage of sightseers. An attempt was made to continue vehicular traffic without interruption, but this became absolutely impracticable after a time, and buses, carts and cabs coming down Victoria Street towards Westminster were at last stopped. As the hour of half-past one approached the air became vitiated and almost suffocating in the centre of the crowd.' Inside the Abbey the crush was now 'unbearable,' and as sightseers thronged the Poets' Corner and the South Transept, occupying every nook and cranny, and clambering up beside the statesmen's statues, it seemed at one moment as though the barrier protecting the privileged guests might crack and give way. When, just as the Abbey clock struck the half-hour, Lord Rosebery and his daughter drove up in their carriage, the crowd burst into roar upon roar of cheering, 'smilingly acknowledged' by the bride as well as by her father. Women in the crowd pressed forward to get a glimpse of the wedding dress, which was embroidered in diamonds and silver-thread in a design of primroses and wheat-ears. Down the length of the choir, where seats were reserved for the Prince of Wales and the other guests, crimson cloth was spread, flanked by palms rising from banks of lilies and marguerites, 'the humbler flower,' as one newspaper kindly explained, 'in happy suggestion of the name of the bride, Margaret.' That afternoon the *Evening News* appeared printed on sheets of primrose-yellow paper.

After a honeymoon on the Italian Lakes and at Venice, Lord and Lady Crewe returned to London, where they settled into the Hill Street house Crewe had inherited from his uncle. In

1901 they bought Wharncliffe House, a metropolitan country-house still standing in Curzon Street to-day, a relic of the old Mayfair that was destroyed between the two World Wars by taxation, private cupidity, aristocratic egotism and a strange lack amongst Londoners of a collective sense of civic responsibility and historical pride. Crewe House, as it was now called, was already capacious, with several drawing-rooms, seventeen bedrooms, a courtyard, stabling and a shady garden. The main entrance, however, was at the back of the house, and approached by a narrow carriage-way winding round into the courtyard. By removing a conservatory on the Curzon Street side of the house, inserting a new front door in its place and reconstructing an old laundry and some of the stables at the back as a large new sitting-room, Lord and Lady Crewe greatly improved the property. In this house, as well as at Crewe Hall—a much more intractable proposition—Lady Crewe was for the first time able to give play to her peculiar gift for arranging houses so that they retain their own strong personality, but seem living, pleasant and happy. In the winter of 1902 to 1903 the Crewes attended Lord Curzon's great Durbar, an experience interesting and splendid in itself, but also of advantage to Crewe (who stayed longer in India than his wife) in giving him first-hand knowledge of a country for which, as Secretary of State for India, he was later responsible for five long years.

Crewe's relations with other Liberal leaders besides Rosebery were intimate. Sir William Harcourt, the son of a Canon Residentiary at York and grandson of 'the gorgeous Archbishop who reigned at Bishopthorpe for forty prosperous years,' was a member of a family with whom the Milnes of Fryston had always been on easy, neighbourly terms. Crewe was baffled by the universal dislike which Harcourt aroused amongst his contemporaries. He remembered Harcourt first as 'a notable figure with the high features and commanding stature with which a novelist might endow the representative of two ancient houses of Norman origin, by a formula which Nature is apt to ignore. Even in later years when increasing weight had blurred the fine outline of face and limb, and massive dignity had replaced active slimness, he stood out in any company with something of eighteenth-century distinction.' On 'Harcourt's alleged unpopularity,' Crewe remarked that this 'was a continual puzzle to the younger generation, especially to those who like myself had received from him nothing but pleasant hospitality and kind encouragement of our start in life.' Dismissing as 'obvious fiction' the famous story of how three friends thought it would be fun to have a dinner of six at their club, each inviting 'the most disliked person of his acquaintance' who in all three cases turned out to be Sir William Harcourt, Crewe admitted that 'there must have been grounds for inventing it.' 'He had strong dislikes,' Crewe continues, 'which he never tried to conceal, and his manner could be overbearing, stressed by his bulky presence and occasional forensic pomposity. But one would have thought that that would be condoned by his innate goodness of heart, his gift of sympathy, and his essential good humour. That this was not so will appear from the tale of his last official days.'

Crewe was amongst those who thought (as did Harcourt himself) that the then Chancellor of the Exchequer should have succeeded as Prime Minister on Gladstone's retirement in '94. The succession lay between Harcourt and Rosebery. In Crewe's opinion Harcourt's claim was plainly the stronger. Born in 1825, Harcourt was almost seventy: 'Rosebery was but forty-seven and his chance would come later;' wrote Crewe, 'a Liberal Premier would lead a miserable minority in the House of Lords; many Radicals, intent on domestic reforms, mistrusted Rosebery's Imperialism. On the other hand, the Exchequer had often been the stepping-stone to the highest place; Harcourt was known to distrust adventure abroad, and was prepared to deal drastically with the drink question. But personal preference prevailed; Harcourt's repute as a *mauvis coucheur* was fatal.' Crewe thought Harcourt inferior in political judgement to Campbell-Bannerman: 'Having known both intimately,' he wrote to Spender, 'I regard C-B. as having been gifted with a far finer political mind than Harcourt was, though the latter had to do with more exciting affairs on a bigger scale, and was probably associated with a greater number of interesting people.'

For the Liberal Party chaos had come with the fall of Rosebery's administration. Rosebery, Harcourt and Morley had each in turn resigned the leadership. Thus Campbell-Bannerman was left, in Crewe's words, 'to drive an unruly team with a light hand.' But when in 1903 Chamberlain's switch to Protection 'again transformed Liberals into a band of brothers' Crewe realised that 'C-B' was 'the ideal man for the hour.' 'History,' Crewe once announced, 'will not write Sir Henry Campbell-Bannerman's name in the very short list, headed by Sir Robert Walpole, of Prime Ministers who can justly be called great, but it deserves to stand high among the rest of his thirty predecessors in the office.' According to Crewe, 'C-B' was not psychologically equipped to understand the foibles and subtleties of some of his colleagues in the Government and the Party. 'The many-sided temperament' of Rosebery 'always baffled his direct inspection,' while 'the reticent aloofness of Grey' and the idiosyncrasies of Haldane remained to him 'rather mysterious.' With the fourth Liberal Imperialist, Asquith, Campbell-Bannerman was on more congenial terms, 'though they diverged widely at times.' In Crewe's opinion Campbell-Bannerman could neither understand nor feel strongly about the British Empire: 'He had no first-hand knowledge of the overseas world for he had never left Europe, of which he had made a leisurely 'grand tour' when he was eighteen, and his imagination never ran loose.' Crewe thought that Campbell-Bannerman, a member of a prosperous merchant family, 'shared in a degree the limitations seen in some of the nineteenth-century Liberals who were great commercial figures, especially those whose devotion inclined them to measure affairs all over the world with a British foot-rule.'

When Campbell-Bannerman took office as Prime Minister in December 1905, after difficulties made by Grey and Haldane, who, inspired by loyalty to Rosebery, would not at first join his Cabinet unless he accepted a peerage, he quickly showed an unexpected gift for that skilful political art, the management of a Cabinet. 'I cannot conceive a more capable or equable chairman of an executive committee than Sir Henry at the Cabinet,' Crewe wrote in an article in the *Manchester Guardian* in 1942; 'He encouraged general expression of opinion, but never allowed time to be wasted, showing patience without slackness. Starting as the subject of some prejudice and with only a few ardent followers, he finished with unchallenged authority and in an atmosphere of universal affection.'

Crewe was convinced that in one particular 'C–B' was singularly fortunate. 'No leading statesman of those days was so congenial to the Sovereign. The King always preferred France to Germany, and so did 'C–B', who knew the language well and whose favourite relaxation was a French novel. And, curiously enough, his limited preoccupation with the Empire was not a bar to confidence, for King Edward, while never shirking Imperial duties, was more deeply interested in the personalities and intrigues of European statesmen. And, lastly, their regular encounters at the Marienbad springs gave rare opportunities for easy intercourse in surroundings free from pomp.' Even so, the Prime Minister did not find King Edward always easy, for that monarch had inherited all Queen Victoria's meticulous attention to detail. The King was watchful and, at times, distinctly touchy:

When writing to the King a very bald account of the last Cabinet I found myself short of matter ['C–B' told Crewe in a typical letter, in July 1907] and put in a sentence about a Commission on the Universities. Tweedmouth reports to me that this has given offence (in a mild way) in the highest quarter. His name should have been introduced, and the decision should have been 'to advise H.M. to appoint. . . .' Perhaps you had better avoid my brusque style when you are interrogated.

Sir Henry Campbell-Bannerman was never one of the very restricted circle of Crewe's close political friends, but he appreciated his gifts, and his value to the Liberal Party, so that, when in December 1905 he formed his administration, Campbell-Bannerman gave to Crewe the position of Lord President of the Council. This post, which carries with it Cabinet rank, was not in those days an exacting one—'it is one of great dignity and importance' wrote a friend in a letter of congratulation; but Herbert Paul was nearer the mark when he wrote: 'My dear Crewe—I can't congratulate you on having nothing to do. But I am heartily glad that you will be in the Cabinet.' In fact Crewe found that the Lord Presidency involved 'rather more work' than was generally assumed and had the advantage of bringing its holder into 'frequent contact with the Sovereign.' Campbell-Bannerman's last act of patronage, when on his deathbed at the end of March 1908, was to offer Crewe the Garter rendered vacant by the Duke of Devonshire's recent death—'a thing,' writes Campbell-Bannerman's biographer, 'done *con amore*, for there was none of his colleagues whom he thought straighter and wiser or more helpful in council.' Crewe was deeply moved by the moribund Premier's attention:

I was inexpressibly touched to get this morning a letter from Nash with a message from CB saying he wished me to have the vacant Garter and might he send in my name for it [he wrote to his wife]. Later Nash came to see me on general business and told me that CB had hesitated for a day if he ought to make the offer, but was so anxious to do it himself that he could not resist writing. Is it not pathetically kind with a sort of personal touch which one can never forget? As a rule no name would be submitted for the moment, and I asked Nash to make it quite clear that it was only CB's illness that made him wish to do it at once.

'What I specially value,' Crewe wrote to Campbell-Bannerman, 'is the idea of receiving it from you with whom I have been so proud to be associated as follower and colleague, and for whom I have long entertained an affectionate personal regard. I am deeply sensible of your goodness in thinking of me in the illness which has been so great a sorrow to me—as to your other friends and companions in the Government.'

As a matter of fact, a stage had been reached at which poor Campbell-Bannerman's infirmities were considerably more than a sorrow to his friends and companions in the Government; they were becoming a grave constitutional inconvenience and even a potential danger to the country. To John Morley, who called on him at this time in Downing Street, Campbell-Bannerman remarked that he was resigned to his fate and had now put all political matters out of his mind—a strange condition, Morley reflected, in which to continue as Prime Minister of the United Kingdom. The King, in Biarritz, was anxious for reasons of personal convenience that 'C–B' should not be pushed into resigning at that moment; but Knollys, Crewe and Asquith were much exercised by the fact that the dying Prime

Minister seemed as incapable of resignation as he was of doing his work. 'I do not believe there has ever been such a political situation before,' Knollys wrote to Crewe. 'Lord Chatham's case when he was Prime Minister 150 years ago is the nearest approach to it;' and, again to Crewe, Knollys wrote that the Prime Minister's Private Secretary, Vaughan Nash, was 'too sensible not to realise that it would be impossible to carry on the present state of affairs much longer. The Country, the Government, & the Party would all suffer from it, and the machinery connected with the Office of Prime Minister has come to a complete standstill. The position of a Prime Minister will moreover be weakened if Asquith is not soon appointed. I quite understand Nash shrinking from saying anything to C.B. on the subject, & it is hardly his business to do so, but either the Dr. or C.B.'s sister ought to speak as soon as possible.' From Biarritz the King persistently replied to Knollys that he had no intention of returning to London for a Privy Council in the middle of April. He suggested holding one at an hotel in Paris, but against this project his advisers stood firm. In the end, after Knollys had twice more sent him messages explaining 'that the duties of the head of the Government had been in abeyance for the last 4 or 5 weeks' and that 'the leading members of the Cabinet feel it is very difficult to carry on the Government any longer under present conditions as confusion and embarrassment exist in consequence' adding that the King would be placing himself in a false position if he pressed for delay in the Prime Minister's resignation, King Edward agreed to accept it, but stipulated that Mr. Asquith must go out to Biarritz to kiss hands. This the new Prime Minister did on the sixth of April. Campbell-Bannerman died in Downing Street on the twenty-second of the same month.

Asquith returned to England with the list of proposed Cabinet changes which he had presented to the King for his approval. These changes included the promotion of young Winston Churchill to the Board of Trade from the position of Under-Secretary of State for the Colonies, a post in which his imaginative views and boisterous speeches had almost wholly overshadowed the lethargic personality of his Secretary of State, Lord Elgin; and the replacement of the latter by Lord Crewe.

6 63

Lord Elgin's tenure of the Colonial Office had been undistinguished; his part in conferences on Colonial matters was often said to consist in tugging at his beard in silence, and on one occasion when he was expected to sum up he surprised his colleagues by carefully putting the end of it into his mouth. But however detached and unemphatic as a Secretary of State, Elgin felt as sorely over his dismissal as a more positive man might have done. He refused Asquith's offer of a Marquisate, and in reply to a letter in which Crewe asked him for advice on assuming office he expressed his sense of grievance openly:

You write in terms for which I cannot but be grateful of my work in the Colonial Office. So have others. But it is forced upon me, if this is all, why cannot I continue my work? I have no answer to that question and I do not ask for one. . . .
Now having got rid of this part of the subject I turn to the Colonial Office itself. There I have absolutely no reservations. I admit at once that there are things which I should like to say to you. Curiously enough my experience goes in the opposite direction. The first executive office I held was the Office of Works, in which I succeeded Morley at the time of the 'reconstruction' of March 1886. I wrote to tell him that if he had anything to say I should be glad to see him. He appeared in mufti on his way to the station & seemed to consider it unusual to discuss matters. But I have always thought he was wrong, and I welcome the opportunity you offer.

'I am particularly glad that you take the view you do as to handing over to your successor,' was Crewe's anodyne reply. 'Indeed I had little doubt that you would do so, as it is not a personal question, but one affecting the public service.'

This was Crewe's first Secretaryship of State; a week later Lord Ripon, who was approaching eighty and was threatened by *angina pectoris*, resigned the Leadership of the House of Lords into Crewe's hands. Six months after that Crewe also succeeded Ripon as Lord Privy Seal. 'I recall with intense gratitude,' Crewe wrote of Lord Ripon, 'his unvarying kindness, his encouragement of any small success achieved by a follower, and his sagacious management of a party nominally in power but comprising only seven or eight per cent of the whole House.'

At the time of the formation of the Campbell-Bannerman

Ministry, Asquith (who constantly sought Crewe's level-headed advice, called him the 'most underrated man in England' and was always one of his most intimate friends and admirers) had told Crewe that, when Ripon resigned, Crewe's natural claims to the succession would be 'most carefully weighed.' In 1908 this promise was amply redeemed. Crewe found himself in charge of the Colonial Empire at a period of great delicacy in its history, Leader of the small and often disunited band of Government supporters in the House of Lords and holder of the ancient and honourable position of Lord Privy Seal. 'I think it must be very satisfactory to take precedence of the Duke of Norfolk,' an old and snobbish Harrow friend, G. W. E. Russell, wrote foolishly when congratulating Crewe on this last honour.

Chapter Six

For Crewe the year 1908—in which he celebrated his fiftieth birthday—was thus the threshold to a period of strenuous and responsible work which did not cease until his resignation from the Government in 1916. Secretary of State for the Colonies for two years, he then succeeded Morley at the India Office in 1910, reverting in the Cabinet reshuffle of 1915 to his old post of Lord President of the Council, and becoming, for a short time, President of the Board of Education in 1916. As Leader of the Government peers in the House of Lords throughout this period Crewe had the intricate task of directing Liberal strategy in the Upper House, and of trying to thrust reforming measures through a solidly hostile and reactionary Chamber.

A notable practitioner of what he liked to call 'the courtesy and charm which make the whole of public life run smoothly,' Crewe was easy as a colleague and friendly as a chief. As political head of a great department of state he proved himself meticulous and exacting. He expected his staff to work as hard as he worked himself, and tended to keep them at it for rather longer hours than those to which, under Lord Elgin, they had grown accustomed. Always a little distant or shy in manner, Crewe was never, on the other hand, austere or grim —'this portrait makes you look grim' his old Harrow head-master, Montagu Butler, the Master of Trinity, wrote to him at about this time, 'and "grim" you have never been for the last thirty years.' In official relations Crewe was amiable, humorous and almost invariably good-tempered. With his detachment there went that Olympian inner calm, that incapacity to be hustled or astonished which seems, as we read their Memoirs, to have marked the English statesmen of that epoch. Theirs was a leisurely and methodical existence, each working week folded between pleasant and often sumptuous country-house week-ends. It was an atmosphere in which impatient and emotional characters like Lloyd George or young Winston Churchill seemed especially noisy and disturbing. Churchill, in particular, would bombard the new head of the Colonial Office with a shower of suggestions, uninvited hints and scraps of unsolicited advice. 'A typical missive, born of froth out of foam,' Asquith once wrote to Crewe of a letter from a younger Cabinet colleague.

Crewe's reign at the Colonial Office was stamped by common sense and dignity. It was neither bold nor revolutionary, and though certain major policy decisions were taken during his two years' tenure of the office he cannot be classed among the very few great Secretaries of State who have had our very great Colonial Empire in their charge. The Colonial Office was not then considered one of the topmost prizes in the political field. The emphasis of both the Campbell-Bannerman and the Asquith administrations was on domestic reform and on maintaining a precarious equilibrium in foreign affairs. The chief imperial anxiety was the anxiety of imperial defence. In the main the vast and steaming stretches of tropical territory, the sub-continents, isthmuses and islands with which Victorian pioneers had presented their countrymen still lay undeveloped and peacefully stagnant.

Nevertheless the problems which Crewe took over from the inert hands of his predecessor, and which Elgin had himself inherited from Joseph Chamberlain and the Unionists, were manifold and complex. About some of them there clung a certain vagueness, not unlike the wispy November fog hanging about the dingy passages of the Colonial Office itself. 'Colonial ideas,' Crewe wrote to Asquith in April 1909, 'are undoubtedly not very clear and there is no complete agreement on ideas, far less on methods.' The salient problem was the union of the South African colonies. Reversing the policy of Milner and the Unionists (who maintained that he had thus allowed the fruits of the Boer War to wither), Campbell-Bannerman had boldly given the two former Dutch republics full responsible government within five years of the peace of Vereeningen. When Crewe took over at the Colonial Office an immediate union of all four provinces was already being actively discussed.

I am following with keen interest the movements for closer union in South Africa [Crewe wrote to General Botha in May 1908]. The difficulties of detail must be numerous and they must seem formidable for the moment, but they should be overcome by the steady determination which I believe exists throughout the country to obtain the great social and political benefits which may reasonably be expected to follow. You may be sure that the effort has the full sympathy of this office, and if a scheme can be carried through while the present Government is in power, nobody will be more pleased than I. As you say, one's sole regret is that Sir Henry should not have been spared to witness this crowning result of his policy.

In October of the same year a convention on union began to meet at Durban and Capetown. By February 1909 agreement on a constitution had been reached, later in that year Parliament passed an act of union and the new self-governing colony was formerly established in May of 1910. Canada, more and more restive and impatient at England's handling of Canadian foreign relations, was another country which called for Crewe's constant and diplomatic attention; while an ever-changing host of other problems—the colonisation of Rhodesia, unrest in Malta, the liquor traffic in Southern Nigeria, fruit development in Jamaica, the seduction of native women by troops in East Africa—called for notice or decision. British opinion on most of these questions was as languid as it has always been on imperial or colonial matters. Only when some sensational subject was exploited by the newspapers did public attention swivel to focus fleetingly on some distant region of the far-flung Empire. The most famous of these bogies, and one which the Liberals had themselves deliberately roused during the 1906 election but which they had since been unable to exorcise, was already hovering in wait for Crewe beside his massive desk. This was the 'Chinese Slavery' question. Crewe's level-headed and sensible attitude to this matter may serve us as a characteristic example of all his Colonial Office work.

The importation of cheap coolie labour to supplement that of the coloured workers in the mines of the Transvaal had been one of Milner's many schemes for increasing the productivity of that area. The Chinese Labour Ordinance, passed in 1904 amidst scenes of unparalleled uproar in both Houses, permitted the importation of this labour. Although Milner said that Asquith, Grey and Haldane had promised him their support in this matter, the whole Liberal Party took up the cry at the 1906 election; 'sandwich-men masquerading as Chinese slaves' marched the streets, and the issue, like its companion war-cry of 'the Big Loaf and the Little Loaf,' proved a popular one, simple to state and easy for even cretins to understand. Once the Liberals had reached power they found that they could not just put the clock back over Chinese Slavery; they could not terminate the Chinamen's contracts and ship them all home in a few weeks. They had in fact to pass an act continuing the system for another four years, although no further contracts were permitted to be made. The contracts already signed remained legally valid, and it was under these that a limited number of Chinese coolies were still entering South Africa, although at home a Liberal Government was in power. At this point Unionists themselves took up the Chinese Slavery cry, accusing the new Government of falsehood and hypocrisy. Many letters were published in the press, and the Secretary of State for the Colonies had on occasion to issue explanations that the only coolies imported were those contracted for during the Conservative Administrations:

We shall probably continue to maintain our respective opinions [Crewe wrote to a violent Conservative ex-Member of Parliament, Colonel Bromley-Davenport, who had attacked the Government on this issue both in speech and in print]. I certainly still think that it was impossible for any Government to cancel these contracts without compensation whatever may have been the opinion of the legal authorities on whom you rely. It was equally impossible to cancel them with compensation, unless we were prepared to take action against the Chinese already on the Witwatersrand. The contract not the whereabouts of the coolie at the moment, seemed to us to be the governing factor, a view which I should have expected would commend itself to a member of the Conservative party.

What we were morally bound to do, having regard to our declarations before the General Election, is a matter for the judgement of the public, rather than for that of political partisans. There is no ground for supposing that the Electors were not perfectly well informed as to the conditions under which the Chinese labour was being carried on, and the precise degree in which these conditions were incompatible with a proper system of indentured employment. The actual conditions were described in a thousand speeches, and the country gave a decisive verdict that it desired the system to be brought to a close. It is being brought to a close, as it ought to be, with as little dislocation as possible of the industry, and with the concurrence of those who are best able to speak for the mining interests. So that we are perfectly satisfied with the result of our action.

Another part of Crewe's work as Secretary of State for the Colonies was the appointment of Governors for our overseas possessions. Much of this was routine work and went with mechanical smoothness, being determined by seniority in the service, but certain cases, such as the selection of Herbert Gladstone to be the first Governor-General of South Africa, needed much thought, and over such cases Crewe was in frequent consultation with the Prime Minister. Moreover the old Victorian idea of patronage was still stubbornly alive, and much of Crewe's daily correspondence consisted of letters from persons—retired generals or admirals, ungifted and unsuccessful peers—who either thought themselves ideally suited to go out and govern a Province of Australia, or else felt certain Crewe would like to appoint a son, a brother or a cousin of their own. The most shameless wrote to Crewe direct, others chose some intermediary of standing in the Liberal Party. To all these postulants Crewe replied courteously, usually in his own hand. Sometimes the King himself made a suggestion for a Governorship, and on rare occasions he would demur to some appointment urged by Crewe and the Prime Minister, or to some such project as the allocation of a barony to the next Governor of New Zealand, which he personally considered premature.

King Edward did not take the vivid interest in colonial affairs with which he watched developments in Europe, nor did he like receiving Colonial Governors as much as Ambassadors or foreign royalties. Governors, in any case, were becoming too mobile:

H.M. is willing to receive any Governors whom Lord Crewe may recommend him seeing [wrote Lord Knollys, the King's Private Secretary in June 1909], but he thinks the line ought to be drawn there as so many Governors now come to England. With respect to Sir Ralph Williams, H.M. says he has no acquaintance with him and he hardly thinks it necessary therefore that he should receive him especially as he is only the Governor of a small Colony.

Suggestions that Colonial officials should track him down in Biarritz were also most unwelcome:

I have been trying to induce the King to see Sir F. Darley [the Governor of Trinidad], and no doubt he will do so before he leaves [Ponsonby wrote from Biarritz in the Spring of 1909], but he is afraid that if it turns out that distinguished men can always see him if they come out here, he may be besieged by all sorts and conditions of men.

In June 1908 the King gave his grudging consent to Crewe's earnest request that a special stand for the accommodation of Colonial visitors should be put up in the Horse Guards parade for the annual Trooping the Colour on the King's birthday:

I quite appreciate His Majesty's point of view in the matter [Crewe had written to Knollys when submitting this request], but I should be pleased for an exception in the case of the Colonists—knowing how extraordinarily strong the feeling amongst them is. It really is not, with them, the question of a spectacle, fine though the spectacle is; but they like the idea of being present when the King is engaged in a Birthday ceremony, and go back to their own part of the Empire with a strengthened sense of the Sovereign's position as its Head. Their disappointment is acute in proportion when they find that only a mere handful can attend. I hope therefore that His Majesty may be pleased at any rate not to dismiss the idea without consideration. I have had so much evidence before me of the strength of the Colonial feeling that I cannot but feel concerned in the matter, and it appears that there is great difficulty in finding accommodation by any other means.

King Edward was not deeply touched by this evidence of colonial loyalty, and gave his consent with an ill grace:

The King . . . desires me to say that he agrees very unwillingly and for this year only to what he considers is the unreasonable demand of the Colonials that a stand should be erected for them. . . . H.M. thinks that the stand should be available for bona fide Colonials only and that they should not have the power of bringing their friends with them.

In all his dealings with the King, Crewe, like Asquith, was infinitely helped by the good offices of Francis Knollys, a convinced and enlightened Liberal who had the royal ear, and whose ability was much above that usual in courtiers.

Ever since the days when he used to shoot at Fryston, King Edward had liked Crewe personally, for they had one passion in common—racing. On one or two occasions the King and Queen actually dined at Crewe House, while Crewe was often at Windsor and Balmoral. The King did not, of course, feel any sympathy for Crewe's politics. Although he had many Liberal friends, such as Knollys, Crewe and Campbell-Bannerman, and could respect such a man as John Burns, King Edward was fundamentally as reactionary as his mother had been—a somewhat natural tendency in monarchs. King Edward would sometimes use Crewe when he wished to express disapproval to the Cabinet of the actions or speeches of one of its members. In July 1909 Lloyd George, then Chancellor of the Exchequer, delivered at the Edinburgh Castle, Limehouse, the famous speech in which he referred to London landlords as blackmailers, and spoke scornfully and humorously of 'the Dukes who harass us.' This created one of the greatest political sensations of the epoch, and aroused the Unionists to frenzy. On 2 August 1909, the second day following the speech, Crewe received a letter from Knollys, who was with the King at Cowes. 'I have purposely,' the King's Private Secretary pointed out, 'not marked my letter *Private*':

I tell you a great deal, & I think I had better mention that the King is so seriously annoyed with L. George's Limehouse speech, that when he sees Asquith tomorrow he intends to speak very strongly to him on the subject, & will probably say that if he does not receive an assurance from him (Asquith) that he will do his utmost to prevent L. George from using such language again, he shall have to consider whether it will not be his duty to write a letter to be read at the Cabinet.

The King thinks he ought to protest in the most vigorous

terms against one of his principal Ministers making such a speech & putting himself almost on a level with Grayson; one full of false statements, of socialism in its worst & most insidious form & of virulent abuse against one particular class, which can only have the effect of setting 'class' against 'class' & of stirring up the worst passions of his audience. It is hardly necessary perhaps to allude to its gross vulgarity.

The King cannot understand how Asquith can tacitly allow certain of his colleagues to make speeches that would not have been tolerated by any Prime Minister until within the last few years, which H.M. regards as being in the highest degree improper & which he almost looks upon as being an insult to the Sovereign when delivered by one of his 'confidential Servants'.

Crewe sat down and wrote two letters; the first a reply to Lord Knollys, the second a note to Mr. Asquith. Both show Crewe's moderation, Liberalism and diplomacy at their best. 'My dear Asquith,' he wrote to the Prime Minister:

I received last night a very strongly worded letter from Knollys conveying, evidently in the King's own terms, a severe condemnation of Lloyd George's Limehouse speech, and telling me the substance of what H.M. intends to say to you on the subject. I have returned as soothing a reply as I could.

Excellent and pointed as the speech was, I personally think all such utterances by Ministers a mistake, as they lose more by alarming the wavering people who might support us than they gain by inspiring those already convinced. Bread, I think, is a better political diet than brandy. In this case L.G. could have produced all his telling instances, and have got as much assent if fewer cheers, if he had attacked the system instead of the persons who profit by it.

As I have said to Knollys, the example of this sort of speaking was first set by Chamberlain, & it succeeds so well at the moment that some of those who shine on the platform cannot resist the temptation of adopting it. I hope you will succeed in somewhat mollifying the King, as it is vexatious that he should be out of touch with the Government & actively hostile to particular Ministers.

To Knollys—that is to say in fact to the King himself—Crewe wrote as follows:

... I need not tell you how distressed I am that the King

73

should take so serious a view of this speech by one of His
Majesty's Ministers and a colleague of my own. I had only
glanced at the speech before, but read it carefully after receiving
your letter.

The observations I venture to make on it are these. I have
always deprecated and disapproved of the class of speech to
which this belongs, by whomever made. I mean *unministerial*
speeches, if one may use the phrase, made by a Minister—
speeches, that is to say, which indicate little sense of collective
responsibility, but simply display the mind of the individual
addressing the audience of the moment. The fashion of
making speeches of this sort was originally set by Chamberlain,
and it has been followed ever since by other politicians of the
same type. To them the temptations of the platform are very
strong, and responsible speech seems to them dull, though there
are plenty of instances, past and present, to show that it need
not be.

As regards this particular case, Lloyd George left the right
line of argument, as it seems to me, by assailing a class of
persons instead of the system which he is engaged in trying to
modify. I don't defend this from any point of view or the
manner in which the attack was made. But I cannot see that
the statements of fact which he made were false, though some
of his inferences may, as is usual with inferences, be open to
question; and it is really only fair to remember that both he
and the Government generally have been the target for any
number of random charges of brigandage and the like, and that
their proposals have been distorted and misrepresented with
little scruple, by some of their opponents. To say nothing of
the manner in which they have been openly threatened with
the possible action of the House of Lords.

I have no doubt that the Prime Minister will do everything
in his power to urge his colleagues to refrain from giving unnecessary provocation on this subject, which arouses very warm
emotions and is liable to be treated with exaggerated colour on
both sides. He, I am certain, will regret most deeply that the
King considers that there is cause to complain of anything said
or done during this Administration, the members of which, I
am sure without exception, would desire to show the utmost
regard to His Majesty's feelings and wishes. I need not say
that my own devotion to H.M., personal no less than official,
renders me peculiarly anxious in this respect.

The frank tone of this letter seems to have annoyed the King still further. 'I have submitted to the King your letter of yesterday,' wrote Knollys in one of the shortest notes he ever sent Crewe, 'and he desires me to express his disappointment with it. His Majesty directs me to add that he regrets that his relations with some of the members of the present Cabinet should be increasingly the reverse of harmonious.' Crewe's point of view on most political subjects, notably House of Lords Reform and the abolition of the veto, mystified and vexed King Edward.

In June 1908 the King and Queen had paid a state visit to the Czar and the Czarina at Reval on the Baltic. Much enjoyed by the royalties concerned, this exchange of compliments had been politically as ineffective as the majority of the royal journeys about Europe which King Edward loved to make, and which led continentals to believe that the royal hand was at the helm of British foreign policy no matter which party was in power. To offset the bad effect in Germany of this Russian visit, as well as to please the Kaiser, who complained that the King had visited Paris, Brussels, Rome, Vienna, Copenhagen, Stockholm and Christiania but never Berlin, it was arranged that in February 1909 the King and Queen should pay a state visit to the German Emperor. This was King Edward's last state visit to a foreign crowned head. The royal suite included Lord Grenfell, representing the British Army, and Sir Frederick Ponsonby, the King's Assistant Private Secretary, both of whom have left vivid accounts of the Berlin visit in their Memoirs. As Minister-in-Attendance the King selected Crewe, an admirable choice since he spoke German, looked distinguished, and cut exactly the kind of figure likely to impress the staid and critical Imperial court. Crewe had never served as Minister-in-Attendance before this, nor did he ever do so again, although he often stayed at Windsor and Balmoral with King Edward and with King George V. The three-day programme was heavy, and the work devolving on him was likely to be considerable and tedious. 'The King told me of his intention to ask you to go with him to Berlin,' Asquith wrote to Crewe. 'Both Grey and I think that he could not have chosen better and that you ought to go.'

The royal party crossed the Channel to Calais on 8 February

in the royal yacht *Alexandra*. The visit, which was marred by
the King's wretched health and (one of its effects) his new
tendency to fall fast asleep at official luncheons and dinners
and even at the Gala performance of *Sardanapalus* at the Berlin
Opera House, began inauspiciously with what Lord Grenfell
calls 'a contretemps.' 'The King was much excited,' Lord
Grenfell continues, 'at seeing the Royal Standard flying on the
flagstaff at Dover Castle, the regulation being that only one
Royal Standard should ever be seen, and that only above the
house, public buildings or ship actually occupied by the King.
It had been hoisted when the King stepped on to the royal
yacht. He desired me to report the error, which I did, by
telegram to the General Commanding at Dover and by letter
to the War Office.'

Further minor incidents increased the comparative dis-
comfort of the journey—the train lurched so violently that a
footman spilled a plate of quails over Queen Alexandra, and,
later in the same meal, the claret fell over and flooded the
table; at Rathenau on the Brandenburg frontier the King's
valet had mistaken the time, and the King, dressed as a German
Field-Marshal, was late inspecting the Guard of Honour; at
Berlin he did not step out of the carriage from which he was
expected to alight, so that the whole Imperial family had to
race along the station in an undignified way; and during the
carriage procession through Berlin the horses drawing the
Queen and Empress jibbed at the cheering of the crowds and
refused to budge, making necessary the transfer of these
ladies to another carriage. 'Even in efficient Germany
intentions and results are not always equal,' the English Princess
of Pless triumphantly confided to her diary.

Suspicious of his nephew's foreign policy, disquieted by
Germany's military and naval programme, often out of breath
and sometimes in such pain that he could hardly walk upstairs,
King Edward was in no optimistic mood and expected few
results from this exacting state visit. 'Friendly and courteous
to all who met him,' the King on the second day won the
Berliners' hearts by a short speech outside the Rathaus, but he
was not well enough to go to Potsdam, and Crewe had to com-
pose a letter of regrets to the Burgomaster of that town.
Indeed in Berlin King Edward, who had only just over one

year more to live, seemed to some of the Englishmen who saw him an object for compassion: 'A *cercle* afterwards,' a young member of the British Ambassador's staff records, 'the King looking very seedy, poor old dear.' At one moment, indeed, the visit seemed likely to end fatally; for sitting on a low sofa after a luncheon at the British Embassy, talking to the Princess of Pless, King Edward, who was smoking in spite of his cough, suddenly fell back in a choking fit, went white in the face and seemed about to die. He had for some years been liable to these attacks, but this was the worst of them that he had so far endured. Certain of his courtiers and physicians were afterwards persuaded that it had hastened his death. The weather of the last two days of the three-day visit proved inclement. The party left Berlin on 12 February. On the arrival of the *Alexandra* at Dover, Grenfell saw to his horror that the Royal Standard was once again fluttering proudly above the kingless castle. King Edward, however, was writing in his cabin; and it was possible to signal for the Standard's removal before he came lumbering out on to the deck. For Crewe, to whom the brazenly military tone then prevalent at the German court cannot have appealed strongly, the Berlin visit was a spectacular rather than a sympathetic experience. After the outbreak of war he recalled that, during the State Ball, the Kaiser had summoned Crewe and Hardinge to discourse to them at some length upon the Germans' love of uniforms and on how odd it was that the British not only did not share but positively misunderstood this passion.

The last year of King Edward's life was shrouded in a close twilight of anxiety. In Sir Harold Nicolson's words the King 'in the final phase was a perplexed and apprehensive man.' From abroad his country was menaced by German military and naval power, and by the Kaiser's dangerous and unpredictable intentions. In home politics anxiety at the now total deadlock between the two Houses of Parliament gnawed at the King's mind night and day. After much reflection—he had hitherto refrained from direct intervention which he held would be unconstitutional on his part—King Edward formed a private plan to solve the deadlock. He decided to reveal it to the Government; and for this purpose he chose Crewe rather than Asquith as his confidant. One evening after an all-male dinner-party at Windsor in the week following the General Election of January 1910 (which had returned the Liberals with a diminished majority) the King drew Crewe aside and spoke frankly to him of the concern he felt at the mutual hatred growing up between the House of Lords and the House of Commons. He then put to Crewe his own tentative solution, explaining that he thought it wiser to accept the House of Lords as it was, making use of all the good elements in it, rather than to create an entirely new Second Chamber. Under his scheme every existing peer would retain his seat and his right to speak, but only one hundred peers, fifty a side, would have the right to vote on any measure. In the King's view there was a great body of moderate independent opinion in the Upper House which would thus still be voiced and which would influence open-minded men amongst the chosen hundred to vote according to reason rather than on a party line. Crewe sensibly riposted that the Leaders of each party might tend to choose nonentities on whom they could rely to vote under a whip, however many independent peers they had heard speak. And what of such brilliant, non-party men as the then Archbishop of Canterbury and Lord Rosebery? Would they not fall between two stools and be omitted from both executive lists? The King felt the bite of Crewe's argument but asked him to consider the proposal carefully. He would send for him later in the year to discuss it again. 'During the conversation I had with His Majesty', Crewe wrote in a memorandum of this talk, 'I was impressed by his shrewd appreciation of the difficulties surrounding the creation of a new Second Chamber.'

The further conference which the King proposed to Crewe did not take place, for later in that year King Edward was lying in his coffin in the vault of the chapel at Windsor, whilst his inexperienced son was anxiously facing one of the most threatening constitutional crises with which any occupant of the English throne has had to deal.

While he did not agree with King Edward's own proposals for solving the House of Lords deadlock, Crewe inclined to believe that had the old King lived the whole question might have been settled more amicably. Replying to Lord Halifax, who wrote to him after reading Spender's *Life of Asquith* in March 1933, confessing that he was 'at a loss to understand

why, in view of general peace and goodwill, the matter might
not have been settled by the personal intervention of the King,
which would surely have done all that was required and
avoided any amount of ill-blood,' Crewe affirmed that:

Nothing could have been more sensible and straightforward
than the King's action at the time of the Parliament Bill, but I
have always felt that if King Edward had been there things
might have been settled as you describe, because of his extraordinary prestige with both parties, and the sense of reasonable
compromise which he never lost.

King Edward's sudden, short illness in the first week of May
1910 took the public by surprise, but did not astonish those
nearest to the Court, who had been observing his decline.   On
the sixth of May the King died.   In her diary for that day Mrs.
Asquith set down an incident at the house of Mrs. George
Cornwallis-West, where she had dined that evening in the
company of her hostess's son, Winston Churchill, the Crewes
and the Harcourts: 'At the end of dinner Winston said: "Let
us drink to the health of the new King."   To which Lord Crewe
answered: "Rather to the memory of the old."'
On the day of the King's funeral Lady Crewe and Mrs.
Asquith were the only women inside Westminster Hall as the
funeral cortège moved out into the sunshine of Parliament
Square.   As it left, Crewe stooped to give a pat to Caesar, the
King's wire-haired terrier, led on a leash by a kilted loader
from Balmoral.
Official history and strict chronology claim the year 1910 as
marking the close of the Edwardian age.   In fact the sentiments, habits, ways of life and thought of that epoch overlapped
into the vortex of the First World War and lingered in quiet
pools and backwaters until the Second.   Superficially secure
and sunny with gaiety, the period had a strong, ominous under-
tow recognised only by those most nearly concerned with
foreign and colonial affairs and not even by all of these.   An
epoch now remembered by some people for the wealth of life
and apparent happiness of the ruling class in England, the
Edwardian age seemed to many who lived through it what we
know it to have been—revolutionary in a humanitarian sense,
and thus passionately exciting.   'I listened to you with much

7   79

interest in the Lords' Debate,' a woman friend wrote to Crewe of one of his speeches during the controversy on the Education Bill. 'Whatever rude remarks History may make upon us hereafter she will have to own that we have achieved some stirring times.'

Chapter Seven

THE character of King Edward VII had been positive and very robust. Both those who had personally liked the late King and those who had not were astonished to observe what a vehement change in the feel of public and courtly life his death had made. Crewe himself had admired the King—'so much kingly dignity,' he once wrote, 'humanised by so much individual geniality, and quickened by such shrewd appreciation of European politics, had never yet adorned the throne of England'—and in common with others who had had close dealings with that monarch during his reign he missed King Edward: 'As in all the places where one saw him often,' he wrote from Rufford Abbey during Doncaster Race Meeting the year after the King's death, 'the lack of his presence and voice gives a sense of strangeness.' 'Having been for a number of years King Edward's guest for this week,' he wrote again, from Windsor Castle, in Ascot week 1911, 'I found it hard to figure it going on without that intense and commanding personality. The impression of his absence was indeed much stronger than it was when I was staying here for the first time last January.' There was altogether less nervous tension about the new régime. 'H.M. does not, at any rate ostensibly, insist so strongly as his Father did on being kept informed in good time,' Crewe wrote to the Viceroy of India over a trivial fragment of Durbar news accidentally released to Reuters before the King had been told of it: 'King Edward would have given you and me a good dressing-down if it had occurred in his life.' On the other hand King George V was, if possible, an even greater stickler in the matter of clothes and uniforms than his father had been. 'By the way,' Lady Crewe had written to her husband soon after he had become Lord President in 1905, 'Papa asked me to tell you that the Prince of Wales is horrified at your always appearing in a short coat in the House of Lords.'

By contrast with his father and his grandmother the new King seemed an enigma to men who had been in public life in the last two reigns, and who had been in the habit of seeing their monarch regularly. A modest and sensible and unassuming man of forty-five, who drank whisky with his meals, liked cocoa and made his own early morning tea, his was the supreme enigma of the commonplace. Neither Queen Victoria nor King Edward had ever appeared to resemble anybody else. Neither had seemed an ordinary mortal nor in the.least like any of their subjects in any walk of life. King George V, on the other hand, was every man. He was the epitome of those qualities and tastes, habits, aspirations and points of view which represent the level ideal of the average English family-in-the-street. This unusual gift of being almost indistinguishable from the great majority of his countrymen enabled George V, by the exercise of a sound British common sense, to navigate safely through the many crises of his long and dangerous reign, and to emerge towards the end of it as the object of a popular affection deeper and fonder than any which had cushioned Queen Victoria or King Edward. It was King George who set the simple, down-to-earth pattern which the British monarchy has followed since.

At first, of course, the new King had to sustain the curious scrutiny of his father's Ministers and entourage. The comparison of his plain, marine nature with his father's genial, cosmopolitan and flamboyant personality aroused inevitable doubts. How did he size up to the King who was dead? 'I do not believe he is at all nervous, though he may not have his Father's marvellous physical indifference to danger,' Crewe wrote when the subject of police precautions during the Indian tour of 1912 was being discussed; or, again, 'He has not got his father's marvellous staying power and indifference to fatigue, and he *looks* tired when he feels tired.' Equally the new King and Queen's demeanour during the Coronation ceremony could be contrasted with that of King Edward and Queen Alexandra: 'The principal personages have got well through their task, with a shade too much of gravity, if one had to ·be captious, but with a full measure of dignity and no aloofness,'

Crewe wrote of the ceremony in which he had participated as one of the four supporters of the canopy: 'In the point of actual manner and bearing we have been somewhat spoiled by the consummate perfection of the last reign, but taking the situation *simpliciter* I do not believe there is a pair in Europe who would have passed through a series of ceremonies so adequately.'

At the opening of his reign King George had to contend with grave constitutional difficulties on the one hand, and with his own lack of experience on the other. In after years he taxed Crewe with having 'taken advantage' of his inexperience over the Parliament Bill guarantee on the creation of new peers; and it has indeed been shown that for many weeks the King could not make up his own mind upon this harrowing and obsessive subject. Like other persons thrust suddenly into positions of great responsibility, the King at first tended to hold out obstinately over small points of detail, and to get the proportions of large questions out of true. He also asked a good deal of advice from a large number of people—in Crewe's opinion he began by consulting too many extraneous people, while Lord Knollys, finding that the pivotal position he had occupied during King Edward's reign had passed to Sir Arthur Bigge, later Lord Stamfordham, in the end resigned.

Crewe soon had ample opportunities to study the workings of the new King's mind, for in September 1910 Asquith asked him to give up the Colonial Office and become Secretary of State for India. This meant that Crewe was closely concerned with the planning of the Delhi Durbar, in which the King took the most detailed interest, and that he accompanied the King and Queen to India for it in 1911. In order to get some idea of the work which preoccupied Crewe for the first five years of the new reign—from his acceptance of the India Office in September 1910 to his resignation of it when the first war-time Coalition Government was formed in May 1915 —it will be necessary to recall briefly the history of Liberal policy on India since the Liberal victory of January 1906.

When the Liberals came into power the Indian situation was causing increasing concern, and, like South Africa and many other parts of the Empire, the sub-continent was high up on the Liberal Party's ambitious programme of reforms. 'The danger,' wrote John Morley in his *Recollections*, 'arose from a mutiny, not of Sepoys about greased cartridges, but of educated men armed with modern ideas supplied from the noblest arsenals and proudest trophies of English literature and English oratory.' Campbell-Bannerman had formed his administration slowly and thoughtfully: 'We came down in the King's train today,' Lady Crewe had told her father in December 1905. 'He told us that he had seen C.B., who meant to take as long as possible making up his Cabinet, as every minister will have to be re-elected, so it will mean practically two elections straight off.' In the end, after much thought, the Prime Minister gave the India Office to John Morley, whose reign there is known in Anglo-Indian history as the period of the Morley-Minto reforms.

The shimmering but embarrassed viceroyalty of Lord Curzon, which Lord and Lady Crewe had experienced at first hand during their visit to his Durbar in 1903, had ended in the Viceroy's resignation; his successor, Lord Minto, had reached India just before the new Liberal Government had come into power. Bent on inaugurating reforms calculated to associate Indians in at least some slight degree with their own civil administration and government, Morley thus found himself with a Unionist Viceroy on his hands. But by good luck Lord Minto, although a man who would never have achieved high office had it not been for his birth and position, and who had just completed a successful term as Governor-General in Canada, was as set on Indian reforms as was Morley himself, and indeed later claimed that it was he who inaugurated the programme of 1909 which goes by their joint names. For five years the Secretary of State and the Viceroy worked in almost total harmony, corresponding with each other voluminously, and constantly taking decisions without reference to their respective staffs. One result of this correspondence and of Minto's anxiety to get on well with Morley was that the powers of the Secretary of State in London increased gradually but imperceptibly, so that by the end of Minto's rule the Secretary of State for India had more control over Indian affairs than had ever been the case before. After the promulgation of the 1909 reforms Lord Minto made it clear that he wished to leave India, and the problem of finding his successor arose.

This was a matter which had perplexed Edward VII, Asquith and Morley. Fairly authoritative gossip was whispering that the position of Viceroy was likely to be offered to Lord Crewe: the offer was never made, nor would he unhesitatingly have accepted it, for a long sojourn in India could not have suited his uncertain health. The strongest candidate was Kitchener, who in conversation with Haldane had 'expressed his *firm expectation*' of being offered the viceroyalty 'with perfect frankness.' King Edward had strongly pressed Kitchener's claims: in May 1909 Morley described the atmosphere 'in high quarters' as 'almost *torrid*' in favour of Kitchener, while in a conversation which he had with the King at Balmoral in October of the same year, and which dealt with a complicated royal project for sending the Duke of Connaught to Ireland and moving the then Lord-Lieutenant, Lord Aberdeen, to South Africa 'to get him out of the way,' Mr. Asquith found King Edward 'still anxious that Kitchener should be the next Viceroy of India.' Asquith and several other members of the Cabinet tended to favour Kitchener's appointment, but in Morley's view it could only arouse Indian suspicions to follow up the mild reform programme of 1909 by the appointment of a notoriously autocratic soldier, a strong man of Empire. Although it did not directly concern the Colonial Office, Crewe, who admired Kitchener's 'remarkable savoir faire,' had had many consultations with Asquith on the subject.

In the event Sir Charles Hardinge, who had accompanied King Edward to Berlin in 1909, was appointed. Newly ennobled as Lord Hardinge of Penshurst, he set off in November 1910. No sooner was this problem settled than Mr. Asquith was faced with a new one: John Morley impulsively declared that the change in Viceroys provided an admirable opportunity for himself to resign his Cabinet job and retire into private life.

My dear Crewe [wrote Mr. Asquith on 14 September 1910] ... here are two problems of a personal kind which require consideration. [The first dealt with making Rufus Isaacs Attorney-General and Simon Solicitor-General; the second was as Mr. Asquith emphasised, 'more serious.']
I have a letter to-day from J. Morley announcing his determination to be relieved of India—on grounds of age, weariness,

advent of a new Viceroy, etc. I shall, of course, ask him to reconsider, but I don't think he will do so; and his place will have to be filled before the opening of the adjourned session.

It is a grave matter in the present condition of India & among our colleagues (& outside) I know of no one but yourself who is *par tantis negotiis*.

Are you disposed to migrate thither?

It is a big & thankless task.

And if you were willing to undertake it, who is then to succeed you at the C.O.—*I know of no one.*

Will you revolve the matter in your mind in your present seclusion and give me the benefit of your thoughts?

I don't think it is necessary or expedient at the moment to speak to the King. J.M.'s letter is strictly private, & I have not said anything about it to any other colleague.

Use your own discretion as to confiding the matter to F. Knollys.

No sooner had Crewe replied to Asquith, and Asquith to Morley, than the last began to hesitate: 'The enclosed highly characteristic document (which please return) absolves us from the necessity of considering an immediate change,' the Prime Minister wrote to Crewe on 22 September. After several weeks of negotiation, Morley allowed himself to be persuaded to remain in the Cabinet as Lord Privy Seal, an office which Crewe vacated for his benefit. It is clear from Mr. Asquith's letters that it had never crossed Morley's mind that his resignation would actually be accepted. The version given in Lord Esher's *Journals*, dated October 1910, thus seems, in the light of these letters, to be substantially correct:

John Morley told me yesterday of his resignation. The truth is that he has been caught this time. Sore at not being asked to Balmoral, inclined to think that he was not being treated with consideration, he wrote to the Prime Minister saying that he was tired out and unable to go on. He did not receive from Asquith the sort of letter he expected, and after a delay, during which he expected *de se faire prier*, he reiterated his wish to retire. He was taken at his word.

Crewe took over the India Office in the first week of November 1910, his first letter to the Viceroy being dated 11 November, a few days after the departure of Lord and Lady Hardinge of Penshurst for the East. In having Hardinge as Viceroy

Crewe was not perhaps so fortunate as Morley had been in Minto. He had known 'Charlie Hardinge' for forty years— they had been at Harrow together—and was much attached to him, but Hardinge, who had begun his career in the diplomatic service, lacked Minto's enterprise, and was in every way a more conventional and less imaginative man, whose career had been architected by his charming and energetic wife. The bulky correspondence between Crewe and Hardinge lacks the glint of Morley's correspondence with Minto.

Amongst the many congratulatory letters Crewe received on his new office was one from the penultimate Viceroy, Lord Curzon. Like certain other people, Curzon had thought Crewe might himself have made an ideal Governor-General:

My dear Bob, I am moving homewards from a little continental journey [Curzon wrote urbanely from the Ritz in Paris] which has been enlivened by exciting telegrams from England none among them so pleasant as the announcement that J.M. having decided to go—and for him I feel the warmest and deepest regard—his place at I.O. is to be taken by you.

As you were not to be Viceroy—a potentiality that we once discussed—I am truly glad that you are to preside at the Office here, for no one knows better than yourself the combined responsibilities and perils of the task. Maybe it will sometimes bring us into contact—never I hope into collision.

I daresay you will occasionally allow me to say or write a thing or two to you about a country and subject to which I gave all the best of my life.

The Morley-Minto Reforms of 1909 had introduced representative institutions to India on a small and deceptive scale. Neither the Unionist Viceroy nor the Liberal Secretary of State had intended them as a prelude to Parliamentary Government in India. Nevertheless King George, who had been captivated by the Indian scene during his tour of the country in 1906 when he was Prince of Wales, secretly disliked this extension of bureaucratic methods in India, believing the paternal system of hereditary chiefs more suited to the Indian people. To counterbalance the growing powers of legislative councils and politicians the King formed a private plan for re-emphasising the importance of the hereditary princes and ruling chiefs: he would go himself to India and publicly assume the Crown at a Coronation Durbar. His scheme, first communicated to the Prime Minister and then to Morley in September 1910, aroused no enthusiasm in the Cabinet: there was the question of expense, the question of security risks, the question of whether the country could get along without its monarch for so long a period as the voyage to India still involved. At the beginning of November, when Crewe had just succeeded Morley at the India Office, the Cabinet sent their rather grudging agreement to the King through Lord Knollys. For the next twelve months the endless details of the Durbar preparations passed across Crewe's desk, adding immeasurably to the work of his new office.

Crewe found the King 'desperately keen' about the Durbar, in which he was to be the symbol of British Imperial power, and very anxious to supervise the plans. On some points he was intransigent. His prime and overweening passion was a simpler one than any of his father's luxurious and complicated tastes, but it held him with what Crewe once called 'an unholy fascination.' This was the sport of shooting. Crewe and Bigge both felt that for the King to refuse to visit Madras because he had no time, and yet to set off six hundred miles from Delhi for a week's shooting would 'give an air of flippancy to the tour' and ill accord with the King's role in India of 'a semi-divine figure.' 'The fact is that it is a misfortune for a public personage to have any taste so strongly developed as the craze for shooting is in our beloved Ruler,' Crewe wrote to Hardinge during these awkward negotiations: 'One may be grateful that the taste itself is not pernicious, but in such a case as this, his perspective of what is proper is almost destroyed.' The new King also seemed too vulnerable to the advice of elder members of his own family: 'Some of the King's family,' wrote Crewe, 'possibly the Duke or Duchess of Connaught, who have just gone to Balmoral, have been trying to terrify him by drawing comparisons, which would more appropriately come from Keir Hardie and Co., between the lavish splendours of the Delhi week and the starving millions who pay for them.' The King had suggested a new Famine Fund, or a substantial gift from the Privy Purse. Such scruples, so alien to the true 'Edwardian' atmosphere, do much to explain the final popularity of King George V.

Besides his heavy administrative task at the India Office, made more wearing by Durbar projects and counter-projects, Crewe was concerned in several important measures which marked the opening of the new reign. One of King George's first actions on coming to the throne was to tell the Prime Minister that he would not open his first Parliament until the anti-Catholic clauses in the Royal Accession Declaration had been altered by Parliament in a sense no longer insulting to his Roman Catholic subjects. This might have seemed a simple matter. It was not. After the death of Queen Victoria in 1901 Crewe had served on a committee appointed by Lord Salisbury to modify the Declaration in some way, but these meetings had proved fruitless. In consultation with Crewe, Mr. Asquith now drafted three alternative formulae, but none of these proved acceptable for, apart from the Anglican bishops, there were vocal religious groups—Nonconformists, Presbyterians, Ulster Protestants—which still felt virulently on the subject. The formula finally adopted by both Houses, and given the King's Assent in August 1910, was one suggested by the Archbishop of Canterbury himself: 'I declare that I am a faithful Protestant and will uphold the Protestant Succession.' In spite of many protests from the North of Ireland, support for the 'anti-bigotry bill' came at the last moment from an odd quarter—a Resolution forwarded to Crewe by Lord Aberdeen, then Lord-Lieutenant of Ireland, and signed by three thousand prominent Irish Protestants. Crewe called this Resolution 'one of the most gratifying events in Irish politics that I can recall,' and felt that it vindicated Irish Protestants 'from the imputation of narrowness and lack of Christian charity which the action of single individuals might have incurred. It has been a happy fact,' he told Aberdeen, 'that the removal of this specific Roman Catholic grievance has helped to create a general atmosphere of good will.' During his years as Viceroy in Ireland, Crewe had already shown marked fairness of mind when dealing with Catholic matters. In this he was acting from moral principle and from fairness of mind. Unlike his father, Monckton Milnes, he had never had any leanings towards the Catholic faith. Crewe belonged, indeed, like his grandfather before him, to that large majority of Englishmen whose religious preconceptions remain those of 1689 and who

would regard with no enthusiasm a direct descendant's
marriage with a Roman Catholic.

Altogether, the first two years of the new reign were exceptionally busy ones for Crewe. In relation to a man less serene
and self-controlled they could readily be called hectic. No
sooner was he settling down to his new India Office work than
the December 1910 Election, the second of the year, was sprung
upon the country. The General Election of the previous
January had been notable as the first in which peers were
allowed to speak from public platforms in support of party
candidates. This, of course, meant that Crewe, who, though
his speeches read well, was a nervous and not eloquent speaker
and never got to like the platform, was considerably used: 'I
am kept flying about the country making speeches,' Crewe
wrote, 'the election having come, as Haldane foretold it would,
like a thief in the night. . . . I believe that our wise men are
hopeful that our position may at any rate not be materially
weakened, with a chance that it may be somewhat improved.'
The Election, in fact, proved 'less acrimonious' than Crewe
had anticipated. Together with Lansdowne, Crewe insti-
gated the holding of the Constitutional Conference between
Unionist and Liberal leaders in the spring and summer of
1910, and he acted as one of the eight members of this body
which tried, but failed, to come to some agreement over
the House of Lords veto. At no moment of his life had
Crewe been at all a strong man physically. In March 1911,
having worked too hard for too long, he fainted at a small
dinner-party given by Lord Morley at Claridge's Hotel on the
occasion of the 'pricking' of the Sheriffs for the following year.
It was after dinner, and the room was hot. Lord Crewe,
standing by himself before the fireplace, was suddenly seen to
sway and fall forwards, hitting his forehead very hard on the
floor. Taken home by John Burns, Crewe was found to have
sustained concussion of the brain. The doctor insisted on a
complete rest from work for eight weeks.

In a lengthy leading article published on the morning after
the accident, headed *The Strain Upon Politicians*, *The Times*
blamed Mr. Asquith for putting 'upon a good man more than
he could bear':

Lord Crewe [this article continued] has had to play a peculiarly harassing and discouraging part, which might well have told upon a man of less perfect temper or less finished courtesy. He has stood practically alone in the House of Lords as the representative of many Government departments, each of which has a separate representative, and generally more than one, in the House of Commons.

The newspaper pointed out that in the Upper House there were then no representatives for the Foreign Office, the Colonial Office, the Admiralty, education and finance: 'Lord Crewe has therefore been compelled, in addition to sufficiently heavy duties at the India Office, to master innumerable details concerning the work of these other Departments.' As Leader of the House Crewe had 'another set of cares.' *The Times* summed up by declaring that the burden placed upon Crewe was the direct result of an alleged policy of the Prime Minister 'to ignore the House of Lords.' 'The whole situation,' it added, 'is extremely unsatisfactory alike from the personal and from the public standpoint, and there is no good reason why it should have arisen, but excellent reasons of public policy why it should have been avoided."

The announcement of Crewe's accident gave rise, of course, to the friendly rumour that he had had a stroke and, his career at an end, was likely also to be incapacitated for life. To counteract this tale Lady Crewe acted swiftly and with decision. She invited the Prime Minister to come and talk with the invalid at the earliest possible moment. 'Mr. Asquith came to see Bob this morning,' she wrote to her father, Lord Rosebery, 'and they had a conversation of several minutes. I gather no changes of any kind are imminent. He is more than surprised at Bob's progress, which is indeed astonishing.' Mr. Asquith remarked that Crewe took up the conversation at the point at which they had broken it off the last time they had met. No drastic changes in the Government proved necessary. Lord Morley—who, *The Times* suggested, was 'not growing younger' —took over in the House of Lords and returned in temporary triumph to the India Office. Writing to commiserate with Crewe on his illness, Lord Knollys said that he had had a letter from the Viceroy 'in despair at your being laid up.' 'I shall,' Hardinge had written, 'of course manage to get on all right with Morley whom I like, but it is not quite the same thing, as

he is very cranky and not so level-headed as Crewe. I do hope
Crewe will come back to the India Office as soon as he is well
enough to do so.' Lady Crewe also received many letters from
Crewe's friends and colleagues, of which one from Sir Edward
Grey will suffice as an example of them all:

Everybody knows how invaluable he is as leader in the Lords,
but only those who are in the Cabinet can know fully how invaluable he is in council [Sir Edward Grey wrote to Lady
Crewe on 5 March]. We are all reluctant to take decisions
without him: he always lights up the difficult places and
explores them for us and has saved us many a mistake. And
you can't think how a man with an unconquerable dislike of
work, as I have, admires the amount of work that Crewe does
and the way he does it: he is a great support to us all and we
shan't get on well till he comes back.

Crewe's accident was not the solitary memorable occurrence
in his personal life that early spring of the year 1911. Three
weeks before his illness, Lady Crewe had given birth to their
first child, a son. The same night Crewe House was almost
destroyed by a great fire, which did what Crewe, with his usual
understatement, called 'a good deal of annoying damage:'

You must forgive a very brief letter from me this week which
to me has not erred in the direction of the commonplace [he
wrote on 10 February to Lord Hardinge]: On Tuesday night
Peggy's boy was born. The event is the greatest possible joy
to us, I need not tell you. Then our house caught fire, from
the old story, I think, of joists running under a hearthstone, a
place which always gets you sooner or later. It was not an
agreeable moment, with what appeared to be the certain
prospect of having to move Peggy to nowhere in particular at
1 in the morning. But this was staved off and she showed
great pluck and coolness.

Newspapers recorded that Lord Crewe took 'the destruction of
a great part of his town residence' with his customary equa-
nimity. 'It might have been a lot worse,' he is reported to
have said, 'I have been going to alter the place for some time
past, and had just made arrangements to do so. This is an
opportunity that is perfectly unique.' Lord and Lady Crewe
moved into Lord Rosebery's house in Berkeley Square, to which
the baby had been taken on the night of the fire.

The child, who was given six Christian names, was christened later in the spring at the Chapel Royal, St. James's, with the King as chief sponsor. Known for a few months as the third Lord Houghton, the little boy was given his father's secondary title Earl of Madeley when Crewe, on the King's own initiative, was made a Marquess in the 1911 Coronation Honours. In the family the boy was called 'Jack.'

When Crewe returned to the India Office, and to intermittent attendance in the House of Lords, he was faced with a mass of detailed decisions about the Delhi Durbar—the first state visit of a reigning King-Emperor to India—as well as with many problems of policy such as the re-unification of Bengal, rashly partitioned when Lord Curzon was Viceroy. Though not shared by the Cabinet, King George's faith in the popularity throughout India of his visit was already proving justified. The very announcement had given pleasure:

Everybody is very enthusiastic on the subject of the King's visit to India [wrote Hardinge in his first letter after his swearing-in], and they prophesy it will have a very tranquillising effect. The Native Princes are simply delighted . . . and consider it the best move that we have made for a long time. I have told them—and laid stress on the fact—that it was the King's own idea.

Yet once the project was accepted as a fact, a thousand difficulties reared their heads: the worst was the problem of boons. 'One's only fear,' Crewe wrote, 'is that the expectations of the masses in India may be only too keenly awakened, and that they may expect some positive results of an extraordinary character from the visit, which a bad year or some other untoward event may disappoint.' In *The Times* Chirol had already raised the question of the special boons which he believed should be proclaimed at the Durbar. The Viceroy initially opposed the idea on the grounds of expense, but subsequently urged the gift of a crore of rupees to India for technical education. Other people thought it would be a good moment to admit Indian officers to commissions in British regiments or to empty the debtors' prisons or either to re-unify Bengal or to raise it to the status of a Presidency. And not only were there these political aspects of the matter, there was also the problem of what the King was to do when he actually held the Durbar. The ancient Indian capital of Delhi was chosen as the site for the assembly, and as the King insisted that as many Indians must see him as possible, a great amphitheatre was built on a plain outside the city walls. But, in this, what ceremonies were to be performed?

The King himself had favoured what Crewe called 'a Napoleonic auto-Coronation.' There were two main objections to this—one, voiced by the Archbishop of Canterbury, was that you could not hold a second Coronation without a Christian religious ceremony, and that you could not hold a Christian religious ceremony before a congregation almost exclusively composed of Mohammedans and Hindus. The second, formulated by Crewe himself, was the danger of setting a precedent:

Is it wise to have a definite crowning ceremony, without which future Kings of England might be held not to be full-blown Emperors of India? What do Eastern peoples think of crowning as a function? It may be all right, and evidently there must be *some* great dramatic moment when the Imperial position is asserted, so to speak, in action, and greeted by a tremendous salute and the homage of all present.

'One's instinct is to avoid the theatrical,' Crewe wrote again in one of his many letters on the subject to the Viceroy, 'but it does not follow that the instinct is sound, as we have got to impress the people of India, not some more or less cultivated persons over here.' Crewe agreed that the King must assume the Crown at some given moment, 'though with nothing which can give the conception of a fresh Coronation. He would advance to the front of the arena with very few attendants, you would bring him the Crown on a cushion, and he would place it on his head in sight of India. Massed bands and general salute. The Crown would be brought from here; what Crown it would be is a matter for future decisions.'

What Crown? Which Crown? The future decisions on this question were not easily approached. When it proved to be illegal to take any of the Regalia, let alone the Crown itself, out of the realm, Sir Walter Lawrence, an experienced Indian administrator by whom the King was much guided in these matters, suggested that a special Indian Crown should be

94

constructed in London, taken out to India and kept there. It was calculated that such a Crown would cost about £60,000, and Lawrence had the notion that the Indian Princes should reduce this price *pro rata* by the presentation of jewels: the Indian Crown would thus be an Indian equivalent of the Stars of South Africa, as the portions of the Cullinan Diamond, presented to the King by the South African states, were officially called. But Crewe and the Cabinet generally opposed the idea of a Crown kept in India, foreseeing it as a precedent for a multiplicity of local Crowns all over the Empire. The Crown, they declared, must be made in London, taken to India, brought back to London and broken up. Here the King intervened with the sensible remark that this might give justifiable offence to Indian visitors to this country. In the end the Indian Crown was made and taken out, the King appeared at the Durbar already wearing it, and on his return to London it joined the rest of the Regalia in the Tower of London.

The Crown controversy settled, fresh problems kept materialising daily: since there was to be no elephant procession would it not at least be suitable for the King and Queen to enter Delhi together on a single giant elephant? (As it turned out, the crowds, expecting to see their Emperor so transported, did not recognise him as he rode by on horseback in the uniform of a Field-Marshal, flanked by Lord Hardinge and Lord Crewe.) Then would it not embarrass the present Commander-in-Chief in India if the King brought the previous C.-in-C., Lord Kitchener, to India with him in his suite as he proposed? Here Crewe suggested an alternative plan for replacing Kitchener by old Lord Roberts, who could be 'carefully carted to Delhi and forbidden to tire himself.' There was also, as we have seen, the problem of the King's obsession with shooting, and the further problem of preventing the royal mind being influenced either by the Connaughts, who were against the whole scheme from the start, or the retired Lord Minto, who went about 'crabbing it' out of what Crewe assumed to be 'the instinctive dislike of the just-retired man for a plan he has not initiated.' Then what was to be done with the Queen during the Nepal shoot? 'It would hardly do, would it, for her to begin in Calcutta without him?'

8   95

Another point, brought up from an unusual quarter, was the question of Queen Mary's real claim to the title of Empress: 'The humble origin of the enquiry,' Crewe explained to Hardinge, 'was a query from Lever Brothers, of Sunlight Soap fame, as to whether the Queen is Empress of India or not. I suppose the information is needed for purposes of advertisement.' The King had at once proposed to issue a proclamation defining Queen Mary's Indian status, but Crewe opposed this, declaring 'that nothing ought to be done to throw doubt on the fact that the Queen derives the title from her marriage, as the Consort of the Emperor.' He added in parenthesis that Queen Alexandra was now the Dowager Empress.

The nearer they got to embarkation day, the more the King became absorbed in minor details of the ceremonial:

The King desires [wrote Crewe] that the 'Standard of India' which was carried at the Coronation by George Curzon, should also be borne at the Durbar, and George, who acquired it by purchase after the ceremony, is willing to lend it for this lofty purpose, only stipulating that the greatest care may be taken of it, which I have faithfully promised. His Majesty wishes you to give your view as to the bearer. To the philosopher it would appear unimportant, but some meaning may be held to attach to the choice, and in my opinion a high civil, not military, functionary should be selected. If you can telegraph your verdict it would be all the better, as the King will like to know before he leaves.

In the end, all was settled on time. On 11 November 1911 the King and Queen, accompanied by the Secretary of State for India and a modest suite, set sail in the P. & O. Line's newest vessel, the *Medina* of 13,000 tons, escorted by four cruisers, for Bombay. 'What with uniforms, and the variety of temperatures we expect to encounter,' Crewe wrote to a friend, 'our luggage has grown to a most indecent amount; mine looks adequate for a married couple taking six children and four servants to settle in the Antipodes.'

The *Medina* drew out towards the Channel in a tempest of wind and rain, so that the travellers' final impression of England was of a mushroom-bank of shining wet umbrellas the length of the receding Portsmouth shore. By nightfall the ship was ploughing her way uneasily through a violent gale. 'The huge bulk of the *Medina* seemed to promise that she would be comparatively still in any sea,' wrote Fortescue, the official chronicler of the voyage, 'but driven against the long rollers of the Atlantic she was sufficiently lively, and pitched heavily. At every plunge she took in green seas over her bows, while the flying spray drenched her from stem to stern.' Built to accommodate six hundred and fifty passengers, the *Medina* now contained only twenty-four. The extra space had been used to provide roomy and luxurious quarters for the distinguished company, but these had been placed so far forward in the ship that the passengers felt the pitch and roll at its worst. In the first few days the rate of sea-sickness was unusual, the sailors being especially afflicted, for in those halcyon pre-war times 'the British sailor,' as Fortescue remarked, 'so rarely left home waters that he had little experience of long heavy seas.' After the Bay of Biscay the ship entered warmer and calmer waters. By way of Gibraltar, Malta and the Suez Canal they reached Bombay on 2 December. Ten days later the Durbar was held in Delhi, and after a shooting party in Nepal and some ceremonies in Calcutta the King-Emperor and the Queen-Empress re-embarked at Bombay on 10 January. On 5 February the *Medina* anchored off Spithead. The King and Queen railed up to London on a cold dark winter's morning to be met by their relatives, by members of the Government and of the Opposition and by almost the whole of the diplomatic corps. 'There were few, I think, among the suite who did not regret the breaking up of a party in which it may truly be said that not an unpleasant word had passed from the beginning to the end of the journey,' the Durbar's official historian remarks.

From the earnest viewpoint of Lord Crewe the Delhi Durbar was of deep and interesting importance. Publicised at that time and ever since as the first visit of a reigning English monarch to the Indian Empire—'Never had a King of England journeyed so far from his accustomed sphere, and only one, over seven hundred years before, had ever set foot within the confines of Asia'—the journey set, in fact, another and an equally significant precedent: it was the first time that a Secretary of State for India had travelled through that country while in office. To us, accustomed to see in our morning newspapers that the Colonial Secretary has flown out to Nairobi for two days and will be back on Friday afternoon, Crewe's journey does not seem odd; but in those days, when the Chief Secretary for Ireland alone was accustomed to visit the country in his charge, it was even more surprising than Jospeh Chamberlain's visit to Cape Town after the South African War.   While the King was shooting and the Queen looking at Agra and watching leopards being shot near Bundi on Christmas Day, Crewe had many long informal conversations with the Viceroy, and could gain living impressions of what had hitherto been problems on paper.   'A quiet unhurried talk with Charlie Hardinge,' he wrote to Lady Crewe about the final train journey from Calcutta to Bombay.   'There are no ragged edges left in our common business I am pleased to think, and until some quite new questions emerge there is nothing to agitate our minds. Thus so far as India is concerned I may contemplate a peaceful voyage home.'   To Crewe's official work the Delhi journey was thus of singular value.   Historically it may be taken as the watershed dividing the old Victorian system, by which Secretaries of State administered distant territories by the advice of remote deputies, and the modern system of close and constant ministerial intervention which air-travel has made familiar.

In another, and a wholly personal, sense the voyage had proved helpful to Crewe, for it was a recuperative experience for a still-delicate man.   'They watch over me with singular care,' he reported to his wife of the King and Queen, who never forgot that Crewe was convalescent and frequently asked him to be seated in their presence.   With his assumption of the India Office, and his sudden illness, the year 1911 had for Crewe proved peculiarly taxing.   Socially that last Coronation summer before the present era of world wars had been brilliant and exhausting for everyone in public life.   For the last time London was swarming with continental royalties and German princelings and their suites.   Like most persons of their position the Crewes had given a series of large luncheon parties for such figures as Prince and Princess Max of Baden, the Grand-Duke and Grand-Duchess of Hesse, the Grand-Duke and Grand-Duchess of Mecklenburg-Schwerin and others of their ilk.   The peaceful progress of the *Medina* to and from Bombay was for Crewe's health a restorative and a contrast to these

formal entertainments. Even so, he was not completely recovered by the time of his return : 'I only hope that everybody
did not find my speech as unutterably tedious as I did myself,'
Crewe wrote to the Viceroy in February 1912, during the
Lords Debate on the Government of India Bill. 'I think the
fact is that though I feel wonderfully well, and am congratulated on all sides for looking so much the better for India, I am
not really in form for making a very long speech, especially as
listening closely to another long speech beforehand, even to one
so clear and agreeably given as George Curzon's, is something
of an effort in itself.'

Introduced into the House of Lords as soon as possible after
the Secretary of State's return home, the Government of India
Bill was skilfully designed by Asquith and Crewe to blunt the
Opposition's claws. Its subject was the legalisation of the
major boons announced at the Delhi Durbar. After much
consultation these boons had been divided into two groups:
minor boons, announced by the Viceroy in the King's
presence, and ˗which included increased expenditure on
education, a grant of extra pay to all civil servants and soldiers,
and the release of certain criminals and debtors; major boons,
unexpectedly announced by the King himself and kept secret
until that moment. These comprised the revision of Curzon's
partition of Bengal and the transference of the Indian capital
from Calcutta to its ancient site at Delhi. The Unionists, who
lost no occasion for abusing the Government for dragging the
Crown into political controversy and using the King 'to shelter
them in acts which without his authority they could not have
carried through,' and who were still seething with sullen fury
at their humiliation over the Parliament Act, saw a splendid
opportunity in the Durbar proclamation. They had, of
course, a certain logic on their side. In one of his frequent
newsletters to his parents (published selectively in his *Politics
from Inside* in 1936), Austen Chamberlain has left a record of a
meeting of Tory leaders early in February 1912, when Lansdowne, Curzon, Bonar Law, Walter Long and Chamberlain
assembled at Lansdowne House to discuss Opposition strategy
for the imminent opening of Parliament. There was to be a
'full-dress debate in the Lords on the Indian changes,' and
Curzon 'made a statement on the subject from his point of view

which I must say was extraordinarily well done.' Curzon spoke from experience but also from harsh prejudices. He had consistently opposed the King's visit to India, and had disliked the criticism of his own aristocratic, exclusive and almost mystical Durbar of 1903 implied in the determination of the King and his Liberal advisers to make the 1911 ceremonies as public and democratic as possible. And in the event the 1911 proceedings had culminated in a royal and public repudiation of Curzon's own action in partitioning Bengal. No wonder that, in Austen Chamberlain's words, Curzon took 'a very strong view on the subject' that morning at Lansdowne House:

First, because whether right or wrong in itself, it was improper that an act of such great political importance, and open under any circumstances to so much criticism, should be made the personal act of the Sovereign and that it should be thus rendered impossible to modify or alter the decision without in some respect lessening his prestige with his Indian subjects. The constitutional impropriety is, it seems to me, singularly heightened by the fact that, as now appears, the changes cannot be carried out without an Act of Parliament.

The King had summoned Lord Lansdowne for the same afternoon. Austen Chamberlain begged him to stress the Unionist viewpoint to the King:

'Do tell him,' I urged, 'in plain language that no Tory Minister, not even Dizzy, at the height of his power, would have dared to make such a use of the Crown. Just imagine what would have happened if Dizzy had caused Queen Victoria to proclaim herself Empress of India at Delhi without a word of prior communication to Parliament, and had come three months later to the House of Commons for the necessary legislative sanction. Mr. Gladstone would have hurried back from his retirement at Hawarden and would himself have moved a vote of censure on the Ministers, which would have been supported by a solid vote of the Opposition of those days.'

Lansdowne told us that the King took a special interest in this policy. . . .

Naturally enough this hostile reaction had been foreseen by men as politically experienced as Asquith and Crewe:

We shall be able, I hope, to bring in the Bill in the House of Lords before very long [Crewe wrote]. Asquith is desirous, if possible, of omitting the formation of the Presidency of Bengal from the measure, and relying on the powers given by the Act of 1854. He points out that the best line of attack upon us is the accusation that we got the King to announce a policy which can only be brought into effect by Parliament. . . . I think myself that the attack could be evaded, but it might be wiser to avoid it entirely, and we shall see what the best legal opinions, in addition to Asquith's own, have to say.

In the subsequent debate on the Government of India Bill Curzon delivered a clever and well-argued attack—'A very able speech, as one would expect,' Crewe termed it, 'but it really suffered, from his point of view, from being what I described it, the work of the Counsel for the prosecution. It was over-prepared and would have been infinitely more effective if the censure had not been so unrelieved, and also more difficult to answer.' Crewe replied to it with his accustomed calm. Although a friend of Curzon's, and sometimes a guest at Hackwood, Crewe was in no way influenced or affected by the former Viceroy's strong sense of the theatrical and of his own importance. Having set his face against the Delhi Durbar, Curzon had pettishly taken the opportunity of Crewe's absence from the India Office in the spring of 1911 to agitate the acting Secretary of State, John Morley. Throughout Crewe's correspondence with Hardinge over the Durbar preparations the necessity for economy had been persistently emphasised: but Curzon, 'romancing' as Crewe politely called it, about the comparative cheapness of his own Durbar in 1903, was determined to alarm both the King and the acting chief of the India Office, a man at once more credulous and more vulnerable than Crewe. On 28 April 1911 Morley despatched a fussy private letter to the Viceroy:

Last night at the House of Lords Curzon talked to me of one or two matters that had come up during a short visit, a day or two ago, to Windsor. He is strongly moved at the huge figure of a million for the Durbar, &c., first, on the ground that it is itself excessive, and second, because, as he is informed, Local Governments are to have £10,000 apiece for their expenditure, and that this or the other high official is to have £5,000 for his *menus plaisirs*, while the smaller men will wear out their boots, destroy their kit & without a sou of compensation. He had

put all this to His Majesty along with the suggestion that His
Majesty should convey to you, through the Secretary of State
or some other public channel, his express desire not to lay a
burden, &c., &c., and so forth.   I told him that we at the
India Office were kept in grim and stern ignorance of the
details. . . . I confess that I quake at the fuss that will arise
by-and-by.   But that is another thing.   I only want to let you
know beforehand that, if economy becomes either necessary
or possible, the ground has been to some extent prepared in the
King's mind.

The Viceroy and the Government of India were, understand-
ably, incensed by Morley's credulity over Curzon's gossip.
In a reply from India it was pointed out that some of the
statements were 'a curious farrago of nonsense' while others
were 'grossly untrue.'   The estimates were being sent to London 'in detail, which is quite unprecedented, and which is in
marked contrast with the entire absence of any previous
estimate which characterised Lord Curzon's Durbar.'   When
Crewe returned to work, his reaction to Curzon's criticism was
typically mild but firm:

George Curzon's peculiar incapacity for understanding what
is, and what is not, the proper occasion for interfering in other
people's affairs has led him on the wrong road in various
particulars.   He had no business to discuss these matters at
Windsor at all, and I am clear that it is necessary to correct
any impression he may have left. . . . I will see that the facts
are correctly understood in the proper quarter.

The matter was closed by a Government of India despatch
'showing the difference between our system of accounts and
that which was employed on the occasion of Curzon's Durbar.'
'Curzon has been talking a lot of nonsense about the expenditure on his Durbar,' the Viceroy wrote with justifiable heat,
'but I am assured by the Finance Department that his accounts
will not bear careful scrutiny or auditing.'

For the most tangible and permanent result of the 1911
Durbar, Sir Edwin Lutyens' New Delhi, Crewe was very really
and very directly responsible.   It was he who pressed the
claims of Lutyens against another architect much favoured by
the Council of India, but whom Crewe judged to be 'of a florid
school' and thus likely to build in 'the very worst style for your

new works.' 'What I know of the simplicity of Lutyens' manner . . . made me mention him in India as a likely card to play. Since he has been seriously put forward here, I have seen photographs of several of his recent performances, and have been favourably impressed.' 'The general impression one collects,' Crewe wrote on a further occasion,

is that Lutyens might prove to be the best ultimate designer of great public structures, as he seems to possess singular purity of taste and contempt for mere ornamentation: but some describe him as extravagant. The extravagance of architects, however, is usually the fault of their employers; and if, as you and I agreed, the work at Delhi must never be allowed to become departmental, there is not much need for terror. I have no doubt that in the House next Wednesday, when G. Curzon has his field-day, there will be loud wails about expense; but I hope to make my views on the subject quite clear and to say that you, and I (so long as I am concerned), mean to pay special and continuous attention to the design of the works and their cost.

In his draft list of Durbar honours, Lord Hardinge had wished to advise the King to give Crewe the Star of India, but Crewe had struck his own name from the list before submitting it to Buckingham Palace. When the *Medina* stood off Spithead in the final stage of the Indian Journey, King George sent for the Secretary of State for India and invested him with the Victorian Chain, a new, high honour invented by Edward VII. Crewe was greatly touched by this attention. The chain, he said, had only previously been awarded in five instances: to Curzon at the time of the 1903 Durbar, to Hardinge on taking up office as Viceroy, to Lansdowne when he had relinquished the Foreign Office and, at the recent Coronation, to the Duke of Norfolk and the Archbishop of Canterbury.

'It seems like the awakening from a wonderful dream to be once more writing a humdrum letter to you from this table,' Crewe wrote to Hardinge four days after his return to London. He added that in his absence his room at the India Office 'has been done up under good advice, and the scheme of so-called decoration, which was of the most garish and offensive sort, has disappeared in favour of cool and soft tones, which make

pleasant surroundings, and also show off to advantage the fine
paintings of the Indo-Persian school which hang on the walls.
... I propose when speaking on the Address to call fresh
attention to the message from India about the visit, which for
some reason does not seem to have attracted the attention here
which its remarkable character demands.'

This message 'from the Princes and People of India' was a
reply to the farewell which the King had read from the canopied
dais on which he and the Queen had sat enthroned before
embarking on the *Medina* at Bombay. The King afterwards
told Queen Alexandra that he 'actually broke down; I simply
couldn't help it' as he read this farewell. 'He was so much
moved at the last sentences, which were simply and touchingly
phrased, that he could hardly finish,' Crewe wrote to his wife
of this episode. 'As he told me, it flashed across his mind that
he would never see India again, and the thought was too much
for him.' In later years, while the planning of New Delhi was in
hand, King George became convinced that he would be held
personally responsible for the merits or defects of the new city:
'He considers the work will be connected with his name in
India. ...This seems an exaggerated view,' Crewe wrote,
'though no doubt the Royal visit will be remembered when,
in Sheridan's words, "all of us are dead and most of us are
forgotten."'

Chapter Eight

'THERE was an unexpected Cabinet hastily summoned at 12.30 yesterday morning,' Austen Chamberlain wrote on 12 April 1910. 'What it was about I don't know, but Winston and Lloyd George looked very glum when they came into the House, and Crewe and Carrington were met in the Park "looking as if Crewe were breaking to Carrington the news of the death of his nearest relation." Such are the joys of office and the resplendent position of His Majesty's Government!'

Austen Chamberlain's news-letters to his family in Birmingham exemplify the *Schadenfreude* with which Liberal Unionists would welcome rumours of difficulty and dispute within the Asquith Government. It was an expression of a hostility both more feline and more meretricious than the open, hearty loathing of the real Tories; and 'Austen's' attitude to the Liberal Cabinet was that of a credulous peeping Tom. 'Balfour and Douglas both confirm my story of the row in the Cabinet between Winston and Crewe,' he would tell them in Birmingham; or 'a lady of high authority said the Government had decided to announce their resignation on Monday.' He lapped up any tale that the strain of office was fretting individual members of the Cabinet: Mrs. Harcourt had told his wife at luncheon that 'Winston's nerves had quite given way after an all-night sitting,' or that 'Lulu was in great need of a holiday.' In the smoking-room of the House of Commons or dining at Grillions, pacing smooth cedar-planted lawns of country-houses on the Itchen or the Orwell, picking wild flowers with Mrs. Colefax at Crowborough or taking part in frustrating Unionist conferences at Lansdowne House, his ear was alert for the preliminary clatter of the longed-for and expected Liberal collapse.

The state of the Opposition after the 1906 Election was described by Lansdowne himself as 'lamentably weak.' In the House of Commons the Unionists and their allies numbered one hundred and fifty-seven, and even this small band were singularly disunited in their views. 'Leaderless and attenuated,' the Party, as Lansdowne's biographer explains, 'did not even possess the merit of homogeneity, since it was composed of Balfourites, Chamberlainites and Unionist Free Fooders.' These disparate elements feuded amongst themselves just as fiercely as the Liberals had been doing until recently. Powerless in the Commons, the Unionist Party had one last resort—enormous and embattled strength in the House of Lords. This was a dangerous weapon to play with, but to use it was irresistible. They did so until it was knocked from their hands by its inevitable recoil.

The Liberals, on the contrary, were exceptionally united. Together with Labour Members and Irish Home Rulers they could muster five hundred and thirteen votes in the Lower House. Many causes had contributed to their triumph, but undoubtedly the basic one was the simple fact that, with one brief interlude, the Tories had been in power for twenty years. It was a cherished theory of the new Prime Minister, Campbell-Bannerman, that to be healthy the political opinion of the British Electorate ought to swing like a pendulum: when the country was in a conservative mood it required a Conservative government, when in a reforming mood a Liberal one. It was on this uncomplicated and convenient hypothesis that Campbell-Bannerman combated the efforts of Rosebery and his sympathisers to modify official Liberal policy so that it might appeal to conservative-minded voters. If you did this, he asked, what would you have to offer the country when it entered on a radical mood?

The very nature of the Liberals' triumph in 1906 branched into thorny difficulties. Internally the Party had been driven to cohesion by Unionist ineptitude—as Crewe remarked, '*quod minime reris*, the enemy saved the situation.' Externally they had inherited a great body of public support overnight from such blocks of opinion as the Nonconformists, and these were but one of many vociferous elements which they now found themselves obliged to satisfy or to placate. The country was

THE NORTH ROOM, CREWE HOUSE

in a reforming temper. The new House of Commons teemed with eager and excited young men, set on making a new heaven and a new earth within the shortest possible space of time. Campbell-Bannerman and several of his colleagues in the Cabinet suspected that the overwhelming majority at the election might be followed by a swift reaction in public opinion. Thus, in their first King's Speech, they tabled as many new bills as they could. And not only had they to redeem generous election pledges to Nonconformists and others: they also had to contend with the heady zeal, and in some cases downright rebelliousness, of a large section of their own M.P.s.

In those days the rank and file of the Party had no direct or personal contact with the mandarins of the Cabinet. Their only means of expressing disapproval was to the Whips, who would soothingly reply that they could 'rest assured that all will be right on the night,' that the Cabinet was 'finding a formula' and (after Campbell-Bannerman's demise) that Mr. Asquith should be trusted implicitly. Sometimes, as in the notorious matter of the contingent guarantees from the Sovereign over the passage of the Parliament Bill, Asquith was lofted forward by the moral pressure of the more advanced among his followers; but in general he did succeed, with sturdy ingenuity, in keeping to his own track even against the views of some of the members of his Cabinet. In all actions Asquith could count upon the intimate support of Crewe, who proved from the outset to be a steadying and moderating influence. The Prime Minister would not infrequently confide to him his exasperation at the indiscretions and loquaciousness of two or three of their younger colleagues. Altogether, Crewe's position in the Cabinet was strong: 'Only a few months ago a junior member of the Cabinet told me that in his opinion Lord Crewe's influence in the Cabinet was second only to that of Mr. Asquith, the reason being that he was conversant with the inner working of so many departments and has brought so much ripe wisdom and rare discretion to his various tasks,' wrote the Parliamentary correspondent of a leading newspaper in 1911. The correspondent added that Crewe 'has never been recognised by the rank and file of the Liberal Party at his full measure.'

As reconstructed after Campbell-Bannerman's resignation

and death in the spring of 1908, the Cabinet was undoubtedly one of the best of this century. It contained many capable and several brilliant men, and there was a neat balance between the almost excessive discretion of Asquith, Haldane, Crewe and Grey on the one hand, and the braying prophetic utterances of Lloyd George, the young enthusiasm and ambition of Winston Churchill on the other. Extreme discretion was indeed the keynote of Asquith's character, as it was of that of Crewe. It was not only Austen Chamberlain and his friends who had to depend on lobby gossip to guess what was being determined in the Cabinet room: the bulk of the Liberal Party in the House of Commons was equally in the dark. This reticence—which in the case of the secret military talks with France prevented most members of the Cabinet from themselves knowing what was afoot—helped to make the whole dramatic episode of the Parliament Bill especially tense and mysterious, and accounted for the consternation of the Liberal rank and file in February 1910 when Asquith revealed to them that he had no pledge from King George in his pocket. It was in this secure atmosphere of confidence that Crewe worked from 1906 until 1916; and it is as an aloof, imposing figure burdened with many secrets that we must see him at this time, moving silently and discreetly against a background of the wildest rumour. We may fancy him entering the doors of the Cabinet Room in Downing Street, where he and his colleagues would sit glancing out at the leafy garden of the Prime Minister's residence, where Mrs. Asquith's little son would scramble up and down the sooty, ivied wall. On what was discussed and decided during those long deliberations in the Cabinet Room, Crewe, unlike some of his colleagues, was to the outside world wholly and wisely mute.

From the first moment he took office Crewe perceived that the only possible way to span the gulf between Conservatives and Liberals in the Lords was by personal negotiation. In this project he was aided by his early friendship with Lord Lansdowne, whose estates at Bowood marched with Crewe's Wiltshire lands at Calne. But though logical, the way of personal negotiation was never easy, and usually, indeed, led to a dead end. In the first great battle with the Lords, over the Education Bill of 1906, a measure in which he took a strong personal interest, Crewe did his best to appeal to moderate Unionist opinion. Passed by the House of Commons, the bill was torn to shreds in the Lords, who returned the tattered fragments to the Commons asking for their approval of the 'amendments.' These the Lower House rejected in a block in December 1906. The battle was joined: but at this point Crewe and Lansdowne intervened, suggesting a private conference. Three representatives from each party, with the addition of the Archbishop of Canterbury, met in Mr. Balfour's room at the House. Nothing came of it. The Conservatives, intransigent as ever, judged that the Liberal leaders had been inclined to give way more than their supporters would permit. 'The general impression produced upon us,' Lansdowne wrote of this meeting, 'was that Lord Crewe and his colleagues felt that they had already gone too far, and were inclined to draw in their horns rather than to advance further.' Here at once is a clear example of the form of pressure which the most ardently radical Liberal Members would exert upon the Government, confident that the country was at their back—for unlike the later and somewhat paternal Licensing Bill, the Education Bill was a thoroughly popular measure, and one which excited passions in the electorate in a way which the legislation for abolishing the House of Lords veto would never do.

Apart from his Cabinet responsibilities—from 1905 to 1908 as Lord President of the Council, from 1908 to 1910 as Secretary of State for the Colonies and Lord Privy Seal and finally, from 1910 to 1915 as Secretary of State for India—Crewe had the constant wearing task of acting for seven out of these nine years as Leader for the Government in the House of Lords. The duties involved by this position are very various and are loosely comparable with those of the Prime Minister in the Lower House—although the responsibilities are obviously less. But whereas Mr. Asquith as Prime Minister could rely on tried and knowledgeable support from Cabinet colleagues in the House of Commons, the Liberal Leader in the Lords had a notoriously weak Front Bench, while the responsibility for expounding all the broader questions of departmental policy, dealt with in the Commons by appropriate Ministers, fell to the Government Leader in the House of Lords. A large segment of his time was eaten up by the arrangements for

debates and by deciding who was to answer which questions for
the Government. Much of Crewe's surviving correspondence
both with Government and with Opposition peers is exclusively concerned with these technicalities of Second Chamber government, made in this case all the more difficult by
the modest number and uneven quality of the Government
minority in the House of Lords. And even this small team
was neither easy to control, nor always dependable. Some
peers would suddenly fall ill before a big debate; others
begged off on the plea of seasonal country occupations;
others again would quixotically embark upon a lengthy
Mediterranean cruise without so much as having warned
Lord Colebrooke, the Chief Whip. And in a situation where
every vote counted, the Liberal peers continued to act with
all the freedom and personal eccentricity which had in the past
reduced the party to a state of anarchy. The excited and
largely artificial unity of 1906 did not bear the test of long years
of office; and Crewe was continually faced with the scruples of
some back-bencher who, while professing the warmest devotion
to the Government, could not see his way to supporting some
individual piece of Government legislation, as well as the
graver situation of certain Liberal peers who were alarmed
over Home Rule and were getting ready for graduated defec-
tion to the other side. These problems he met day after day
with his unusual combination of patience, fairmindedness,
commonsense and charm. Moreover for Crewe personally the
frequent delivery of long and elaborate speeches expounding
or defending Government policy was in itself a source of inner
tension, for he was a hesitant, unemphatic and at times stam-
mering speaker: 'Crewe,' Asquith once remarked to a woman
friend, 'is an excellent teapot but a bad pourer.' 'I only hope
that everybody did not find my speech as unutterably tedious
as I did myself,' Crewe wrote, as we have seen, of one Indian
occasion; and there were undoubtedly many other times at
which the identical thought flitted across his calm mind, for
Crewe was the least conceited or self-satisfied of men.

A Junior Whip under Lord Granville in the eighteen-eighties,
Crewe already had a quarter of a century's experience of
House of Lords procedure when in March 1906 he agreed to
act as lieutenant to Lord Ripon, who, still leader of the House,

was much enfeebled by age and by recurrent illness. For two years this rather unorthodox and unwieldy condominium persisted, but by it Crewe gained invaluable experience for the future. Ripon expressed himself as fully satisfied with Crewe, whom he openly regarded as his successor-designate. 'You can have no difficulty in filling up my place as Leader in the House of Lords,' he wrote to Campbell-Bannerman in an attempt to resign after his wife's death in March 1907, 'for Crewe proved himself in last session to be perfectly fit for the post and obtained a hold on the House on *both* sides which would make him a thoroughly good leader.' When, a year afterwards, his second resignation offer was accepted by Asquith, the new Prime Minister, Ripon admitted that though the two years of dual leadership—'of the Two Kings of Brentford description,' as he called it—had proved cumbrous on occasion, this was through no fault of Crewe's. 'Nothing could be kinder than Crewe is to me in every way—if he were my own son he could not treat me with more consideration . . . (but) it is not fair to him to let him take almost all the work and give him none of the honour.' Thus from April 1908 onward, as chief Government spokesman in the House of Lords, Crewe led and directed the defence againt massed Unionist attacks on every liberalising Government measure. But though small in numbers, the band of Liberals which Crewe headed in the House of Lords were not perpetually on the defensive. They could and did at times take the initiative, most notably in the famous historical episode of the passage, in August 1911, of the Parliament Bill.

The history of the Liberal victory over the Parliament Bill has been told finally and well in two recent books, one by Sir Harold Nicolson, the other by Mr. Roy Jenkins. There is no call for recapitulation of factual sequence here, yet it is naturally integral to this study of a personality to recall Crewe's own vital part in the destruction of the Peers' right of veto. The biographies of statesmen should not be so generalised as to become the histories of their times; but there are instances like this one in which the man and the historical event are intimately, indeed inextricably, linked. Crewe's firm, sagacious attitude through the Parliament Bill controversy shows us his character in daylight and shows it at its best,

9

III

while the papers which he kept from that period afford us an oblique view, a peep from the wings, at this great scene in English political life. Throughout this difficult, tempestuous episode the Prime Minister took care to keep in step with Crewe, and would in fact seem to have relied upon him to expound the Cabinet's view to Edward VII and to help him to persuade that King's successor to give the pledges which they felt they must demand.

Crewe's views upon the abolition of the veto, and upon the separate question of House of Lords reform had never varied. It was a matter to which he had given much grave thought. In 1907 he had produced what Asquith termed an 'admirable memorandum' with which the Prime Minister was 'in almost complete agreement' on the subject. In January 1910 he had, as we have seen, been consulted by and argued with King Edward, who had privately unfolded to him his own scheme for reforming the House of Lords. At about the same time Crewe and Grey also discussed the question of the creation of peers with Lord Knollys. Publicity on this subject was now reaching a crescendo: 'How your unofficial people and most of our Press seem to be discussing the problem before us without any attempt to think it out and with a strong desire to run their heads against a brick wall, which is evidence rather of the thickness of their skulls than of their intelligence,' Edward Grey wrote to Crewe early in February. And on 19 April 1910, just over two weeks before the King's collapse and death, Crewe wrote a long memorandum for the Sovereign, in the time-honoured, unofficial form of a private letter to the King's Private Secretary. In this he laid out his own view (which was also doubtless that of the majority in the Cabinet) 'of the present constitutional controversy, particularly with regard to the position of the Crown, as to which some rather unfortunate and inaccurate language has been used.' This memorandum, a model of restraint and blunt good sense, is of historical interest. It also gives us an excellent notion of the quality and lucidity of Crewe's brain.

Crewe begins by remarking that there was no need for him to remind Knollys of 'the double issue raised by the treatment accorded to the Government's general legislation by the House of Lords and by their rejection of the Budget.' He then sets out three points to be borne in mind: firstly that 'the House of Lords and the Opposition generally deny that any constitutional crisis exists'; secondly, that 'the House of Lords, and presumably the Opposition also, affect to deny the existence of what W. Bagehot called "the safety valve," i.e. the prerogative to create peers in the last resort, on the advice of Ministers, if the House of Lords continue to resist a reform of which the country clearly approves'; and thirdly that all the schemes of Lords reform put forward 'whether Rosebery's or any other' aim at the abolition of this royal prerogative 'because they all propose to limit the number of Peers or others who are to sit as Lords of Parliament.' 'In these circumstances,' he continued:

our supporters all over the country, some of them angry and impatient, others nervous and beginning to be despondent, ask 'How is this business ever to be concluded? What reason is there to suppose that the Lords will give way in this matter after a second Election or a third?' The pressure thus put upon us not only in the House but in the country is thus very strong and I cannot pretend to be surprised. If nothing is going to happen our supporters may well ask what is the use of returning a majority to Parliament; and it must be remembered that if Ireland is left out altogether, which it is scarcely reasonable to do in this connexion, we have a majority of 63 in Great Britain.

This then is how the idea of the ultimate action of the Crown has come into being, really by force of circumstances and not by any deliberate intention. I regret it deeply myself because, in the rather random discussions of the platform, people are liable to wander from the abstract constitutional point on to the forbidden ground of the King's personal action in such or such a contingency. I know from a letter which I had from Ponsonby a few days ago, in which I had His Majesty's commands to mention the matter to the Prime Minister, how distasteful any discussions of that kind must be to the King. I can only say for myself that I would do anything to avoid making His Majesty's views a matter of public discussion, and when I have strongly impressed this, my colleagues have all heartily agreed. But what is the best way to effect this object? Assuming, as one must, that the *possibility* of the exercise of the prerogative cannot be ignored—because it is mentioned in every text-book, the newspapers were full of it before the Budget was rejected, and it has been a matter of common talk all over the country—I think that the best course was taken in the Prime Minister's declaration last week. The wording of that statement was most carefully considered in order to prepare people's minds for what is most likely to occur. If and when the House of Lords rejects the proposals contained in the Resolutions, the Prime Minister must lay the situation before the King and point out the various possible courses. This is technically 'giving advice' because a Prime Minister cannot tell the House that he will talk the situation over with the Sovereign. If you carefully consider the various possibilities, I think you will agree that the really undesirable situation, that of a Government with a majority (even though composite) in the House of Commons having to resign because it has asked for something which it cannot get, is less likely to come about in this way than in any other. That would be a great national misfortune, because the Crown would then be almost necessarily involved in party politics, and personally I would far sooner retire from public life than that such a calamity should happen.

In my forecast of events it is not in the least likely to occur, because in the first place I do not believe in indefinite obstinacy on the part of the Lords and in the second because I have a profound faith in the good sense of the country.

Lord Knollys forwarded this lucid exposition of the Government's case to King Edward at Biarritz. The King returned it with a message of thanks: 'He expresses himself very kindly about you as regards your private personality,' Knollys wrote ambiguously. In the same letter, dated 24 April 1910, Knollys enquired of Crewe just what he had meant in a recent and widely criticised speech which he had made upon the constitutional question at Winchester. Knollys explained that the speech had caused 'some misapprehension among people' as to Crewe's attitude to the 'guarantee question' and the Crown: 'Some say that you wished to imply that the King would be obliged constitutionally to accept the advice of the Cabinet on the "guarantee question," while other people are not quite sure what you exactly meant.' Knollys knew the King, and knew also that the speech was 'sure to be discussed' before him after his return from France in three days time: 'I cannot help thinking,' he wrote, 'it would be satisfactory if you could in a letter to him or to me explain what you really intended to convey.' In response to this hint, Crewe wrote Knollys a second letter restating his views on 'the royal prerogative for the creation of peers at a time of crisis between the two Houses.' Stating that he regarded it as a 'duty to make the matter clear,' he emphasised that:

The point, I conceive, is whether a Prime Minister in recommending such a creation 'gives advice' in the technical sense, which the P.M. on his side definitely presents for acceptance, and the Sovereign by constitutional custom accepts—or whether the P.M. makes a request which the Sovereign can grant or refuse at will.

My answer would be that I can imagine a hypothetical case, of a kind which I trust is never likely to arise, in which, after a definite refusal by the House of Lords to act upon the express desire of the country, the Sovereign might find himself, as the *Spectator* said in a rather interesting article last Saturday, in the position 'of an Institution rather than an individual' (or some such words) and so playing a constitutional part into which his personal view would hardly enter.

But as a matter of fact when speaking at Winchester I was not thinking of this aspect of the subject. My object was to address a warning to those supporters of ours who seemed to think it is the simplest thing in the world to approach the King with a request of this sort—as if H.M. were to be asked to open a new hospital—quite forgetting the tremendous importance of the issues involved. I desired to point out that if such a step were taken, it could only be in the last resort as the definite advice of H.M.G., certain that the country was at their back and unable to carry out administration without it.

Accordingly when speaking of 'advice' I was thinking of the responsibility which Ministers would undertake in bringing forward the subject in a formal manner. Personally I cannot conceive of such 'advice' being given without an agreement having been reached between His Majesty and His Ministers that the country demanded the production of this final weapon.

This letter was written on 27 April, the day of the King's return to London from France. At Biarritz King Edward had latterly been adumbrating a compromise scheme to solve the constitutional deadlock by giving peerages to the eldest sons of Liberal peers. Whether this scheme would ever have been accepted remains dubious, for within five days of his homecoming the King fell ill and four days after that he was dead.

With him died any real possibilities of compromise on the issue of the Parliament Bill, which had had its first reading in the House of Commons on 14 April.   As long as King Edward was alive Mr. Asquith 'had been able to postpone a collision by mingling procrastination with occasional pronouncements, designed to assuage, or at least bewilder, his diverse antagonists, supporters and allies.'   The new reign, like a well-lit, empty stage, seemed set for dramatic and decisive action.

King George V's open-minded, candid attitude towards many problems and personalities for which his father had expressed nothing but the strongest prejudice is constantly reflected in the many letters which Lord Knollys, up to his resignation in 1913, dashed off to Crewe, a correspondence afterwards carried on in much the same intimate terms by King George's own Private Secretary, Sir Arthur Bigge, later Lord Stamfordham.   These letters incidentally make clear Crewe's unique position both as an official link between the Crown and the Cabinet and, perhaps more important still, as the Sovereign's confidential adviser on any personal matters which King George did not wish to discuss with the Prime Minister. What sharper contrast, for example, to King Edward's petulant rage over the Limehouse Speech of 1909 than King George V's first invitation to Lloyd George to stay at Balmoral, three months after Edward VII's death.   'I am glad to say that the King has consented to ask Lloyd George to Balmoral,' Knollys wrote to Crewe in August 1910.   Crewe answered that Lloyd George 'and his friends will regard it as a real compliment, and he has shown such good feeling that it is a compliment well deserved.'   In May of the next year Knollys told Crewe that the King had directed him to write to congratulate Lloyd George on his famous Insurance Act—a measure which Knollys declared would 'keep the Government in office for another 15 years unless they get into trouble over the Home Rule Bill.'

The shock of King Edward's sudden death, and a natural sympathy for the new King's inexperience, combined to lessen political tensions for a brief while.   The Prime Minister scrupulously took advantage of this atmosphere to suggest to Mr. Balfour a series of secret talks between Government and Opposition leaders to try to reach a compromise on the Constitutional crisis and to avoid a second General Election.   This

Conference, which dragged on (with a summer intermission) for six months, consisted of Asquith, Crewe, Lloyd George and Birrell for the Liberals, Balfour, Lansdowne, Austen Chamberlain and Cawdor for the Unionists. The Conference began to meet in June 1910. By November it had solved nothing, and had merely served to emphasise the differences between Government and Opposition on many matters besides the House of Lords veto.

In its earlier stages it seemed possible that the Conference might succeed. Asquith told the King it had 'indicated a desire for *rapprochement*,' while at the beginning of August the King thanked Crewe for his report on the Conference and was 'very glad to think that the prospects of the success of the Conference are hopeful.' But by the end of July, when the Conference adjourned until October, pessimism had gathered. At the adjourned meeting of the Conference, Crewe tried to break the tension by suggesting that when the meetings were resumed in the autumn they should be held at Crewe Hall. Most of the eight participants shared Lansdowne's view of London in the early autumn—'I detest the idea of being in London in October,' he had told Crewe—and the invitation was gratefully accepted. The Conference disbanded to reassemble in the autumn at Crewe. But doubts of the wisdom of this plan soon developed: Lloyd George hinted to the Prime Minister that for the opposing parties to meet in a large Liberal country-house would lead to misconstruction, while Lord Lansdowne roundly declared that he had never heard, and therefore had never accepted, Crewe's invitation at all:

At the last meeting of the Conference [he wrote to Crewe], it was decided that we were to meet during the first week of October. It was not until two or three days afterwards that I became aware that it had also been decided that we were to reassemble under your roof. I must have been inattentive or deaf, but I gather that I was the only one of the members who failed to realise that your hospitality had been not only offered but accepted.

It occurred to me at once that there were serious objections to this alluring proposal. The arrangement would, in my opinion, be certain to provoke hostile comments. The Conference is already regarded, I fancy on both sides, with a certain amount of suspicion and this would, I am afraid, be increased if, instead of transacting our business under the ordinary official conditions, we were to assemble under your hospitable roof. It would at once be said that the whole affair was a picnic, and that business of such importance ought not to be transacted in such a distracting environment. Any agreement at which we might conceivably arrive must, from the necessities of the case, meet with severe criticism, probably at the hands of your supporters as well as ours. That criticism would, I cannot help thinking, be much more severe if the arrangement had been come to under such unusual conditions. For these and other reasons it seemed to me that we ought to stick to Downing Street, and retire to our own tents after each encounter.

Lansdowne added that Chamberlain and Cawdor both agreed with him, while Mr. Balfour, who was undergoing a cure at Gastein, had written that 'he has no strong feelings on the subject one way or the other.' 'While Balfour is evidently indifferent on the question of *venue*,' Lansdowne continued, 'he expressed with considerable emphasis a wish that 'the whole thing might be put off till November,' especially as the King 'has bitten another slice out of my home time by bidding me to Balmoral.' This dilettante attitude of Balfour confirms the findings of the most recent and thorough study of the failure of the Constitutional Conference—that it was not just due to insurmountable differences between Liberals and Unionists but also to the personalities and varied individual aims and motives of the eight men involved.

Historically the chief interest of these unsuccessful inter-party talks lies in the opportunity they gave Lloyd George to produce his splendid and imaginative plan for a Coalition Government to face up to and deal with the accumulating dangers of the domestic and foreign situation. This plan, rejected by Mr. Balfour, who declared that he could not become 'another Peel' in his party, was always believed by Lloyd George to have been capable of averting not only the Irish revolution but the First German War. Dictated by Lloyd George in the month of August, the Memorandum was shown to the Prime Minister in the third week of October but seems previously to have been made the subject of talks between Balfour and Lloyd George. Both at the time and subsequently Lloyd George was accused of double-crossing Asquith, and there have been many conflicting reports on such points as how his Memorandum reached Balfour, whether Asquith knew of it before it was shown to the Opposition leader, and whether Asquith consulted his colleagues. The only evidence existing amongst the Crewe papers is a short letter from Lloyd George to Crewe, dated from the Treasury Chambers, 20 October 1910:

At the Prime Minister's request I am sending you a Memo: I dictated on the desirability of co-operation with the Unionist leaders on a wide programme of National reconstruction.

Although I dictated it in the month of August, I had no opportunity of showing it to the P.M. until last week. You know what has happened since.

I ought to add that in my conversations with B. I assumed that as a condition precedent to such an understanding, a compact on the Constitutional issue was essential.

I also gave it as my opinion that an agreement as to the lines of settlement of the Education and Welsh Church questions was a necessary preliminary to any Coalition. The Nonconformists could not come in on any other terms.

He raised difficulties about Home Rule; but he was quite willing to consider any proposals for a federal arrangement.

Please return this copy as soon as you have read it. Are you likely to be in Town next week? I should like to talk it over with you before the Conference resumes.

In October the Conference resumed its sessions in London, Crewe's offer of his house having been, perhaps wisely, overruled: 'My own view,' he had replied to Lansdowne's letter, 'is that the whole transaction is so far out of the run of ordinary political controversy that the anomaly of opponents meeting for discussion at a private house might have been excused within limits. That is to say, that while it might have seemed improper to conclude a final arrangement under conditions so informal, it had not occurred to me, nor am I convinced, that to make some progress in this way during the holidays would have discouraged our well-wishers, or have given a handle to those who are hostile.' He added that there was no possibility of himself and his colleagues agreeing to a postponement or respite. Lansdowne punctiliously thanked him for this letter: 'Public opinion on both sides is no doubt rather highly strung,' he suggested, 'and it was really for that reason that I leaned to Downing Street rather than Crewe Hall.'

Lord Crewe

The optimism about the results of the Conference which Crewe had shared with Asquith at its opening, slowly diminished. Looking back on its deliberations after a lapse of twenty-five years, Crewe admitted that its failure was inevitable:

The Constitutional Conference was bound to fail [he wrote in retrospect], and the two Houses faced each other like gladiators in the arena. In ordinary times the current of Royal duties and occupations flows smoothly in a majestic stream, unbroken by obstructing rocks or by seething rapids. The British Constitution, with the vagueness of outline which has been its chief protection, has left the operation of the Royal Prerogative to settle itself throughout the changing conditions of two hundred and fifty years. But every now and then Governments, baulked by parliamentary stagnation, have invoked its aid from the Crown. In the turmoil of the great Reform Bill William the Fourth had reluctantly agreed to a possible creation of Peers far larger than that which carried the Peace of Utrecht under Queen Anne. Queen Victoria had no such difficult decision to make; but in 1871 the purchase of Commissions in the Army was abolished by Royal Warrant, a stroke described by Disraeli as 'an avowed and shameful conspiring against the privileges of the House of Lords' which had declined to proceed by legislation. Now, before Parliament was dissolved in November for a fresh Election within the year, it was evident that the position of 1832 might be reproduced on a more formidable scale. Party passion, still more excited by the financial policy of the Government, flared up higher than it had on the Eastern Question in 1877 and 1878, or even over Gladstone's first Home Rule Bill of 1886.

It was universally felt to be a hard fate for the Sovereign, not only that his reign should open in an atmosphere so disturbed, but that he should at once be confronted by a constitutional problem more puzzling than any that his illustrious Grandmother had had to solve during her reign of more than sixty-three years. It was impossible for the King to give any pledge to an outgoing Minister to support him in a new Parliament. He might not achieve a majority at all, or a majority so insignificant as to render doubtful the country's approval of his policy. Therefore, anything that the Sovereign could say must be purely hypothetical. But the Prime Minister's path was also difficult. It had been formally announced in February, and repeated in April, that the powers of the House of Lords would be in some respects curtailed, and after the break-down of the conference Parliament was dissolved on this issue. Unless there was a fair prospect that the certain resistance of the Peers would be in some way overcome sooner or later, the fervour of keen Liberal supporters would be damped, and the centrally minded voter, the man who creates a large parliamentary majority, would not trouble to assert himself. The main preoccupation of Ministers was to prevent the Crown, and the possible use of the Prerogative, from becoming a principal topic of discussion in the heat of the Election, and in the event the danger was, on the whole, avoided. It was agreed that the Sovereign had said as much as he could say, and nothing that he should not have said, constitutionally speaking. . . . The King must have been gratefully aware that whatever changes in domestic policy the future might hold, he was never likely again to be troubled by a domestic question so harassing and so unpleasant. Nor was he. The coming years produced sensational events for the United Kingdom, but none that imposed on the Sovereign the burden of a decision so arduous as this.

The deadlock in the Constitutional Conference, patent to all its members during the resumed sittings in the autumn of 1911, thus left the Cabinet with no alternative. Even Asquith's gifts of prevarication and delay could no further adjourn the evil hour of decision. The Government must now arrange, speedily and with the King's connivance, that the Parliament Bill be passed into law by the House of Lords. On 10 November, the day the Conference finally collapsed, Asquith went down to Windsor. By a curious mixture of delicate feeling, discretion and subtlety he left upon the King's candid mind the false impression that the Cabinet never were going to ask him for a formal promise to create sufficient Liberal peers to swamp the Tory Opposition in the Upper House. In fact the Prime Minister merely regarded this talk at Windsor as a preliminary or warning discussion; and when a few days later he did demand the 'guarantees' in the name of the Cabinet he was bewildered to learn that both the King and Bigge, his private secretary, felt that this almost amounted to a confidence trick. The King was mystified, and angry.

At the instance of Lord Knollys, whose influence in the first year of the reign was stronger than that of Sir Arthur Bigge, the King came up to London to give an audience to Asquith and Crewe. This was the famous 'scene in the Royal Closet' over which Opposition peers and Tory newspapers were so indignant. The two men explained to the King in clear terms that they were now under an obligation to hold a second General Election, but that they could not take this step without the King's expressing himself willing to create peers if necessary. At the close of the interview the King agreed, in his own words, 'most reluctantly to give the Cabinet a secret understanding that in the event of the Government being returned with a majority at the General Election' he would use his prerogative to create peers. 'It is obvious,' Asquith wrote to Crewe later in the same year, 'that our resignation in such circumstances, with a dissolution following, would have been in every way more damaging to the authority of the Crown, and this consideration may well have weighed with him.' The secrecy clause, probably inserted to spare the King's feelings, in fact incensed him more even than the actual demand for a guarantee. 'I have never,' he told Lord Esher in the autumn of that year, 'in my life done anything I was ashamed to confess. And I have never been accustomed to conceal things.' It is unfortunate that Crewe has left no personal memorandum of this interview, or that if he wrote one he subsequently destroyed it, an act in keeping with the extreme reserve and discretion of his character. Although the King never allowed his personal affection for Crewe to be impaired by this episode, there is evidence that to the end of his life he felt a sense of grievance, a suspicion that advantage had somehow been taken of his inexperience. Asquith has been criticised for bringing Crewe to the audience, as though he had felt the need for an independent witness. Whatever his motives—and n fact it seems only logical that Crewe should have attended the meeting in any case—he could not have chosen a witness of greater integrity or one less disingenuous or furtive. In an article which he wrote for the *Contemporary Review* on King George's Jubilee in 1935, a quarter of a century after these events, Crewe showed that he felt in retrospect neither doubt nor regret for his part in persuading King George to create peers.

The December Election—in which peers once more pursued the novel policy of speaking publicly in support of Party candidates—did not materially alter the Government's position. It left them with a convenient if composite majority in the House of Commons. Oddly enough, public opinion, so readily inflamed over matters like Chinese Labour or the Suffragettes, remained relatively calm upon the House of Lords issue, as though failing to appreciate either its drama or its import. Commenting on the previous election of January 1910, Crewe wisely remarked: 'It is curious that when the issue is by both sides admitted to be a supreme one, the polls in many places are smaller than can be accounted for by the fact of the old register.'

But if the voters remained lymphatic, the newspapers were crammed with letters of protest or support. These increased in number and vehemence as the Bill was first passed through the Commons in the spring, and then went up in early summer to the Lords, who were busy throwing up a defensive stockade in the shape of the Rosebery Resolutions for the reform of their House. Reports of Liberal speeches in Opposition papers, at no time notably urbane, now became frankly offensive: 'Faltering in his delivery, Lord Crewe was no less faltering in his arguments,' runs a typical sentence from a *Daily Mail* Parliamentary reporter's piece. Angry letters speculating on 'what had passed in the Royal Closet' abounded, alternating with reports of histrionic telegrams from Liberal peers such as Carrington, addressed to Liberal gatherings: 'We are engaged in the fiercest constitutional struggle since 1832. Again we have to secure that the will of the people shall prevail.' As the Lords debate upon the Bill dragged on through the summer, tempers rose. The thermometer was also rising, and the final August debate took place in a subtropical heat which even invaded the cool and shadowy corridors of Barry's Palace of Westminster. The Opposition peers rallied around Lord Halsbury, an unfortunately aged, infirm and reactionary symbol for them to have chosen. One fervent admirer sent the *Morning Post* verses addressed to Halsbury, verses which had in themselves an old-world, Regency ring;

> Thou antique bantam of a fighting breed,
> Holding with all thy lore this simple creed—
> To hold the right and fight and hold the right
> And fight and hold the right and fight and fight.

Crewe himself combined great admiration for Lansdowne's valiant moderation with contempt for the Halsburyites:

The 'Die-hards'—as they call themselves rather arrogantly taking the title of one of the Peninsular Regiments [he wrote to Hardinge]—include most of the names that one would expect to find.   I am not surprised that Selborne was one of their leaders, having had experience at the C.O. of his astonishing unwisdom and obstinacy on occasions, as well as of his sounder qualities.   Rayleigh alone gives some distinction to the list; but he is no politician, even in theory; and with nearly all the others 'I would not be seen dead at a pig fair.' as they say in Ireland.   The King, whom I saw for a long time yesterday, was greatly vexed at these hot-headed people, and keenly anxious for their defeat, in order to be saved from the very unpalatable necessity which would have been forced on him and us.

To the Die-hards not only the contents of the Bill but above all the manner in which it was being forced through were anathema.   The plan for 'lightly' creating several hundred peers shocked them beyond words, although many of them, including the *Morning Post* versifier, strove to put their anger into written form.   It was the idea of Liberal commoners lying dormant like leather-jackets in a summer lawn that drove these traditionalists to frenzy:

> Like caddis-worms, unseen, unknown, they lie,
> Ready to burst into the butterfly.
> One touch from Asquith and the grubs arise,
> A cloud of splendour to the crimson skies.
> But, Asquith, will those painted gawdy things,
> Spreading the glory of their ermined wings,
> Will they, flying far above the turgid flood,
> Remember that they rose from *Liberal* mud?
> Some change of state, like death, might break the bond
> Even of the high-souled, ultra-mundane Mond.
> Ah, there's the horrid doubt!   Who can deny
> When Peers are born that Liberals must die?

Even Crewe, himself a living and active contradiction of the last couplet of this jingle, greatly disliked the publicity of these fevered days, and the implied criticism of the King for acquiescing in Asquith's demands.   Although, as we have seen, he

124

had long played a leading and intimate part in the preparation of the Parliament Bill—what is clearly the very first rough draft, scribbled on House of Lords notepaper in Lord Loreburn's hand and addressed to Crewe is among his personal papers—he did not at all look forward to steering this contentious piece of legislation through the House of Lords. Thus in one sense his accident of March 1911, with its subsequent concussion enforcing a temporary retirement from public life, was almost welcome to him, for he was automatically relieved of taking the chief part in what he publicly named an 'odious business.' His illness meant the temporary return of John Morley to the India Office, and that 'our newest Viscount' (as Curzon called him) would for the time inherit the Government leadership in the House of Lords as well. Here Morley showed, again according to one of Curzon's letters to Crewe, 'quite excellent skill and flexibility.' To Esher, Morley confessed that he 'loved' leading the House of Lords and that he would not 'like it a bit' when Crewe came back.

In fact Crewe returned to his India Office desk some months before his doctor permitted him also to resume his work in the House of Lords; but, although thus forbidden to take part in the debate on the Parliament Bill, Crewe toiled ceaselessly in that first week of August to try to ensure its passage. On the first of August he had conferences with the Archbishop of Canterbury, and with Lord Cromer, both of whom were influential supporters of Lansdowne's policy of bowing to the inevitable by letting the Bill slip through. Crewe wrote a record of these two interviews, for the eyes of Asquith and Morley alone. This memorandum reveals Crewe's powers of conciliation, as well as the acute embarrassment which the Halsburyites or Die-hards were causing Lansdowne and his sympathisers:

I saw the Archbishop of Canterbury this afternoon on the question of the Division in the Lords [wrote Crewe]. He had issued at Lord Lansdowne's request a form of enquiry to the episcopal Bench. Three bishops had not replied, Manchester, Worcester and Bangor. All were strong Tories, but the strongest, Manchester, had stated orally that he would abstain, and the Archbishop expected that the other two would do the same. Three bishops, Chester, Hereford and Birmingham, would almost certainly vote with the Government and the Archbishop thought that seven or eight in all would do so sooner than see carried the negative to the Government motion. But we must remember that bishops sometimes have engagements which it was difficult to break, as they often affected large numbers of people, so that it would not be safe to count on the presence of these extra recruits, though probably some of them might be there. The Archbishop said in conclusion that though he could not act as a Whip to get bishops to vote, yet he would help generally as far as he could.

Later I saw Lord Cromer. His view was that Lord Lansdowne's last letter had added to the difficulty of the situation, by making it harder for Opposition peers to vote with the Government. A careful examination, made by a process of exhaustion, led him to place the possible danger at 106; but he believed that as a matter of fact not nearly so many would vote with Lord Halsbury. On the other hand he had reason to believe that some of those on the Lansdowne list would be irritated into voting with the revolters by the mere fact of Unionist support being given to the Government. He knew of one or two such, but did not think there would be many. On the other hand, if a single peer were created, the revolters would doubtless receive an uncertain but very large accession of strength, while most of his friends would not vote at all in such a case. His view was that the Government peers, plus some bishops, ought to muster close on 80, and that therefore an accession of 50 or 60 from the Opposition ought to make matters safe. He would consult two of his way of thinking, who would actively interest themselves in getting promises to attend.

I explained our position, and said that though an accession of 60 might, and probably would, ensure the carrying of the motion, they must be 60 people actually in the lobby, not merely well-wishers, and that a larger margin would be needed if distinct pledges to be present were not forthcoming in every case. It must be clearly understood that we could not run any real risk, though it was true there must be some element of uncertainty, in the absence of a list of revolters. It was therefore not possible to leave things till the last moment, because a man who had walked out could not change his mind at the last moment, even if he then regretted the probable defeat of the Government and wished to prevent it. A margin was therefore required beforehand. He said he would come again later in the week.

The Archbishop of Canterbury had also suggested that, if the Government were defeated, it might be possible to arrange to have the subject debated all over again so that any 'rebels' who regretted the defeat—the Archbishop thought there would be many of these—could have a chance to vote the other way. Although it seemed to Crewe that this was constitutionally legal and feasible he was firmly against such a solution. On 2 August he wrote to the Archbishop to explain why:

There seem to me to be two practical obstacles to any such sequel to a hostile division, both insuperable:

(*a*) Even if the Government desired to give an opportunity for reconsideration, it is most doubtful whether in the present temper of their supporters in the House and the Country, it would be possible for them to do so.

(*b*) There could be no guarantee that advantage would be taken of such an opportunity to reverse the Lords' decision. It is not to be supposed that Lord Lansdowne and the other leaders, having deliberately abstained for the first time, would then turn round and support the Government; and nobody can say that their followers would go with them, even if they were prepared to take such action themselves. Even if a certain number of peers were prepared to vote with the Government in order to reverse the decision, they would probably be counterbalanced by at least an equivalent number of those who abstained on the first occasion, but would vote on the second with Lord Halsbury and his friends, in order to avoid a *volte face*.

In these circumstances it is clear to me that every peer that desires to avoid the creation of such a number of peers as will override all possible opposition to the measure when it again comes before the House, must understand that he will share the responsibility for such a creation, if he abstains from supporting the motion not to insist on the crucial amendments made by the Lords, and it is thereby defeated.

As he proved later at the Paris Embassy, Crewe was innately conscious of the difference between the conciliatory and the prevaricating. When a point had been reached at which honest compromise was not possible, he was quick to say so. This quality comes out strongly in his reaction to the Unionists' next move—an attempt to strike an ambiguous bargain with the Government.

On the day following what the Unionist leader called 'our purely informal conversation' of 1 August, Crewe received a letter from Cromer informing him that 'a private meeting of some Unionist peers, many of whom at all events are, it is believed, anxious to avoid any fresh creations' would be held at Lord Bath's house next day. He therefore asked Lord Crewe to reply, for the Government, to three questions. How many Unionist votes would the Government require to ensure the passage of the Bill? Secondly, could Cromer be given 'a distinct assurance' that if this number were mustered in support of the Government 'no peers will be created?' Thirdly, could Crewe give the exact number of Liberal peers to be created if sufficient Unionist support were not forthcoming?

Cromer followed this semi-official letter with a private note in his own handwriting which makes it clear that even those moderate Unionists who did not think the Government was bluffing were startled and alarmed at the idea of a very large creation:

I would again urge the desirability of your stating in your letter to me that there will be no substantial difference, under the alternative possibilities, in the number of peers who will be created, and indicating clearly that the number will, in either case, be large. (I understand that this is the Govt's view.)

You mentioned to me 300. It may be unnecessary and undesirable to state any exact number in your semi-official letter to me, but I am not sure, if you really mean 300, that it might not be as well to state the figure in a private letter to me of which I could make a discreet use. My reason is that the figure was quite a new light to me. The general impression is that the new creations would, in any case, be far less numerous. The *maximum* figure I have ever heard suggested in Unionist circles is 120. If it were noised abroad on fairly good authority that you meant to make 300, there would of course be an outburst of indignation. The practical effect would be two-fold. On the one hand it would rejoice the hearts of the extreme 'no surrender' men who want to push you into a large creation. On the other hand it might make many, who expect a relatively small number of creations, pause. I cannot hazard a conjecture as to which of these influences would be the strongest, but I hear on good authority that

Selborne has been going about pledging his word of honour that the number of creations will be small.

Cromer added that he was not, of course, offering any opinion as to the Government's actual policy, of which he could not approve; but that he wanted to 'be of some use' in letting his Unionist friends 'know what are the real facts with which they have to deal.' As we have already noticed, an impenetrable secrecy shrouded the Cabinet room under Mr. Asquith's Administration.

Crewe drafted a careful reply to Cromer's letter, and submitted it to Mr. Asquith for emendation. The Government, he wrote, would undertake not to advise the creation of any peers for the Parliament Bill division only if a specific number of Opposition peers guaranteed to support the Government. On the subject which so tantalised the Oppostion—the probable numbers of new peers to be created—Crewe politely but firmly refused to pronounce:

It will [he wrote of this final alternative] become the duty of His Majesty's Government to advise His Majesty to create such a number of peers as will ensure the passage of the Bill in the form approved of by the House of Commons when the Lord's amendments are considered.

I ought to make it clear that if a creation of peers has to take place either before or after the Bill returns to the House of Lords, the number cannot be limited by any supposed estimate of the number of those peers who are now prepared to vote in favour of insisting on the Lords' amendments. The situation will have entirely changed, and many of those, who in existing circumstances are prepared to abstain, will consider themselves free to give a vote which would then be directed not against the creation of peers but against the measure of H.M.G. The Government would therefore be compelled to advise such a creation as would definitely safeguard the Bill against any opposition it could possibly encounter in the House of Lords.

But after further consideration this semi-official letter was never sent. Instead Crewe had a second meeting with Cromer, in which he explained why the Government did not propose to send a formal answer to his letter and to make it clear that there was 'therefore nothing in the nature of a bargain between the Government and any section of the Unionist

peers.' On 4 August Cromer wrote again to Crewe to tell him
the result of the meeting of Unionists at Lord Bath's. It had
been unanimously agreed that 'no attempt should be made to
organise a Unionist vote in support of the Government.'
Cromer hoped for a large-scale abstention by Unionists when
it came to the vote:

But I would venture to urge upon you the necessity of making
certain of all your own men—getting a few Bishops if you can
—and the Court votes. It may be, and probably will be, a
near thing, and it will really be perfectly monstrous if a step of
such enormous importance is taken by reason of the votes of a
few peers who are personally of no great importance.

As regards publicity. I said that nothing whatever had
passed between you and me which might not be proclaimed
on the housetops, but that although the general result was
public property at the same time the details of the negotiations,
of which I informed the meeting, were confidential, and I
trusted to the honour of those present not to make any indis-
creet revelations. I think this will be all right, but really if
some partial accounts leak out, it does not very much matter.

These parleys with the Opposition over, Crewe could not
yet wash his hands of the 'odious business.' Not for Asquith
only but for King George also, the fact that Crewe would not
be able to conduct the great debate for the Government was
worrying. Crewe shared with the King and the Prime
Minister the exclusive knowledge of just what had taken place
at the famous audience of the previous November, and he was
a man whose word commanded absolute and instantaneous
belief on both sides of the House. At the instance of his colleagues, therefore, he agreed to speak for the Government
during the debate on the Vote of Censure, which preceded the
final voting on the Parliament Bill by two or three days. He
did not welcome the task or feel physically up to it:

I curtail my letter today [he wrote on 4 August from the India
Office, to which he recently returned], as the political crisis
has invaded my retreat here, and I have been obliged to take
a somewhat active part, much against my will, as I hoped that
the adjournment of Parliament would take place without my
being dragged there. As it is, I shall have to attend the Vote of
Censure debate on Tuesday, and to say something by way of

apologia pro vita nostra as a Government, in reply to George Curzon's attack on us. It is vexatious to have to combine this work with my business here, which I am able to cope with in the main, but which does not leave me much spare energy available.

To Lord Knollys he wrote a letter for the King's information, explaining why he was going to speak:

As you know, I have been keeping away altogether from Parliament as I have found my daily work here as much as I could undertake [he wrote from the India Office]; but as this Vote of Censure has been put down for Tuesday I think it my duty and my principal colleagues think the same, that I should attend and make a statement of what actually took place. I saw your letter to the Prime Minister in which you said that the King desires that a plain statement should be made; I think I can do this without in any way dwelling on His Majesty's personal attitude in the matter as distinct from his action as Sovereign; and without entering into any needless detail. Care has made me distinctly better and I don't dread or anticipate any ill results from this temporary plunge into the arena. I shan't take any part in the Parliament Bill debate, beyond voting, or in any other business that may come on before the adjournment.

Lord Knollys replied from the royal yacht *Victoria and Albert*, on board which at Cowes he then was with the King, that he thought Crewe wise to refrain from taking part in the Parliament Bill debate, adding:

I am very glad however that it is *your* intention to make a statement of what actually took place in connection with the King's consent to give the guarantees, & H.M. has the greatest confidence in your judgement and discretion.

I hope you think he was right to let Asquith know, that as far as he is concerned, he (Asquith) was at liberty to make a 'clean breast' of the transaction.

I cannot help believing that there will be a small majority in favour of the Government on Wednesday. I should have much liked to have voted, but Asquith thinks that in view of my position about the King, I had better not.

While preparing notes for his speech, Crewe had been in close touch with Vaughan Nash, the private secretary to the

Prime Minister who was himself at that moment 'in a more or less voiceless condition.' Crewe had particularly asked whether, in his House of Commons statement during the vote of Censure, Asquith intended to make use of the word 'guarantees,' which, freely bandied about by Opposition and Government supporters, as well as by most of the newspapers, had acquired a very sinister implication, suggesting (as the Unionists freely did) that King George had been held up to ransom by Asquith and Crewe:

As to the word 'guarantees' he says he has never used it and doesn't propose to [the Prime Minister's secretary wrote to Crewe on 4 August]. He favours the word 'understanding' as a correct expression of the result of the interview with the King. As to what passed at the interview he is rather disposed to deprecate any details being given. He thinks of saying himself not much more than that you and he saw the King, and that H.M. consented to a Dissolution, and that an understanding was arrived at . . .

Crewe's speech was not long, but it took a great deal of careful preparation, and he could not cast it in a final form until the actual debate was under way and he had heard the chief accusations by Curzon, to which his speech would form a reply. This was the reason he alleged for refusing a direct request sent by the King through Knollys to submit his speech to Buckingham Palace before he made it:

I would have of course obeyed the King's wish and sent a statement if I had one, but I have not prepared it in a readable form because it is not possible to say on what particular point Curzon will lay stress in connection with this part of the subject in the light of the debate of yesterday and Asquith's speech [he wrote on August 8].
But speaking generally I propose to state His Majesty's wish that the circumstances should be clearly described and that I have also objected to the phrase 'guarantees,' because in November last two things remained hypothetical (a) whether we should have an adequate majority and (b) whether the ultimate difference between the Houses would be of sufficient magnitude to justify the giving of advice to create peers. That we could not advise a dissolution without knowledge that the contingency might possibly be thus met, and that a resignation

of our offices would not have helped matters, but the contrary. And, in particular, that it is my belief that if the late King had been spared, though it is impossible to say if the Conference would have taken place, the general course of events would have been the same as that which has actually occurred.

The speech of Lord Curzon to which it fell to Lord Crewe to reply proved a stinging attack on the Government. Curzon twisted Junius's epigram by declaring to the bench opposite: 'You began by coercing the King and ended by betraying the people,' and alluded sarcastically to the 'mercenary host' by which the Upper House was threatened with invasion. According to one Opposition newspaper Crewe in reply 'spoke like a man who was not in sympathy with his brief,' a contention which seems almost justified when we read his speech today:

The question of the interview with His Majesty has been made the subject of so much comment that the King naturally desires that the facts should be plainly stated. The effect of that interview was that we ascertained His Majesty's views. We suggested that if the opinion of the country was plainly ascertained upon the Parliament Bill, in the last resort a creation of peers might be the only way of putting an end to the dispute. His Majesty faced the contingency and entertained the suggestion as a possible one, but with natural and— if I may be permitted to say so—with legitimate reluctance. His Majesty naturally entertained the feeling, which we shared, that if we resigned office having, as we had, a large majority in the House of Commons, the only result would be an immediate dissolution in which it would practically be impossible, however anxious we might be, to keep the Crown out of the controversy. The mixing up of the Crown in a controversy such as that was naturally most distasteful to its illustrious wearer whom we regard as the express guardian of its prestige, but scarcely more distasteful even to His Majesty than to myself and my colleagues. It is altogether inaccurate to state that any time we asked His Majesty for guarantees. . . .

The noble earl [Curzon] has complained of the Government's reticence with regard to the conversations with the King. I wonder what he would have said if we had attempted to use those conversations as a lever for the general election last December in order to secure votes for the Government? Those conversations were of a formal character and were not of a nature which should have been made public at the time. . . .

The allegation is that our action in presenting the views of the Cabinet last November was premature. Our answer is that it was not action at all. It was a conversation dealing with a purely hypothetical set of conditions. . . .

I do not pretend that as a party we are all of one mind on the question of the creation of peers. We, therefore, resemble the noble lords opposite, some of whom seem to look forward with positive enjoyment to the idea of a forced creation. If we are to be forced into giving advice as to the creation of peers, we cannot pretend that the number to be so created shall necessarily be limited by any newspaper lists, nor would necessarily have any reference whatever to the division lists of this House. . . . The whole business, I frankly admit, is odious to me.

The phrase which drew most notice in this speech was that in which Crewe had referred to the King's 'natural and legitimate reluctance' to consider creating peers. Some Unionists took it as proof that the Government was bluffing. In fact, this phrase seems to have emanated from Buckingham Palace itself, since Knollys wrote to Crewe suggesting the phrase 'with whatever reluctance'—a noun, in fact, the adverb of which the King had himself used in his own journal account of the November interview—as the most suitable to 'meet the case.' The King had been displeased by Asquith's explanation during the Vote of Censure debate in the House of Commons as well as fussed by the speeches of radical M.P.s and by criticism in the Carlton Club. He looked to Crewe, to whom he would sometimes appeal as 'a lifelong friend' to repair the damage:

It appears [Asquith wrote to Crewe on 8 August] that the King thinks that in the case, as presented by me, he looks too like a willing accomplice in our nefarious doings. So I see no objection to your saying that he entertained our suggestions last Nov. with 'natural & legitimate reluctance.'

As late as that July, when he described the King as 'obsessed by the House of Lords question,' Crewe had felt fairly confident that the Bill would be passed and the new creations avoided: 'The position,' he wrote, 'now seems easier, and it seems pretty clear that we shall avoid a creation of peers, greatly to the disappointment of many, probably the majority, of our party.' But on the steaming night of 10 August, when the Bill was finally passed amid scenes unparalleled in the history of the

House of Lords,[1] even Crewe felt doubts, as he admitted in an account of the scene which he wrote the next day:

It is a comfort and relief to us to have got rid of the Parliament Bill at last. Last night's scene in the House of Lords was striking and novel: most of the dramatic episodes I have witnessed there, such as the rejection of the Home Rule Bill of 1893, and of the 1910–11 Budget, were foregone conclusions, and carried therefore no genuine thrill with them—yesterday it was otherwise, because the best prophets could not tell up to the end which way the event would go, and the excitement was patent and universal. I did not attempt to sit through the proceedings, having done as much as I dared by attending the Vote of Censure debate on Tuesday and making a speech. This was a duty, because I had been so intimately and continuously mixed up with the earlier phases of the struggle, that if I could get to the post, even on three legs, it was necessary to run. I was none the worse, though desperately tired that night and the next day.

But I attended last night's division, of course, and watched before the end the working faces and tense expression of our generally apathetic members. One of my early recollections is of going as a schoolboy to some of the 1869 debates on the Irish Church; I can remember the effect produced by such speakers as the old Lord Derby and Bishop Wilberforce, but have not carried away the memory of any scene like yesterday's.

This habit of historical comparison, of setting modern events into the long perspective of time, gave wisdom and serenity to Crewe's attitude towards the shouting and scurry of contemporary life. He was firmly convinced that no ameliorating effort is ever wasted; 'apart from religious beliefs,' he once wrote to his wife, 'one can maintain the faith that life is continuous and that nothing that has once been real ever dies. We all go on and so does any work that we have done.'

---

[1] The tellers announced the final figures at 10.40 p.m., when it was learned that the Government had won by a majority of seventeen votes. Apart from their own eighty supporters, they had received the votes of thirteen prelates and thirty-seven Unionist peers. Lord Lansdowne and his supporters had abstained.

Chapter Nine

FROM our present stand-point in time the two years 1912 to 1914—in Crewe's life the period between his return with the King and Queen from the Delhi Durbar and the tormenting decision of the Asquith Cabinet to declare war in August 1914—are not easy to get into a just perspective, nor indeed to contemplate attentively at all. Far too frequently referred to as a canyon or a chasm, the First World War seems, as we look back at it, more like some evil mountain range, rearing into a black sky and blotting out of view everything upon its further, sunnier slopes. Crewe himself, of course, never felt this. Not only had he lived and worked through the decades before the war, but he also persisted in regarding life, and particularly political life, as what he termed 'a continuum.' 'I do not myself in the least sympathise with those who regard pre-war politics as out of date,' he wrote in reply to an historian's enquiry for information in the early nineteen-twenties. But to us it is almost impossible not to look at the last years of world peace in the light of the subsequent world conflict, and perilously difficult to try to reconstruct the mood of leisurely optimism of those pre-war days. For those in charge of public affairs in this country in 1913 and 1914 had no special reason to suspect that the outbreak of a continental war was imminent. It was the fear of a Civil War in Ireland which was then obsessing the minds of the King, the Cabinet and the Opposition leaders, while as a background to the long deliberations on what should be done about Fermanagh and Tyrone when the new Home Rule Bill passed into law, the surly muttering of the discontented coal-miners mingled with the strident and distracting cries of the heroines of Mrs. Pankhurst's Woman's Suffrage campaign.

Like most other public figures, from the King downwards,

Lord Crewe was periodically threatened by the Suffragettes and had recourse at times to police protection. 'My Lord,' begins an 'urgent and private' letter from a total stranger, a fair example of others he received in these years:

In the course of a letter from a Suffragette friend to me received this morning I gather that something is to be attempted this evening by the militant suffragettes as regards yourself.

I have looked in vain in *The Times* for any announcement of any public engagement of yours, and assume therefore that something may be attempted at the House of Lords, or at your private house. It is possibly something desperate, a flaming advertisement for the Suffragette cause in the papers, as my young friend anticipates going to prison for 'encounters and skirmishes at Lord Crewe's.'

Lord Crewe returned 'warm thanks' for this friendly warning, and told his private secretary to inform Scotland Yard.

Crewe's attitude towards Female Suffrage was not sympathetic. He believed that no Government could or should give the vote to women without an appeal on this issue to the electorate. On one occasion he was taken to task by Mrs. Pankhurst herself, who wrote him a peevish letter about his answer to one of a suffragist lady's questions after a speech which he had made at Brierley Hill. Crewe had then declared that anybody who fancied that the Government could introduce a bill 'to bring forward a greater Constitutional change infinitely than that suggested by Home Rule or the Reform Bill of 1832' was so 'deplorably ignorant' of the way public affairs were carried on in this country as to 'encourage one to doubt the fitness of such a person to exercise any political functions at all.' On such occasions Crewe was not incapable of delivering a sharp retort.

In the matter of coming out publicly against votes for women, Crewe felt himself somewhat shackled by his father's memory, for typically enough Lord Houghton, a zealous devotee of every new and unpopular cause, had been one of the earliest enthusiasts for the movement, allowing John Stuart Mill to use his own and his wife's name as members of the General Committee of the Women's Suffrage Society when this was founded in the eighteen-sixties. In 1911 Lord Curzon had written to Crewe enclosing a draft of a letter which he

and Lord Cromer intended to publish, announcing the
foundation of their Anti-Woman-Suffrage Appeal. Ten
thousand pounds had already been subscribed by private
persons—£3,000 from the Rothschilds, £1,000 each from Lady
Wantage, Lord Iveagh and Sir Ernest Cassel, while other
subscribers included Lords Rosebery, Durham and Joicey,
'Lulu' Harcourt and Sir E. Stern. Would Lord Crewe
contribute to this good cause? Crewe replied that he would
like 'to think over the question':

I have always been unfavourably disposed to the idea of
Women's Suffrage [he told Curzon], but I have never so far
taken an active part against it, largely because my Father (in
more placid times) was one of those who helped the cause in
public and private. Circumstances have changed but I should
like a little time for consideration before committing myself to
the Campaign.

It is characteristic of Crewe's total lack of prejudice that after
1918 he entirely changed his views about female suffrage, on
the grounds that the work done by Englishwomen during the
four years of war abundantly proved that they deserved, and
ought to exercise, the Vote. Crewe was throughout his life
open to conviction: 'For myself,' he wrote on one occasion, 'I
care little for the imputation of changing my mind, for it is
often the wisest thing a man can do.'

Crewe took the national coal strike of February to April
1912 with his accustomed detachment. Although he knew a
good deal about mining conditions, having been reared at
Fryston and at Crewe, and himself owning some small coalmines, he took no part in the direct negotiations with the
strikers which Mr. Asquith was instituting. The Government
'*conférenciers*' as Crewe called them were Asquith, Buxton,
Lloyd George and Edward Grey. Crewe merely observed
what was going on:

The remarkable features of the whole business [he wrote in
March 1912] have been (1) the extraordinary good humour
with which the war has been carried on, (2) the apparent
callousness of the miners, who are essentially the best of working
men, in contemplating the shortage of a necessary of general
life, and (3) the littleness of the points at issue. This last fact
explains the first; but it will not be admitted by those who see

in the strikes a profound Socialist or Syndicalist plot (and many of these critics seem to be unaware that the two things are not only different but are in direct antithesis one to the other).

The year 1912 brought an increase of party hatred; and in the words of Sir Harold Nicolson, 'as the year drew to its end, the King was saddened by the new bitterness of party conflict and by the presage of further strife to come.' Crewe shared King George's anxieties. After the unseemly row in the House of Commons in November 1911, when a Unionist member had seized a book from the table and hurled it at Mr. Winston Churchill's head, Crewe commented in one of his routine letters to the Viceroy of India:

You will have seen what excitements have been thrilling the House of Commons. I cannot say that our moral position is impregnable, because we are undoubtedly trying Parliament high in pressing three first-class measures to a conclusion at once and within a brief time. I hope that the peculiar conjunction of the stars which in our opinion makes this necessary may not recur in my time.

The most important of these three first-class measures, and the one which aroused party feeling to quite new extremes of frenzy, was the Government's Bill for giving Ireland Home Rule.

With regard to Irish Home Rule Crewe remained what he had always been—a strong Gladstonian. In his youth he had learned from his father to distrust the English attitude to Ireland, for Lord Houghton interested himself in Irish affairs and took the unorthodox—or as his friends preferred to call it, the 'paradoxical'—view that England was largely to blame in the matter. In 1845, indeed, Monckton Milnes had been reproached for his views on Ireland by his own constituents in Pontefract, after he had published a pamphlet urging his compatriots to look at Ireland from 'an *Irish,* not an *English* point of view.' Crewe's subsequent, first-hand experience of the country over which for the three years 1892–1895 he ruled as Lord-Lieutenant confirmed his previous opinions. If anything he left Viceregal Lodge a more convinced Home Ruler

than when he had gone there. Since those days he had continued to study the Irish problem, publishing articles on it in
such periodicals as the *Contemporary Review*, in which he combated the Unionist assertion that a country which had been
occupied for seven centuries had no claim to be regarded as a
nation. He would point out the odd and hypocritical anomaly of England, 'a sworn crusader of the national idea,' the
champion of oppressed minorities, occupying Ireland by force
and refusing to recognise its nationhood:

During the last century [England] showed sympathy, genuine
if sometimes rather helpless, with unredeemed Italy, with
Poland, with Hungary, and with some of the races subject to
the Sultan's rule. She had words of admiration even for
hopeless risings against a foreign occupation:

> You said (there shall be answer fit),
> And if your children must obey,
> They must; but thinking on this day
> 'Twill less debase them to submit.

But through these vague campaigns of authentic sentiment it
was never imperative for Englishmen to formulate a precise
definition of what a nation is, or the measure of its claim to
self-government.

With his customary fair-mindedness, Crewe admitted that the
fault was not all on England's side: 'There are indeed many
crimes and many revenges in the last four hundred years that
both countries will do well to forget when the gates of Janus
are closed for good,' he wrote in 1922.

Crewe bore, of course, the burden of arranging the Home
Rule debate in the House of Lords in January 1913, but he
seems to have had little to do with the planning which preceded the presentation of that measure or with the negotiations
of the following year. In September 1913, at Balmoral, the
King, who was beset with anxiety about the whole Home Rule
question, consulted various of the Ministers and statesmen, who
passed through the castle that month, on the possibility of
arranging an inter-party conference on Irish Home Rule.
While some of his Ministers made satisfactory and even
enthusiastic replies, the King thought Crewe only 'fairly sympathetic' to this conference scheme. As we have seen, Crewe

had great faith in the value of negotiation and of compromise, but he did not believe in fruitless negotiation and he knew when a point had been reached at which compromise was out of the question. The Buckingham Palace Conference of July 1914 proved as abortive as Crewe had supposed that it would. In September 1914 the Irish Home Rule Bill was given the royal assent, and then shelved until the termination of the war.

In April 1913 King George's personal friendship with Lord Crewe was publicly affirmed by his acceptance of an invitation to stay at Crewe Hall during a visit with Queen Mary to the Potteries. This expedition to the Midlands was in keeping with King George's own interpretation of his royal duties: that he should travel about the country, be seen by people who might never have a chance to come to London, and himself obtain a close-up view of living conditions. He toured mining and industrial areas, talked to men at work and called on families in their homes, generally using some house such as Wentworth Woodhouse or Crewe Hall as a convenient base from which to motor round the county. On this occasion he and the Queen visited the Minton factory at Stoke, the potteries at Fenton and Longton, Wedgwood's Etruria works, the silk mills at Leek, and a colliery at Kidsgrove, as well as railway workshops and orphanages in the town of Crewe. Each evening they returned exhausted to Crewe Hall, to be revived by the Crewes' superlative food and—in the case of Queen Mary, since the King drank whisky only—wine. Glees were sung in the evening by local choirs, the King planted a tree in the grounds, and on Thursday, 24th April, the royal visitors entrained for Euston Station, much gratified, as they wrote, by their stay. Like all royal displacements, this brief visit had required complex and tedious organisation. It has left behind it a solid residue of paper parcels containing letters, papers, maps and plans. 'I am busy with the preparations for the visit which the King and Queen are going to pay us at Crewe next month,' Crewe wrote in March 1913 to a friend. 'Though it only lasts three days it seems to take almost as much arranging as the Durbar.'

A few months before the visit of the King and Queen to Crewe Hall its owner had entertained there, for two days in September 1912, the Russian Foreign Minister, Sazonov, who

was on a tour of the capitals of Europe. Sazonov had been
invited to Balmoral by King George, and it was on his way
back South that he and the Russian Ambassador, Count
Benckendorff, stopped at Crewe Hall, where they held conversations with their host and with Sir Arthur Nicolson of the
Foreign Office. From both the India Office and the Foreign
Office viewpoints there was much to discuss—the Persian
situation generally and the Russian bombardment of Meshed
in particular, Russian intentions towards Kashgar and in Tibet,
and the eternal matter of the Afghan frontier. More conscious
than people in England of the dangerous proximity of Russian
power to the frontiers of India, the Viceroy and the Government at Calcutta maintained the greatest vigilance. Diplomatic conversations do not make very interesting reading; but
a quotation at this point from the account of the Sazonov talks
which Crewe sent to Hardinge in India will show the manner
in which Crewe dealt with an awkward topic and thus illus-
trates one further facet of his competence. A subject, chosen
here at random, can be the recent bombardment of the ancient
Persian city of Meshed, and local difficulties between the
Russian and English consuls there:

I in no way concealed my opinion [Crewe wrote of this part
of his talk with Sazonov], and he expressed great regret that
there had been any bombardment. We were to take it that
Prince Dabija would not trouble us any further, though
Sazonov avoided saying in so many words that he was retired
on the spot, because he was trying to find out if Major Sykes
could not be moved. The line he took was that we both had a
certain number of officers of the old school, who respectively
could not get rid of the notion that England or Russia is the
enemy and conducted their policy on that basis. He had
himself removed from Teheran one man of this kind. (This
was the consul whose name I forget, but he figures prominently
in Shuster's book.) I said that there had been a great deal of
friction at Meshed, but that I did not think that Sykes had
worked in any underhand way against Russia; we thought
him a very good man (if not one of the coolest, such as for
instance Cox) and it might be difficult to promote him on the
spur of the moment. However I would tell you what the
Minister said. He went on to urge that civilians and not
soldiers should be sent to these posts, because the latter often

had the hostile tradition of which he had spoken. I replied that this was not true of a very large proportion, and did *not* admit to him that there may be a certain foundation for this classification. On the particular case, if a good place could be found for Sykes, which he would like, I should not mind his being moved, would you? On the other hand, Russian doings in Khorassan have been atrociously bad, much worse than those in Tabriz of which so much capital has been made by the partisans of Shuster and the Persian Nationalists in this country.

At Balmoral the royal family had been 'charmed' by Sazonov, so the King wrote to his cousin the Emperor Nicholas. Crewe, who had invited 'a few sociable people' as well as his foreign guests, was less enthusiastic. He thought the Foreign Minister of the Russian Empire not quite up to his job:

Do you know Sazonov? [he asked Lord Hardinge, reporting to him on these questions]. I suppose that when you were in Russia he was a quite inconspicuous figure. I thought him capable and well-poised in mind, but he seemed either tired or below par, giving the impression of a man with too little vitality to care as much as a Foreign Minister ought how events shape themselves. I enclose a copy of the note I made after our conversation, which was not striking, though he was evidently well up in the various details.

While Sazonov, Benckendorff and Arthur Nicolson were at Crewe they received the sinister news of Bulgarian mobilisation. Three weeks later the First Balkan War was well ablaze.

The First Balkan War, which ended in May 1913, was soon followed that June by the Second Balkan War, and this in its turn by the universal catastrophe of August 1914. The suddenness with which the 'Great War' burst over Europe astonished certain members of the British Cabinet, including some of those most intimately acquainted with Foreign Affairs. 'Looking at the whole business,' Crewe wrote a few days after our declaration of war on Germany, 'one cannot avoid the conclusion that panic, more than aggression, is at the bottom of it. Russia no doubt has never forgiven the way she was hectored by Germany over the Bosnian affair five years ago, but Germany herself has been haunted by the idea that she is hated and hemmed in, the first of which is true enough, though the latter is not. It was very maladroit of her not to get on better terms with Belgium, if she meant to use her as a highway to France.'

Born two years after the signature of the Treaty of Paris, which ended the war in the Crimea, Crewe had as a child been fascinated by stories of that conflict, all the more so since Miss Florence Nightingale had been one of the closest friends of his parents, and godmother and namesake to his sister Florence. While the boy was at Harrow, the Franco-Prussian war was raging. He would recollect in later years the feverish interest with which he and his companions followed the campaign upon school maps, and how in 1871, when his father crossed to Paris to see the ruins of the Tuileries and other buildings burned during the Commune, 'Robin' would pore over the albums of photographs of charred buildings and desolate battlefields which Lord Houghton brought back for his children. But this was all in the distant past and, like many other of his contemporaries, Crewe could not, in 1914, seriously believe that the folly of general war would ever again be indulged by the civilised nations of Europe. So late as the very end of the month of July 1914, Crewe was writing with a faint surprise that 'the European situation has developed in a remarkable way,' but the notion that the Sarajevo murders could lead to war offended his sense of logic: 'Even though the Archduke was the victim of a plot hatched in Servia there can be no direct implication of the Servian Government; nor was he, poor fellow, so much of a national hero that the whole crowd must spring to avenge him,' Crewe remarked.

But soon the speed of events was bewildering. All sense of reality seemed to dissolve. On 6 August, two days after the British declaration of war, Crewe found the sequence of events 'changing like a kaleidoscope,' their development being 'so amazingly rapid that we all feel as though we were living in a novel by Wells, and in no real world.' Some months later, in November, he remembered that at about the same period of the previous year he had been to a peaceful shooting-party at Windsor: 'The poor Archduke Franz Ferdinand was the central figure of the party,' he wrote to a friend, 'and when one reflects on all that has happened since, of his murder and its ostensible sequel, the ordinary flow of time seems to disappear in a mist, and count of everything is lost.'

Of his colleagues in the Cabinet, it seemed to Crewe that it was Edward Grey who, during these days of acute crisis, showed the greatest wisdom and good sense:

> Grey [he wrote to the Viceroy] has been a tower of strength and patience, the latter all the more striking because he became convinced that we must be driven into support of France some time before most of us were. Not a few thought that Germany would accept the conditions of neutrality of Belgium and abstention from attack on the French coast which would have been so advantageous to France as to offer almost complete payment of our debt to her. But it has been clear that Germany, maintaining the Bismarckian standard of public ethics, never meant to keep her treaties. If it had been left to Lichnowsky I believe that things could have been settled.

Once war was declared, Crewe, like other leading members of Mr. Asquith's Government, was plunged into many new and strenuous administrative activities and faced by novel and unprecedented problems. A chief preoccupation, of course, was to coax the Government of India into agreeing to the despatch of as many trained men as possible to Europe, while simultaneously trying to prevent the War Office, under Kitchener, from depleting India of soldiers beyond a certain margin of safety; in particular Crewe agreed with the Viceroy that it was essential that at least some British soldiers should remain in India. Observing the rather hectic tempo at which Kitchener kept the War Office, Crewe came to the conclusion that the latter was not 'the great organiser' he had in peace-time been assumed to be, but rather 'a man with an amazing capacity of getting work out of people, to an extent which I have never seen equalled.' The apparent inability of the Admiralty to ensure the safety of convoys on the Indian Ocaon and other seas also gave Crewe food for reflection:

> I do not think that the Admiralty have come out very strong all over the world in the arrangements for shadowing the hostile cruisers and so hunting them down [he wrote before the close of the year 1914]. We were formerly allowed to believe that coaling necessities would make it impossible for these highwaymen to keep going for long: but in practice this theory seems

to have broken down, and they disappear for a long time, turning up like giants refreshed at the end of it. It is true that the sea is a large place, as Winston is fond of pointing out; but we pay fifty millions a year for our Navy in order to reduce its area to manageable dimensions.

Apart from his specifically Indian responsibilities—which now included a sharper concern over those Arab countries adjacent to the Indian frontiers, and liable to invasion if Turkey declared war on the Allies, as well as keeping an eye on arrangements such as those for the reception of Indian contingents in France and in this country, and the transit of Indian wounded to Egypt—Crewe also worked with Lloyd George during the first weeks of the war over financial arrangements, 'a vast and complicated job' which involved concerting plans with the Bank of England and many private banks. But the most interesting of Crewe's secondary war-time tasks were his frequent turns of duty at the Foreign Office, where he took over from Sir Edward Grey whenever the Foreign Secretary retired to Fallodon or to The Glen to rest. Grey's confidence in Crewe's judgement was as complete as that of Asquith: 'I cannot sit here,' he wrote from his Foreign Office desk one day in 1915, 'without sending you a line to say how deeply grateful I am for the relief, which but for your presence here I could not have had, not at any rate with such confidence.' In order to make it easier for Crewe to take over the Foreign Office at a few days' notice, Grey gave him free access to Foreign Office telegrams and despatches. Some of these Crewe studied with detached amusement:

Grey has had a harassing time of it lately with Greece and the Balkan States [he wrote in 1915]. Their mingled greed and coyness is that of a set of cocottes offering themselves with no sort of disguise to the richest bidder; and anybody who has entertained lofty ideas of national ethics ought to study the correspondence and telegrams. One does not expect very much in the way of morality from King Ferdinand; but so far perhaps Roumania must be awarded the prize both for avidity and duplicity.

On the much-debated question of whether the war would last a short time or long one, Crewe inclined to the view that all

Europe was embarked on a prolonged war of attrition. In the very first weeks the terrible nature of the new war proved hard to realise. In its early days it seemed to Crewe to imply a profound dislocation rather than a severe demolition of normal life, an impression evident in a comment he made to one of his daughters, whose husband was leaving for France. 'Military necessities,' he wrote, 'seem to involve a vast amount of individual inconvenience.' But by the onset of the first winter it was clear that more than 'individual inconvenience' was concerned, and as death after death amongst the sons and nephews of Crewe's friends filled the ever-lengthening casualty columns of *The Times*, his reflections upon this appalling wastage of young life were as melancholy as those of any sensitive and peaceful man must be in such conditions: 'The heavy toll goes, taking so many, as it seems, who have every- thing to make life delightful, and a brilliant future never to be realised.' In November 1914 'the inferno of shell-fire' at the Front engulfed his eldest daughter's husband, Arthur O'Neill, leaving her a widow with five children, while later in the war Crewe's brilliant brother-in-law, Neil Primrose, was killed in the Middle East. The daily news of fresh losses, and the dulling sense that this holocaust might well go on for many years, worked powerfully on Crewe's imagination. When, in March 1915, the schoolboy editor of *The Harrovian* asked him to contribute a brief note to a memorial number containing the names of Harrow boys already slaughtered in France, Crewe returned suddenly to the practice of his youth, and produced the verses, *A Harrow Grave in Flanders*. These verses are among the best which Crewe ever wrote. Constantly reprinted during the first war, they deserve to survive today:

> Here in the marshland, past the battered bridge,
>   One of a hundred grains untimely sown,
> Here, with his comrades of the hard-won ridge,
>   He rests unknown.
>
> His horoscope had seemed so plainly drawn:—
>   School triumphs, earned apace in work and play;
> Friendships at will; then love's delightful dawn
>   And mellowing day;

Home fostering hope; some service to the State;
    Benignant age; then the long tryst to keep
Where in the yew-tree shadow congregate
        His fathers sleep.

Was here the one thing needful to distil
    From life's alembic, through this holier fate,
The man's essential soul, the hero will?
        We ask; and wait.

Many people assumed that Crewe was thinking of some
particular young friend or relation: he was not. 'I have given
up writing any verses', he told an old friend, 'but I did not like
to refuse this invitation. The lines do not refer to an individual,
but to a type of popular and successful schoolboy, with the
vista of a happy and useful life cut short, as so many have been.'

In May 1915 the Prime Minister attempted to remedy
general dissatisfaction with the conduct of the war by inviting
Unionist leaders to join a Coalition Ministry. His decision,
caused by what Crewe discreetly termed 'simultaneous crises
at the Admiralty and the War Office,' was taken entirely on
his own initiative, and without even Crewe's advice. 'There
are of course countless inaccuracies in the published reports;
but the general effect is well-known,' Crewe wrote to Lord
Hardinge. Like the Prime Minister, Crewe believed that 'a
new régime' had become necessary at the Admiralty. The
War Office matter, he added, was a different one:

At the War Office, the failure entirely to solve the problem of
supplying munitions—in particular high explosives—proving
as it did the undue burden laid on one man, even so good a
worker as Kitchener, brought about a situation of a different
sort. It was evidently a more difficult task than was imagined
for a first-class soldier at the War Office to carry on in concert
with the commanders at the front; and a most unscrupulous
press campaign, mainly conducted by Lord Northcliffe's
papers, has added to the difficulties. I say deliberately that
there can be no spy here in German pay, however ingenious,
who has done or is doing a tithe of the harm to his country than
Lord Northcliffe and his newspapers are. The War Office
difficulty will I trust be solved satisfactorily; but it became
evident to Asquith that we could not carry on thus, so *proprio
motu*, and with no preliminary discussion with one of us, even

the most intimate and influential (in which he was absolutely right) he decided on reconstruction.

All the members of the Cabinet automatically placed their offices at the Prime Minister's disposal. In doing this Crewe himself added some words of unselfseeking advice, which he likewise recounted for the Viceroy's benefit:

The Unionist leaders, with whom we have been discussing things in the most friendly spirit on both sides, are clearly entitled to a considerable share of the higher offices, such as Secretaryships of State, and I thought it my duty, besides generally placing my office at Asquith's disposal—as we all did —to point out what sort of change here would be prejudicial to India and be likely to create an undesirable and even dangerous agitation among the most loudly vocal class; and on the other hand what kind of successor could safely sit in this chair.

The result of these negotiations was that Austen Chamberlain succeeded Crewe at the India Office, while Crewe himself reverted to the post of Lord President of the Council, which he had filled from 1905 to 1908. He said that he ended his official connection with India 'with poignant regret.' After the Cabinet changes had been announced, he received a warm personal note from Mr. Asquith:

Now that this chapter is closed, I should like to assure you of the deep gratitude and affection, which will always be engraved in my memory, for your wise counsel, and your loyal and unselfish help.

In the following year, 1916, Asquith asked Crewe to move across to the Board of Education as its President. For this post Crewe was ideally suited in every way, but he did not have the chance to occupy it for long. In December 1916 the Prime Minister was ousted by an intrigue of Lloyd George, who, taking advantage of Unionist dissatisfaction with Asquith's lack of a more vigorous war policy, succeeded him as Prime Minister of a reconstituted Coalition Government. Crewe and Grey followed Asquith out of office. Later in the month of December Crewe sat down and wrote a factual, sober-minded and

convincing account of this crisis. Both as an historical document, which Asquith himself declared to be the most accurate
record of the incident, and as showing Crewe's gift for expressing himself obliquely and without invective, I have printed
this lengthy memorandum, *The Break-up of the Coalition Government*, as an appendix to this book.

In this memorandum Crewe implies, without ever directly
stating, that Lloyd George had behaved in a manner which
Crewe himself could not condone. It was seldom Crewe's
habit to condemn a man outright, and he would always make
an effort to understand or at least analyse conduct alien or
inferior to his own ethical standards. He had never either
liked or admired Lloyd George, and it is characteristic of
Crewe that amongst the many books in his library which cover
the period of the First World War the fat volumes of Lloyd
George's *Memoirs* do not figure. Crewe always refused to read
this somewhat imaginative work, 'not caring much,' as he
wrote on the subject to Herbert Paul in 1933, 'about the
cooked-up recollections of the Statesmen, British or foreign, who ·
appear to have foreseen everything at the time; but to have been
unable to point out the more excellent way while everybody else
was thundering along.' In the nineteen-thirties Crewe was
approached by other friends of Edward Grey to assist them in
preparing a denial of the accusations against Grey contained
in Lloyd George's book. Crewe agreed, wryly remarking:
'It could be done, no doubt, by making reckless counter-
charges against Ll. G.—like a Rivarol or a Tim Healy in his
best days—but I fear that none of us is up to that form.' He
contented himself by repeating a judgement on Lloyd George
which he had come across in a German review of the *Memoirs*
in the *Berliner Monatschefte* for October 1933: 'He was the most
insular of English statesmen, and knew less of foreign countries
than any other Minister at that time.'

Now out of office, Crewe had more time on his hands. In
1917 he was elected Chairman of the London County Council,
a position which had been created in 1889, when it had been
held by Crewe's father-in-law, Rosebery. In the same year
also he was elected Chancellor of Sheffield University, in
succession to the 15th Duke of Norfolk who had lately died.
Crewe had already taken part in the negotiations between

Sheffield and the Imperial College of Science and Technology, of which he was Chairman of the Governors. In February 1918 he was ceremonially installed, and conferred honorary degrees on distinguished men including the Ambassadors of the Allied Powers. He continued to act as Chancellor until his resignation, from ill-health, in 1944. Apart from this work, from speaking in the House of Lords, and from other activities of a political and patriotic nature, Crewe used his new leisure in literary directions. During his term as President of the English Association in 1916 he delivered a scholarly, instructive address, *War and English Poetry*, which he subsequently polished, and had printed as a pamphlet in 1917. Spanning five hundred years, this survey begins with such early English ballads as Minot's rhyming tale of the fight at Neville's Cross in the reign of Edward III, but perhaps the most interesting part of it discusses the poetry inspired by the Crimean War: 'The Russian campaign,' Crewe reminds us, 'was singularly picturesque in its setting; war was a novelty to most men under sixty; and the band of Victorian poets was at its fullest height.' He recalls now-forgotten but stirring war poetry of that period —work of the brothers Lushington, of Sir Francis Doyle, of Archbishop Trench, of Sydney Dobell, and of his own father Lord Houghton, contrasting this wealth of verse which the war in the Crimea inspired with the paucity of that produced by the Indian Mutiny and other Colonial wars. This was the kind of essay, suggestive, well informed, yet never boring, at which Crewe excelled. Lord Revelstoke had sent a copy of it to Sir Owen Seaman, editor of *Punch*, a good poet and knowledgeable critic as well as an accomplished satirist. 'I have sat late into the night reading the delightful monograph,' wrote Seaman. 'I am amazed at Crewe's erudition, and still more at the astounding perseverance which seems to have carried him through some of these portentously tedious works. I like too the personality that shines through his criticism and the charming humour that is never far away.' Lord Curzon also had read the pamphlet by night: 'Lying sleepless last night I sought to console myself, and did, by reading your admirable essay on War Poetry,' he told its author. 'I racked my brains to discover anyone whom you had left out—but failed.' 'Nothing in the world,' wrote Arthur Balfour, 'is so difficult as to give unity and interest to these rapid surveys of great tracts of Literary (and other) history. You have done it with excellent success.'

Amongst those who wrote to congratulate Crewe on *War and English Poetry* was Sir Walter Raleigh, whose letter of approval concludes with a passage both very characteristic of the mood of that moment and of the unchanging, wishful attitude of eminent civilians towards the ordinary fighting man and towards war generally:

I go about the wounded camps, lecturing on the war. I find (1) they are all as keen as a knife to hear bare facts about history—Germany's or ours, (2) they are a perfectly sympathetic audience for my three-ply optimistic views, which are not really shaken if it were proved that we cannot get a so-called decision against the Germans. We can, but probably it won't be dramatic, any more than blood-poisoning is dramatic. But it will be a good, slow, real decision.

I'm not sorry not to be in London. All the dreariest blighters I meet are in possession of privileged bits of blue information upon public affairs. They have no perspective. Nor have I, perhaps, for our two soldier sons (County Regiments) are in this push. *I think they are happy.*

The war dragged on, as it seemed, interminably, but like everything else it came, at long last, to its end. Crewe and his wife reoccupied Crewe House in Curzon Street, a building which they had placed at the Government's disposition early in the War, and which had been used as the head office for official propaganda.

One effect of the armistice on domestic politics was that, although the Coalition Government continued to operate, it once more became necessary to organise a proper Opposition in both Houses of Parliament. Curzon wrote to Crewe upon this subject in January 1919. Bent on restoring unity amongst the Liberals, Crewe sent him the following reply:

As you surmise I find that there is a general wish among the Liberal peers that a distinct organisation with Whips should be reinstated, and I am accordingly taking this in hand. At the same time I have made it clear to the Liberals who belong to the Government or the Household that while of course I don't attempt to rope them in in any way their position as

Liberals remains unchanged, as they and their counterparts in the House of Commons no doubt desire.

As a matter of fact, while we take up the position of a regular Opposition, we shall no doubt very often act in support of the Government policy and measures; only, as you point out so clearly, whereas during the War we regarded general support as a positive duty, now it will rest on the general agreement which we hope may exist. From time to time, of course, we may find ourselves definitely opposed.

I don't know what line the Unionist non-official peers propose to take, and if they will maintain any distinct party of their own. Midleton said something to me on the subject not long ago; but he takes a rather independent view, and I suppose that Salisbury is more the mouthpiece of 'the stern and unbending' division.

Thus, from early in 1919, Crewe resumed his old role of Leader of the Liberal Party in the House of Lords; only now his role was to criticise rather than to defend or explain the actions of His Majesty's Government.

During the War a second child, a daughter, christened Mary, had been born to Lord and Lady Crewe. Meanwhile their son, Jack Madeley, born in 1911, was proving, in his father's words, 'a boy singularly perfect in character and bearing.' On this boy all his father's hopes were centred, as years before they had been on the son of Crewe's first marriage, Dickie, who had died in childhood in the year 1890. So many of the Crewes' closest friends, so many families throughout the length and breadth of Britain, had lost their sons in the War: the deaths in battle of youths like Raymond Asquith and the Grenfell brothers were deemed to have fatally impoverished the England of the future. His child, at least, Crewe might have thought, was safe to carry on into another generation the ideals and traditions, the interests and the tolerant beliefs that had inspired Crewe's own career.

In March, 1922, after a short and agonising illness, the boy died. 'For us, his parents,' Crewe wrote years later, in one of his few public references to this stupefying blow of Fate, 'it was the tale told in the grave, unadorned lines of Callimachus:

Δωδεκέτη τὸν παῖδα . . . .

. . . . τὴν πολλὴν ἐλπιδα.

Chapter Ten

THE death of his son extinguished Crewe's hopes and projects for the future. For the time being, also, it dimmed his interest in current affairs, and although even amongst his friends he treated his loss with customary reticence, it seemed to them that, now in his middle-sixties, he neither wanted nor hoped for further public office. 'Any personal ambitions I may ever have entertained,' he wrote a few months after the boy's death, 'have long since been satisfied or quenched lately.'

In a mood of bleak but thoughtfully camouflaged despair he continued his mechanical round of regular duties, such as his constant and important work as chairman of the Delhi Committee or at the Imperial College, an institution which, as Secretary of State for the Colonies, he had helped to create. In mid-October of that same year, 1922, a predominant section of the Conservative rank and file had finally broken into open revolt against Lloyd George's Coalition Government. At a meeting at the Carlton Club they passed a resolution stating their intention to fight the next election as an independent party once again. Lloyd George immediately resigned. Bonar Law, a sick man and an exact contemporary of Crewe in age, was called back from voluntary retirement to head the new Government and to prepare for a General Election in November. It was widely recognised that in this election the Liberals, cleft by Lloyd George into two opposing camps, would have little chance of victory.

Despite his mourning Crewe got ready to play his part in the General Election, and agreed to make, as usual, a series of public speeches. He did this from a sense of party responsibility, finding perhaps distraction in the routine work of politics which he knew so well. But at this very moment, when

BAKST
1921

LORD CREWE in 1921
From a drawing by Bakst

the interest as well as the pleasure of life might have seemed to him to have vanished for ever, he received one morning in late October a letter which changed his whole way of life for the next six years, forcing him into the turmoil of post-war international politics and bringing him face to face with new and alien problems. The writer of this letter was Lord Curzon.

Before considering this letter itself, it is illuminating to recall the background against which it was written. 'George Curzon,' who had been in charge of the Foreign Office for exactly three years (having succeeded Balfour in October 1919), was a life-long friend of Crewe, but their relationship, like most of Curzon's relationships, had not been smooth. Abnormally touchy, alert to any whisper of criticism, Curzon was also vindictive and long-memoried. To his party's natural, inbred hatred for all the Liberals' proceedings he added a bitter sense of personal resentment over their Indian policy—the reversion of his plan to partition Bengal, the move of the capital to Delhi, even the royal Durbar of 1911—which he regarded as a public affront to his own tenure of office as Viceroy. For most of these objectionable steps Crewe, as Secretary of State for India, had been directly or indirectly responsible; and he was perfectly aware that Curzon had never forgiven either the Liberal Party or himself. 'Party feeling no doubt animated the large majority of Curzon's supporters,' he wrote, for instance, over Unionist opposition to the Indian measures of 1914, 'but with him it was supplemented by the unabated annoyance over Delhi, which lately he has had no chance of exhibiting, and by an irresistible inclination to deprecate any Indian measure in which he has not had a hand.' At other times he would refer privately to Curzon's 'unwisdom' or to his 'peculiar incapacity for understanding what is, and what is not, the proper occasion for interfering in other people's affairs.' They had clashed in the House of Lords on many occasions, most notably over the Parliament Bill, when Curzon had accused Crewe and Asquith of bullying King George. As Government Leader in the Upper House, Crewe would often receive petulant notes from the former Viceroy: 'I found it exceedingly difficult to speak yesterday afternoon because though I was answering a direct challenge from you to explain why I was against the Bill . . . you scarcely paid me the compliment of affecting to listen but were talking to Morley the whole time. It was noticed by the whole of your Bench and must have been noticeable to the entire House. . . . Pray do not think me hypersensitive.' Again, when the Coalition Government of 1915 brought Crewe and Curzon together as colleagues, Curzon would complain that he was given nothing to answer for in the House of Lords, nor allowed to treat any of the many subjects of which he was convinced (and often rightly) that he knew more than anyone else. Crewe took these outbursts quietly, sending soothing explanations and replies; but in fact it is hard to conceive of two characters more dissimilar—Curzon arrogant, brilliant, showy, self-important and ready to take offence—Crewe restrained, modest, tolerant, intelligent in his calm distinguished way. Yet this very contrast seems to have attracted Curzon towards his opposite. Writing of Curzon in one of the notes on personalities with which he prefaced the published volumes of his Berlin journals, Lord d'Abernon, a shrewd observer, remarked: 'Perhaps Crewe, though opposed to him in politics, was the man with whom [Curzon] was most in sympathy. He appreciated Crewe's reticence and reserve—the complete absence in him of the facile, the florid and the exuberant—a character outwardly in direct contrast with his own.' It was this recognition of Crewe's powers that led Curzon, in his search for a new Ambassador to France at this most delicate period of Franco-British relations, to do something unprecedented for a Conservative Foreign Secretary—to ask the official leader of the Opposition in the House of Lords to take charge of the British Embassy at Paris.

Curzon, of course, was fully aware how unorthodox his offer would seem to the recipient of it. 'I am going to submit to you a proposal which may at first sight surprise you,' he wrote to Crewe on 30 October 1922, 'but for which I think I can offer excellent and sufficient justification. Hardinge is resigning, for personal reasons only, the Embassy at Paris and wishes to vacate at the end of the year. My experience, which is now rather long, convinces me that Paris is the pivot upon which our Continental policy depends and that there, more than anywhere else, we want authority, influence, distinction, power.

Ordinarily I might hope or expect to find these in the ranks of the Service. I cannot at present do so: and looking round for someone who will speak with the voice of England to Poincaré or his successors, and who will at the same time maintain the dignity and prestige of a very high office, I have come to the conclusion, in which Bonar Law concurs, that no one would satisfy that criterion so well as yourself if you are disposed to consider it. The presence of Lady Crewe would add a further element of popularity and charm which would be of the highest value. I hope that you will both seriously consider the suggestion, even though it means an uprooting for a time of political and social ties at home.' Foreseeing Crewe's most likely objection—that he could not guarantee to carry out a Conservative foreign policy—Curzon assured him that such fears were not warranted: 'I do not think you need have any doubts as to the policy of which you would be the exponent since I know of no divergence of opinion between Unionist and Liberal in the matter. The supreme need is to re-establish the peace of Europe, of which a clear and solid understanding between France and ourselves is an essential condition.'

Gratified by what he termed 'the friendly and most flattering suggestion,' Crewe at the same time expressed doubts. 'I regard this as one of the two or three most distinguished offices that any Englishman can hold,' he assured the Foreign Secretary, in a letter of 3 November written after a long discussion with him, and in which he recapitulated the arguments he had then used—'I ventured to urge,' he reminded him, 'that for a man in my position to accept from his opponents of the past a high appointment like this in the early days of a General Election would painfully affect my political friends. They would regard it, if not as a desertion, at least as a significant withdrawal from the field—presumably on the grounds that their cause is already hopeless. I hope I don't overstate my importance as a party figure; but I asked you to think what you would feel if our positions were reversed, and I feel confident that the P.M. will not dispute this. There is also the possibility, though I myself consider it a slender one, that the result of the Election and the balance of parties might not leave you a fortnight hence in the position to implement your offer, or me to complete my acceptance of it. I therefore said, and still say, that I can only with all gratitude accept the offer on the definite understanding that the fact of its being made remains absolutely private until after the result of the General Election is known. If by any chance it should leak out, I should thus feel justified in contradicting it as a misstatement. . . . I have no love of secrecy, but this is a peculiar case.'

In the course of this conversation Curzon had himself raised a delicate matter on which he had asked for Crewe's co-operation. If Crewe were to 'take an active part in the Election campaign as a Liberal speaker,' even criticising the past acts of the Coalition rather than the future projects of the Tories, Curzon might find it 'difficult to justify' to his friends the 'offer of a blue-ribbon appointment to a man who had just been working to turn the Government out.' As a *quid pro quo* for his request for secrecy, and aided by Providence in the form of a laryngeal cold, Crewe therefore privately agreed to abandon his engagements for public speaking in the Liberal cause. 'I hope,' he explained, 'you will recognise my wish in so doing to offer real reciprocity for the privacy I have asked above.'

In this way the obstacles to Crewe's acceptance were removed by what Curzon called an agreement of 'mutual abstention— you from platform speech, I from public announcement during the next fortnight.' 'The only persons,' Curzon added, 'who have the slightest idea of what is happily impending are the King, who asked me point blank yesterday what I was doing and who thought your appointment if it could be effected a brilliant inspiration, but on whom I impressed absolute secrecy—Bonar Law, Crowe, and my wife. So that, if it gets out, the culprit can be found in a narrow circle, though I quite agree with you that in the event of its doing so before the Elections are over there will be no alternative but to deny.' He added a word of personal congratulations to Lady Crewe 'who will make a splendid Ambassadress.' The result of the General Election was a fair Conservative majority. Bonar Law remained Prime Minister, with Curzon at the Foreign Office. On 20 November it was announced that Lord Crewe had been appointed the new British Ambassador to France.

The announcement released upon Crewe House a cataract of congratulatory letters, including a private note from the

King to say with 'what great pleasure' he had approved the appointment to Paris—'where I know that from every point of view you and Peggy will do admirably and keep up British prestige. I also like to think' (the King continued, striking a note which many of the other letter-writers also struck) 'that it will bring fresh interests into your lives which have been so clouded by sorrow. Both you and Peggy know Paris well, she has relations there and you will both make new friends.' Lord Stamfordham wrote that 'the country also is to be congratulated on a choice so universally applauded,' while Lord Salisbury described the appointment as 'from a public point of view ideal'—'to have secured a man of your great position as a statesman and otherwise to represent England in Paris is not only a singular advantage to the nation but will be taken I need not say as a great compliment to France.' Crewe's Liberal colleagues also wrote, though in more sombre vein; for though his acceptance of the post did not mean a betrayal of his Liberal principles, it did mean that the party, split into factions as it was, would now be deprived of one of its leading and most respected figures. 'I felt a pang when I read that you were going away—it marked another fall in the fortunes of the Liberal Party & of the old association in which I was so carefully brought up!' wrote an old Liberal peer; 'The white robe in which I used to walk about the garden takes on dark stains and if I live I shall die a Tory. It is a process of rapid consumption.' 'We shall miss you in the House of Lords,' wrote Haldane. 'You exactly suited it, just as Lansdowne did, and have been a great figure there. But I feel that you are right to have accepted this great post. It gives you the future which the circumstances of our time threatened to withhold in politics.' 'I assumed that you would now take the Paris Embassy and I think you are quite right to do so,' was Lord Grey of Fallodon's unenthusiastic comment, while Asquith naturally minded most of all. 'I need not tell you,' he wrote, 'that your removal to Paris is to me a personal and political loss of the heaviest kind. It is quite impossible to replace you. But I quite appreciate the force of the considerations which have influenced your judgement, and I could not have controverted your conclusion.'

Except for these Liberal leaders, the majority of people who wrote to congratulate the Crewes did so in a vein of polished optimism, as though to take charge of the Paris Embassy at a moment when our relations with France were almost at break-ing-point—'la rupture cordiale' as it was beginning to be called in Paris—would prove a gay and prolonged continental holiday: 'You will probably dislike leaving home,' wrote Lord Lansdowne, 'but if you are to go abroad, I can conceive nothing more interesting or attractive.' Herbert Fisher alone ex-pressed some understanding of the difficulties of Crewe's new task, though he believed that 'if anybody can succeed in bringing the two nations together in spite of the underlying and persistent grounds of variance which now divide them you are the man, for you understand the French spirit in life and literature as few Englishmen do and have all the personal qualities which command their admiration.' Fisher called the appointment 'a fine conclusion to your brilliant public career.' Another friend, Sir Theodore Morison, Principal of Arm-strong College, Newcastle-on-Tyne, and later Director of the British Institute in Paris, wisely emphasised the importance to this country of being represented by a man of Crewe's culture, at a moment when Frenchmen were beginning to judge England by the vulgar and abusive anti-French policy of the Beaverbrook and Rothermere Press. 'It is only by personal contact with Englishmen who represent the better mind of this country,' wrote Sir Theodore, 'that the mischievous impres-sions created by newspapers can be corrected. The mass of people on both sides of the Channel are still friends at heart, but their warm feelings must in time cool if something is not done to counteract the pernicious influence of the press which envenoms every disagreement.'

Fisher, of course, was right. Crewe had inherited from his father a love of France, and he knew the country well. At Crewe Hall he possessed an extensive library of French history and literature, and to this he was constantly adding while at the Embassy. He read much French and spoke it better than many Englishmen. His appointment undoubtedly pleased the French official world, particularly as Lord Hardinge of Pens-hurst, whom he succeeded as Ambassador, had been a widower with a formal point of view and manner, and altogether lacked Crewe's outstanding qualities of highly cultivated mind and quiet charm. Crewe was the last eminent English landowner and peer to be sent to represent his country in France, and his appointment was in the tradition which had, in the nineteenth century, provided such distinguished if amateur English Ambassadors to Paris as Lord Normanby, Lord Granville and Lord Lytton, and during the recent war, Lord Derby. Had Curzon not been in charge of the Foreign Office, it is unlikely that Crewe or anyone else of his status in this country would have been sent to France. In July 1919 Curzon had sounded Crewe as to the possibility of his being willing to go as British Ambassador to Washington, and had been nettled by Crewe's refusal, based on the plea of 'obstacles that cannot be surmounted.' His selection of Crewe for Washington then, for Paris now, was the outcome of those cherished theories of the supreme importance of wealth, breeding and worldly position which made Lord Curzon seem to many of his colleagues and all of his numerous enemies an anachronism in post-war, democratic England. When writing to Crewe to explain why he was going over the heads of career diplomats in choosing him for the Paris Embassy, Curzon had used the significant words 'authority, influence, distinction, power.' These four words sum up Lord Curzon's views on the conduct of international relations, as well as on that of daily life itself.

Lord Crewe's arrangements for taking over the Paris Embassy were conceived to accord with the old-fashioned scale on which he always liked to live. It was not the scale on which he had been brought up, for Monckton Milnes' establishments at Fryston and at Upper Brook Street had been run in a somewhat slap-dash manner; nor was it at all times the scale on which Crewe could afford to live, for he was both generous and amiably reckless about expenditure. In many ways this last official appointment was reminiscent of his first one—when in 1892 at thirty-four years of age he had been sent to Ireland as Queen Victoria's Lord-Lieutenant, and had shipped over carriages and horses and had ordered state liveries to be made for his household. Free with money, and a perfectionist in comfortable living, Crewe determined to keep up the Embassy in what he felt to be an appropriate style. He sent to Paris a number of the famous Crewe family portraits, a quantity of his books, some of the specially fine French and English bindings from his father's collection and his own, together with all his gold and silver plate, his china and glass, and the Irish state liveries for his servants. At the Embassy he found that Hardinge had left a staff comprising a French groom of the chambers, four men in livery and three men out of livery, a French chef with three assistants, four English housemaids, two chauffeurs and two odd men. This establishment Crewe supplemented by his own housekeeper from London, his butler and his valet, his chauffeur, a steward's room-boy and most important of all his English cook, the skilful and expert Mrs. James, who worked as *adjointe* to the chef. About food, Crewe cared as much as his father Lord Houghton, one of the most notorious gourmets of his day, had cared, but to it he brought a finer taste. He would often complain that hardly anyone in England realised that vegetables should only be eaten when very young and small, and he had a considerable reputation for his knowledge of the pleasures of the table. 'Gracie has just gone to Paris,' wrote Lord Curzon to Crewe on one occasion, 'but before she left she asked me to beg your advice on a point on which she says you are the greatest master in London. We have a chef whom, though he came with the highest credentials, we think very poor. To what place or authority do you advise me to go in her absence with a view to finding a competent successor? The whole class of French chefs in London seems to me to have greatly deteriorated in the last 20 years.'

Crewe had no high opinion of Hardinge's taste in food, which he found heavy and elaborate; and while he kept on his predecessor's head cook he recognised that the man was by no means perfect at his art: 'He is a decidedly economical cook,' Crewe told Tyrrell in 1928, when handing over the Embassy. '. . . Before he came here to the Derbys he was in Prince Murat's kitchen, which is an extremely good one, but I do not consider him by any means in the first class, and I have had more than one distinctly better than him in former days in England.' For transport Crewe relied on the official Embassy car, his own car which he brought from England and a Rolls-Royce which he purchased from Lord Hardinge and sent to have a new limousine body bearing his own crest and monogram fitted at once.

It had at first been agreed that Crewe should not take up his appointment until the New Year, 1923, but the adjournment of the Prime Minister's Conference to Paris, which meant that Bonar Law would be arriving in the French capital on 2 January, led the Foreign Office to ask Crewe to advance this date. He finally left London, with his wife and daughter, on 28 December. Two days later he presented his letters of credence to the President of the Republic, Monsieur Millerand, making a speech which showed that like his father before him he was at home in French. To the customary diplomatic banalities about the unity of France and England—under the current circumstances almost ironical in sound—Crewe added a personal touch recalling that he had been present at the first Anglo-French political and military conference of the War, held at Calais in 1915, where he had deliberated with the British Secretary of State for War, Lord Kitchener, who was now dead, and his French counterpart, Millerand, who was now occupying the highest office in the French Republic. Crewe also expressed suitable misgivings as to his capacity for succeeding his old friend Lord Hardinge—'Je connais trop bien sa valeur et son expérience pour ne pas éprouver une crainte légitime en envisageant ma tâche'—and diffidently pointed out that his lifelong Parliamentary experience might hinder rather than help him in his new career—'Peut-être aussi la vie Parlementaire n'est-elle pas la meilleure avenue pour aborder la carrière diplomatique.' This ceremony over, Crewe returned to the Embassy and began to face his real task—that of preventing a grave Anglo-French split, and of acting as a kind of buffer between the angry and mutually antipathetic temperaments of Lord Curzon and the French Prime Minister, Monsieur Poincaré.

While it is, of course, an error to succumb to the biographer's weakness for attributing undue importance to the purely personal reactions of heads or representatives of foreign States to one another, there can be no doubt that the sense of private rancour against Poincaré which Lord Curzon harboured did help to envenom Anglo-French relations at that time. After the Chanak crisis of September 1922—a disastrous muddle which had precipitated the fall of Lloyd George's Coalition Government—Curzon had involved himself in a series of violent and undignified scenes with Poincaré at the British

Embassy in Paris. After one of these the British Foreign Secretary, from sheer frustration, had burst into tears. Curzon was also convinced that Poincaré was to blame for the failure of his negotiations with Turkey, which were taking place at Lausanne at the very moment at which Crewe was settling into the Paris Embassy. Curzon's exceptional capacity for hatred and suspicion, notably exercised twenty years before at the end of his Viceroyalty in India—when he had written to Crewe of Kitchener's 'unblushing lying and intrigue' ('there is nothing too low for that man to stoop to'), and of St. John Brodrick's determination to make the Viceroy 'eat mud'—was now applied to loathing the Prime Minister of the French Republic.

This strong obsession taints many of the private letters which Curzon would send regularly to Crewe. Like almost all his correspondence, Curzon's letters to Crewe were written in his own complicated and at times illegible hand. 'Both Derby and Hardinge used to write to me regularly from Paris—at least twice a week, sometimes oftener. That is the real way in which Anglo-French relations are managed, for St. Aulaire is a great duffer and has not the confidence of his chief,' he wrote to Crewe when the latter took up his Paris appointment. 'In these critical times,' he wrote again, 'I am always very glad to hear from you in a private letter what is going on in the background, whether about the Ruhr or Turkey or Memel or anything else; and I very frequently pass on the letter to the Prime Minister. It keeps us in touch. Derby in particular was very active and very useful in this respect. I will give you an illustration. We have been having a rather pointed exchange of notes with the French about their conduct at Angora and Lausanne. But I have no idea whether our closing replies have produced in the French indignation, compunction, fury or remorse or any other emotion.'

In his first weeks at the Paris Embassy Lord Crewe received much advice from Curzon on how to deal with the French Prime Minister: 'The right prescription for Poincaré is firmness and fearlessness. He is rather a disagreeable and bad-tempered man—and does things no gentleman would attempt. But when firmly handled he is amenable.' 'I think you hardly appreciated the gravity of Poincaré's conduct since you have not assisted at all my previous conferences with him or heard the nature of the pledges as to common action all through Lausanne and up to a treaty by which he bound himself,' he wrote again. Or he would refer to 'the eternal and (to me) most repugnant Poincaré,' or to a note drafted by the French Premier as 'an enormity . . . equally packed with malevolence and lies,' or would simply comment: 'I wonder whether Poincaré is capable of a generous gesture or a genial thought!' It was in this heated atmosphere that Crewe began his thermo-static task of Anglo-French reconciliation: 'It is not pleasant to point out to a man that he is a proven liar,' Curzon wrote to him, on the same recurrent theme, 'but if anyone can do it with grace it will be you.'

And indeed that talent for urbane and wise diplomacy which Crewe had signally shown throughout his political career—as Lord-Lieutenant of Ireland, as Leader in the House of Lords, as go-between at the time of the Constitutional Con-ference and of the contentious Parliament Bill—was exactly what was now required in the British Ambassador in Paris. The immediate history of the years after the First World War is well known, and, particularly to persons of the generation born during that conflict and thus in time to fight in the next war, it makes melancholy and usually exasperating reading, diminishing any inborn respect for the British or foreign poli-ticians of that epoch. All that is here necessary, fortunately, to set off the figure of Lord Crewe during his six years' Paris mission is to emphasise the extreme delicacy and difficulty of the task which he was daily called on to perform. Disarma-ment in Germany and swift demobilisation in this country had left France the major military power in Europe. The attitudes of France and England to the German problem were often opposed to each other, as were points of view on Turkey. Curzon inclined to attribute all blame to the French: 'The French Government,' he wrote to Crewe in November 1923, 'will be responsible for pulling down the Entente. It has been tottering for months and will not need a very big crowbar to bring it to the ground.' It contrast to his knowledgeable and imaginative Eastern policy, Curzon's European policy was unsure and at times unsteady. A case in point, in which Crewe was directly involved, was the mysterious 'Corfu Incident' of September 1923.

Lord Crewe

The murder, probably by bandits, of an Italian General, who was then a member of the International Delimitation Committee working on the Graeco-Albanian frontier, had been made by Mussolini the excuse for an Italian bombardment of the defenceless chief port of Corfu and the brutal occupation of that island by Italian troops. Greece appealed to the Hague Court and to the League of Nations, at that moment in Session, yet the Italians succeeded in persuading the Ambassadors' Conference (then meeting in Paris and of which Crewe was automatically the English representative) that the case fell under the Conference's own jurisdiction, and demanded as the price of withdrawal from Corfu a large fine from Greece. Curzon himself was intensely anxious at first that the case should come up before the Council of the League, since he sensibly regarded it as a first test case for that new international body's strength:

Very many thanks for your letter of the 8th and for all you have been doing about Corfu [he wrote to Crewe from Geneva on 13 September 1923]. I have not yet heard exactly what you have done today in the Conference of Ambassadors. Opinion here is very uneasy on the subject. The Delegations, particularly from the smaller nations, are beginning to wonder what the Council is doing about it and to urge them to action, and I feel our position is not very defensible. So I expect tomorrow at latest we shall have a meeting of the Council to take some action. Indeed, quite apart from all questions of the feelings of the Assembly and so on, I do hold very strongly that unless we get the Italians out of Corfu pretty quickly a great blow will have been struck at the public law of Europe.

Meanwhile the Ambassadors' Conference had suddenly decided the case in favour of Italy and against Greece. As Crewe pointed out in a despatch and a telegram to Curzon, this left no alternative solution. In after years Crewe declared that the Government were afraid that Italy would walk out of the League unless the Ambassadors' decision was favourable; and, for whatever reason there may have been, Curzon changed his mind. He had at first thought, he wrote to Crewe on 26 September:

that the attitude of the French was all wrong, and that the Ambassadors were about to condemn Greece in the face of the

166

evidence to pay the full penalty for an offence which there was
no proof that she had ever committed—and all this to prevent
a fresh display of lawless bravado and duplicity on the part of
Mussolini. But when I began to look carefully into the text
of your note of September 13—and of Avezzana's declaration
of the same date, I found (I wish I hadn't) that your colleagues
had apparently given the case away, whether consciously or not
I cannot say. . . . That you can ever have meant to compel
the Greeks to pay the full fine—even increased—and to drop
the reference to the Hague (except on the point of costs of
occupation) I can hardly believe. But that seemed to me the
actual result of what the Ambassadors had done, tho', being no
lawyer, I have no authority in interpreting texts. . . . It is
rather a humiliating finale (if indeed it is that) of the episode.
But I daresay even the Greeks would sooner pay than see the
Italians remain in Corfu.

Historians have seen in this incident the first attack on the
League's influence and prestige. 'The lawless duplicity and
bravado' of Mussolini had paid rich dividends, a fact of which
Japan and certain other countries were not slow to take note.

Meanwhile Lord Curzon's nerves were badly frayed by his
failure to become Prime Minister, a post to which, even at this
late period of his life, he still aspired. In May 1923 Bonar Law
resigned the Premiership owing to ill-health, dying shortly
afterwards. Curzon expected to succeed him, misunderstood
a message from Lord Stamfordham as being a summons from
the King, rushed up to London from Hackwood, and discovered
that Stanley Baldwin had already kissed hands. This was a
mortal shock to Curzon's ambition and his pride. Crewe
sensed what he must be feeling, and wrote frankly to him in
the wise, quiet tones of an old friend:

Bonar Law came and spent a considerable part of the afternoon
with us on Thursday and told me the whole situation as far as
it affected him. He was his pleasant self to the utmost, but
was in a very low key, as indeed was natural, and it was a
pathetic moment which we shall not easily forget.

Of course I had anticipated that you would be asked to
succeed him, and, except for what one sees in the papers, I am
still quite in the dark about the causes of the actual selection.
The two reasons stated in the press are of course the obvious

ones. The first does not seem to me overwhelmingly strong, that of your being in the House of Lords, though in these days it would be an absolute bar to a Liberal. The other reason appeals to me more strongly, I confess. I do not see how, as things are, you could have combined the retention of the F.O. with being Prime Minister. That constitutes a real consolation to your friends, most of all those who, like myself, serve under your Department. I think it must also be a solace to yourself, in what must surely in other respects mean such a deep disappointment both to you and to Lady Curzon. You have such astonishing powers of work, and of arriving at decisions, that you may well think that the double task would have been a possibility; but I cannot help thinking that no man's health could really stand it. Poincaré seems to be an exception, but he is a man of amazing physique, with no outside tastes or amusements of any sort, and concentrates on his job in a way which is really inhuman. And I do not think that the strain here is of the same kind which an English Minister has to face.

Curzon would have none of this. Although in constant physical pain, and always complaining of overwork, he had been perfectly prepared to shoulder the double burden of the Premiership and of Foreign Affairs:

I was knocked out, not at all because it was thought impossible that I should combine the 2 offices of P.M. & For. Sec. because I had made up my mind—if invited—to try it at least for a time, but because the Opposition party in the H. of C. being in its majority a Labour Party—the King thought that the head of the Govt. must be there to answer them. This as I pointed out is tantamount to a perpetual ban upon Peers since the Labour Party is never likely to be less numerous in the H. of C. than now, and this contention—however cruel in its implications—was not disputed. Hence my loss of the prize.

Of course it is a great disappointment. But public life is made up of such: and the only thing is to go on and do one's best as I shall try to do.

Curzon remained on at the Foreign Office, watching the new Prime Minister's activities with a wry interest. 'When you read of the glorious policy of Baldwin—common sense—courage—etc.' he told Crewe, 'it may amuse you to know that so far he has done nothing but read out in the H. of C. the answers which I have prepared and that in the Cabinet he has not said a word except to endorse my policy. I do not complain. But I am amused.' Two months later, however, Mr. Baldwin took a step of which Lord Curzon soundly disapproved. He insisted on what was, in Curzon's view, 'a premature and unnecessary dissolution.' Perfectly confident of a victory at the polls, and influenced by Ramsay MacDonald's conviction that the Labour Party would lose seats, Baldwin found that he had led his party into heavy defeat. 'As you know,' wrote Curzon to Paris, 'I deplored the ill-judged action of Baldwin which has met with a crushing rebuff that has placed the country and its foreign interests in grave peril. But the party must pay the penalty and work out its punishment in the manner prescribed by our system.' On 23 January 1924, Curzon wrote to tell Crewe that he had that morning handed over his seals and was now '*functus officio.*' He told Crewe that he wished to emphasise what pleasure he had found in his co-operation with him during his period of office, how much he regretted it had not been longer, and 'how much I and HMG have owed to your tactful and efficient conduct of affairs at Paris.' He went on to relate what he had heard of the plans of Ramsay MacDonald (who proposed to combine the office of Prime Minister with that of Secretary of State for Foreign Affairs) for conducting Foreign Office work:

May you be equally successful with my successor, although what I hear from Crowe of his opening talks in the F.O. appals me as to the methods of business which he proposes to adopt. . . . The P.M. is neither to read papers, nor to see Ambassadors (he can neither speak nor understand nor read French), nor to record interviews, but is to devolve the whole of this upon A. Ponsonby his Under Secy while he sticks to the Front Bench in H. of C. All I can say is:
(a) Good God!
(b) He will soon learn wisdom in a sharp school.

To this letter Crewe despatched a warm and graceful reply, thanking Curzon for his 'unfailing kindness and consideration' and paying tribute to his 'wonderful power of grasping a difficult subject, and of getting to the heart of it,' as well as to his patience in carrying on negotiations 'even on the very edge of hopelessness.' Indulging in an altogether characteristic understatement, he referred to the new Foreign Office arrangements which had excited Curzon's scorn as 'rather startling.' To Crewe these seemed more traditionalist than revolutionary 'for it does not seem as though the P.M. is going to do much more than direct policy in the broadest outlines, as some of his predecessors have done or tried to do.' He suggested that foreign ambassadors would probably resent always having interviews with the Under-Secretary instead of with his chief.

In fact, Ramsay MacDonald (whose first action on assuming office was to write a letter to Monsieur Poincaré so personal and friendly that it aroused the protests of the Governments of Italy and Belgium) was a not unsuccessful Foreign Secretary during his first Labour Government's short tenure of office. In October 1924 the Government were defeated. A General Election returned Baldwin and his followers once more to power. But Curzon was not asked to resume control of the Foreign Office. Instead, the efficient and self-confident Austen Chamberlain was chosen. He continued in charge of the Foreign Office for the remainder of Crewe's time at the Paris Embassy, just under four years.

After Lord Curzon's petulant and sometimes brilliant conduct of affairs, the rule of Austen Chamberlain introduced an element of common sense. He spoke of himself as the most Francophile member of Baldwin's Cabinet, and he never ceased to support all Crewe's efforts to improve Anglo-French relations. 'You know me well enough to know how earnestly I desire to work closely and harmoniously with Monsieur Herriot in all matters of common concern to our two countries,' he told Crewe in his first semi-official letter in November 1924; and for Briand Chamberlain felt a genuine affection. He took care to keep Lord Crewe, in Paris, and Lord d'Abernon, our Ambassador in Berlin, in touch with the complex of negotiations then going on between the three capitals. 'A three-handed game, such as is now going on between Paris, Berlin and London, is not an easy one to play, but I do my best to keep both Crewe and d'Abernon fully informed,' he wrote.

The story of the negotiations leading up to the evacuation of the Ruhr, and the Locarno agreements, is well known, and, although Crewe was closely concerned in them, their description would only lumber up this attempt to portray his character and his career. It might here be relevant to remember the entertainment side of the Embassy which he had to keep up, with luncheon and dinner-parties of fifty or sixty persons, as well as entertainments on such occasions as the visits to Paris of the Prince of Wales. Crewe made many friends among the French, and would also go shooting with the President and with other French acquaintances. Amongst those whom he learned particularly to respect and like was Briand. Crewe has left a charming account of a high-summer's day in 1927, when he and his wife visited the French statesman on his property in the Eure-et-Loire:

Last Saturday Peggy and I motored down to luncheon with Briand at Cocherel. Quinones and Leger were the only other guests. He has a delightful little property along the banks of the Eure:—not so very little either as it must be some 1300 or 1400 acres, including one or two woods. There is a quite small pavillon right on the river from which he can fish, but he occupies a larger one, formerly a presbytery, some little way up the hill. There we had an excellent luncheon of local produce, including a matelotte of eels from the river, and one of our host's own lambs. After luncheon we drove and walked to his large farm on the plateau, which is well appointed in every way, with some good stock of different sorts; altogether a very enjoyable day. Briant seems pretty well himself again though he still has to rest a good deal. . . . He leads a sort of Edward Grey life down at Cocherel, getting up at 4.30 or 5 in the morning, and keeping company with the birds. He gets golden orioles to answer from the trees in the early morning when he calls to them from his bedroom window. I have never, to my knowledge, seen a golden oriole, though I believe they come to the south of England now and then in the summer.

By 1927 Crewe felt that he had been out of England long enough. He was in his seventieth year and wished to spend the remainder of his life in his own country and his own houses, amongst his own compatriots and friends. He therefore sent in his resignation to Austen Chamberlain, who persuaded him to stay on in Paris until midsummer 1928. On his departure from the Embassy he received the usual formal despatch from the Foreign Secretary thanking him for his six years of ambassadorial work.   He also received a less official, and a very sincere, personal tribute from the Foreign Secretary himself:

I cannot be content without saying to you in a more personal form how much we owe to you.   You have enhanced the dignity of a great post.   You and Lady Crewe have won the hearts of the Parisians, but you have done more than this: in the early days of your Mission, relations with France were difficult and sometimes came very near to breaking-point.   I believe it to be largely owing to your judgement and courage that even then our differences were kept within bounds, whilst since those relations have improved you have at every turn contributed to the restoration of confidence and to the close co-operation which it was essential for us to secure. For all this I am grateful, not only as Secretary of State and as such the mouthpiece of His Majesty's Government, but because I could have had no more able and willing helper in the post which you have filled.   Nothing could have been more delightful than my relations with you, both public and personal.
  You have taught me to understand Asquith's saying that 'Crewe has the best judgement of all my colleagues.'

Epilogue

ON his return to England Lord Crewe prepared to retire into the welcome tranquillity of private life. 'It is perhaps cowardly,' he wrote from Paris to Lord Grey of Fallodon, who had asked him to resume an active part in the counsels of the disintegrating Liberal Party, 'but after six years or more of absence from public life at home, I feel the wish to obtain what they would call here a correct orientation, before deciding whether I should take any further active part in it or not.' There was one brief interruption to Crewe's withdrawal from official life. This was in August 1931, when he served as Secretary of State for War in Ramsay MacDonald's first National Government. He held office barely three months, for after the General Election of November 1931, which confirmed the new coalition in power, Crewe, Austen Chamberlain, Reading and Amulree all resigned their posts, to give a chance to those younger men in whose hands the future of the country would lie. After the Ottawa Conference he joined Reading and Grey in a public letter supporting Sir Herbert Samuel's retirement from the Government, and reiterating the old sacred Liberal faith in Free Trade. In 1936 he was re-elected Leader of the Liberal Opposition in the House of Lords, and to the end of his life he was ready to help and support the genuine Liberal cause. Until 1944 Crewe continued as Lord-Lieutenant of the County of London, as well as retaining the Chancellorship of Sheffield University, to which (as we have seen) he had been elected in 1917.

From now on Crewe led the dignified life of a trusted elder statesman, an old man universally respected and consulted frequently. 'I should be very grateful if I might consult you as an old servant of the King on a very private matter in which your counsel would be of great value,' Stanley Baldwin wrote to him, for example, during the early stages of the Abdication crisis of 1936. In London and in the country Crewe's time was spent amongst his books, re-reading the Greek and Latin classics, talking to friends and indulging with enthusiasm in his passion for racing. From time to time he would produce an article for the *Manchester Guardian* or the *Quarterly* on some current topic. These articles, irradiated by a serene mind and informed by a lifetime of political experience, often contain glimpses of earlier days—recollections of what Mr. Gladstone really thought about Ireland, or of Lord Ripon's attitude to Bengal. He would also on occasion review important political biographies or books of memoirs for one of the Sunday newspapers or for the *Spectator*, besides himself superintending the Royal Society of Literature's annual publications.

When he left Paris for good, Crewe was seventy years old. At the most he might have looked forward to another decade of life and thought; but as it transpired he lived on, as mentally alert as he had ever been, until the considerable age of eighty-seven. This in a man who had always been physically delicate, and who had been several times dangerously ill, was in itself strange. Crewe reflected upon the contrast between his own longevity and the spans of his father and his grandfather, both of whom had died of old age in their seventies. 'It never occurred to me in my younger days,' he wrote to a friend who had sent him greetings on his eighty-sixth birthday, 'that I should live to such an age, and certainly not that I should do so with such few infirmities, comparatively speaking. No doubt people live much longer than they did, particularly in the comfortable classes who, as a doctor once told me, have to be regarded as at least ten years younger physically than the working population. As an example, I think that more than a third of the K.G.'s are over eighty, which I am sure never happened two generations ago.'

A political career like that of Crewe is to be regarded as a form of self-expression, and, as we cast our eyes over it, provides us with an understanding of his personality just as surely as the impression which we gain of some author's character by reading his book. In Crewe's case politics was not his only, but his chief, form of self-expression. He had never set up to be literary, for (thinking perhaps of his father's life) he did not believe that literature and politics could be successfully combined. His own verses he took modestly, treating them more as a civilised pastime than as anything of consequence. His newspaper and periodical articles, like his letters, official or private, his drafts and his minutes, are exceedingly lucid and well expressed. In 1929, however, Crewe embarked upon a task which needed somewhat specialised equipment, or at least some earlier practice—that of writing a biography. His father-in-law and friend Lord Rosebery had died in May 1929. Rosebery's son and successor invited Crewe to undertake the intricate business of composing the official biography of this original and extraordinary man. Published in July 1931, the book absorbed all Crewe's time and energy for eighteen months. 'I fear I must refrain from taking any active part in the Coal Bill,' he wrote to Lord Stanmore in March 1930: 'I find it difficult, while I am engaged on the biography of Rosebery, to divert my attention from it by taking up any political or other work which demands close study, as a question like the Coal Bill certainly does.' On the face of it Crewe had every qualification for painting a life-like, full-scale portrait of his subject. 'My own friendship with Lord Rosebery and his family,' he wrote in a letter concerning the American edition of his book, 'dates from far back, and indeed dates from an earlier generation still, as his mother, the Duchess of Cleveland, was an intimate friend of my father and mother, and I was several times a guest at Raby Castle in my young days. I therefore became well acquainted with Rosebery fifty years ago; and as it happens I knew his wife at an even earlier time. My father was intimate with all the Rothschilds, and Miss Hannah Rothschild was a friend and contemporary of my elder sister. . . .Thus when I became his son-in-law we were by no means strangers.' Throughout the remainder of the year 1929, and all through 1930, Crewe worked his way steadily into the great mass of papers which Lord Rosebery had left. The material was of the first interest, yet when the book emerged it was disappointing. The reasons can easily be analysed. On the one hand there was Rosebery's brilliant and hypersensitive personality, hard for the most accomplished biographer to recapture or to make convincing. On the other there was Crewe's lack of experience in the mechanics of biographical composition. Also, his wish to make the best possible use of the papers at his disposal was hampered by his own innate discretion and his great anxiety to avoid any comment which might wound or even bruise the feelings of persons then alive. An honest and conscientious work, Crewe's two volumes on Lord Rosebery's life form a useful source-book for students of that period.

By the early nineteen-thirties, the shape of life in post-war England was becoming devastatingly clear. Few people would ever be able to live again on the scale on which they had lived before 1914. Lord Crewe set about modifying his way of living accordingly. With no direct male heir to succeed to the place and name, Crewe Hall had become a stately incubus. In 1931 its owner offered it as a gift to the Cheshire County Council, who refused it. Determined that his tenants should not suffer from a change of ownership, Crewe next entered into sale negotiations with representatives of the Duchy of Lancaster. Crewe Hall, with the bulk of the estates, passed under the control of the Crown. Crewe retained certain farms and villages, several local livings and Madeley Manor in Staffordshire.

Crewe Hall disposed of, Lord and Lady Crewe began to seek a small country house within easy reach both of London and of Epsom. They had at one time lived in a house belonging to Lord Rosebery at Epsom, but on his death they decided to buy a house of their own. After looking for many weeks at many houses, most of them too big and none of them sufficiently appealing, they chanced upon West Horsley Place, a low, sixteenth-century house built of small red bricks, which lies at the end of a sloping avenue, and with walled gardens and orchards behind it, near Leatherhead in Surrey. Although larger than they had intended their new house to be, West Horsley, with its singular quiet charm, airy well-proportioned rooms and fine staircases won their hearts. They bought it, and settled there in 1932, filling the house with pictures, furniture and objects from Fryston Hall, and installing in a long, dim bookroom hung with curtains of red brocade the great library collected by Lord Houghton and amplified by Lord Crewe. So large is this collection of books that it overflows into several other rooms and lobbies of the house.

THE MAIN STAIRCASE AT WEST HORSLEY PLACE

In keeping with the Whig traditions of Crewe Hall, two bedrooms at Horsley were re-christened the Buff Room and the Blue Room and furnished in these colours.

Some years after the sale of Crewe Hall, Lord Crewe determined also to give up Crewe House, for to live in so large a mansion in commercialised Mayfair had become both an anachronism and an expense. As though to emphasise the severance of old, Edwardian ties with that part of London, the Crewes moved to Chelsea, where they bought Argyll House, a rambling building designed by Leoni, standing back, behind gates, from the King's Road. Here they re-hung the famous Reynoldses, Romneys and Lawrences which are part of the Crewe heirlooms; and here, up to the outbreak of the Second World War, they would entertain in an ample, old-fashioned way which seemed to one very young man when he first dined there to provide a spectacle of almost historical interest, with the table laden with gold plate, and attended by several footmen.

Meanwhile foreign and domestic politics filled Crewe with hopeless gloom. The slightest apparent loosening of the tension gave him hope: 'May I be permitted to add that the pleasure of the week was greatly enhanced by the fact that the horizon has at last become a little clearer in public affairs,' he wrote to the King in a letter of thanks after staying at Windsor during Ascot week in 1933. 'It is impossible to get the fruition of any success or of any amusements when the atmosphere of the whole world is as gloomy as it has been of late. And I feel sure that of no one in the country is this more true than it is of Your Majesty.' In 1936 the death of King George V saddened Crewe deeply. In 1937 he performed the role of Lord High Constable at the Coronation of King George VI. He had now lived in five reigns.

The advent of the Second World War did not surprise Lord Crewe. Nor did the fall of France, on which he wrote a wise and fair-minded article in a series he was then contributing to *The Sunday Times*, sounding a true and sympathetic note at that moment of acrimony. Lord and Lady Crewe spent most of the war years in London, where they endured many of the worst air-raids, and at West Horsley. Towards the end of the war in Europe his doctors considered that Lord Crewe should leave London. He went first to his mother's old home, Madeley Manor in Staffordshire, and later to his brother-in-law's house, Mentmore, which had been built by Paxton and was filled with the marvellous possessions of Baron Mayer de Rothschild. Much of the house at Mentmore was lent by its owner for purposes connected with the war. 'Somehow the changed aspect of these great places brings home to one the reality of the war almost as much as the sight of the bombed areas in the City of London,' Crewe wrote about this time. Mentmore was a house which recalled for him happier days of long ago—his engagement to Lady Peggy Primrose, and house-parties presided over by her father, with his brilliant eyes and ravishing smile and his devastating humour. 'We dined out on the terrace under the full moon last night,' Crewe had once written to his wife from Mentmore at the turn of the century. 'It really was perfect.'

With the increasing imperfections of mid-twentieth-century life Lord Crewe was not asked to cope much longer. On 20 June 1945 he died at West Horsley Place, in a room overlooking the flower-garden and lined with books.

Appendix 1

LORD CREWE'S INTEREST IN RACING: A NOTE BY THE EARL OF ROSEBERY

CREWE was devoted to horses, and his outdoor relaxations were almost entirely concerned with them. He hunted as much as possible in Ireland and in Cheshire until about 1900, when he gave it up. In the meantime he had built some paddocks at Crewe and had bought a few brood mares, whose produce were trained by John Porter at Kingsclere. He had a few winners, but none of them of much merit, the best being St. Lundi.

He had at that time acquired Maid Marion, a mare who was destined to become famous as the dam of Polymelus who became one of the greatest stallions of his generation. He was head of the list of stallions for several years. I well remember him coming out at Ascot in 1904 in one of the big two-year-old races. His fame had preceded him and he started a hot favourite; but he was weak and backward and finished second.

For various reasons Crewe decided to sell his horses in 1905 and Polymelus was bought by Faber. Thereafter Crewe's interest as an owner on the Turf was very small. During the last few years of his life he had a few horses trained by Ted Leader, at Newmarket, but without much success.

He became a Steward of the Jockey Club in 1899—a three-years' appointment. Shortly before this time there had been what was known on the Turf as the American invasion. Lord William Beresford had imported Tod Sloan, the American jockey. He was a brilliant horseman, but not at all the type of person that was wanted on the Turf in this country. He had small regard for the Rules of the Jockey Club, and was followed across the Atlantic by a mass of professional gamblers of the worst type. The night after the Cambridgeshire of 1900 Crewe was dining with Leopold de Rothschild at his house at Newmarket. He took a cab from The Rooms, where he was staying, and gave Captain Machell a lift. Captain Machell, probably forgetting whom he was talking to, said that Sloan had told him that if he had won the Cambridgeshire on Codoman, who was second, he would have won £40,000 in bets. Crewe made no reply to this remark, but the next day Sloan was had up and told he need never apply for a licence to ride in this country again. By this means the gang was broken up, and the horde of undesirables gradually returned to their native land.

Always after this, right up to his death, although not again a Steward, he was a power behind the scenes. If there was any difficulty or trouble, he was always consulted, and indeed frequently spoke at meetings of the Jockey Club on matters of importance; and I can remember no Steward in my time who did not treasure his friendship and value his wise counsels.

Like my father, what he really liked about the Turf were the people he met and the gossip of the racecourse. No one had a wider circle of friends or a greater capacity for friendship. He had the facility of being able to understand the viewpoints of people much younger than himself, who were never afraid to come to him and ask him for advice. It is as an administrator and true lover of the Turf that Crewe will be remembered rather than as an owner of horses.

Appendix 2

LORD CREWE'S MEMORANDUM ON THE BREAK-
UP OF THE COALITION GOVERNMENT,
DECEMBER 1916[1]
(See page 150)
The Break-up of the Coalition Government

IT had for some time been becoming evident that strong currents of dissatisfaction were affecting the smooth flow of the Coalition Government, and this unrest found vent, as is usual with Cabinets, by the issue of several suggestive or warning memoranda. Possibly the veritable *causa causans* of the final break-up is to be traced to Lord Lansdowne's striking paper of November 13, 1916.[2] It has been rumoured that the present Prime Minister regarded this document as the danger-signal marking an obstruction in the road, the barrier being a supposed invitation to the 'Elder Statesmen' or soberer spirits of the Government to anticipate an enforced conclusion of the war. Study of the memorandum does not confirm this fear.

---

[1] This memorandum was published by Lord Oxford in his *Memories and Recollections* 1852–1927 (Cassell and Co., 1928). It is reprinted here both for its intrinsic interest and as an example of Lord Crewe's fairness of mind, commonsense, and gift for understatement.

[2] Lord Lansdowne's memorandum, prepared in response to the Prime Minister's request that members of the War Committee should express their views as to peace terms, urged that owing to the gravity of the war situation and to the fact that 'we are slowly but surely killing off the best of the male population of these islands' earnest consideration should be given to the possibilities of a negotiated peace. Lord Robert Cecil took, in his memorandum, the opposite view but suggested that something should be done, such as the closing of 'rich men's clubs' to ensure that 'the comfortable classes do not escape their share of privation'. 'We cannot,' he added, 'expect the working class to undergo fresh burdens unless they feel that all are treated alike.' Both memoranda make, today, illuminating reading.

It is, rather, to be regarded as a plain and courageous exposition of the facts, perhaps erring somewhat in the direction of mistrust, but displaying no poverty of spirit or lack of determination. Lord Robert Cecil's paper of November 27, 1916[1] struck a note of anxious warning; and it is certain that no member of the Government was undisturbed by a conviction that a prompt change in methods was demanded. The recent lack of progress on the various fronts, the Roumanian disaster, and the crisis in Greece, might stand in no direct relation to such a change; but ill-success in war always encourages heart-searchings at home. And the increasingly venomous assaults by part of the Press on the Government as a whole, and particularly on the Prime Minister, Lord Grey, and Mr. Balfour, made it clear that the atmosphere was becoming more and more highly charged. Amongst ourselves there existed a general feeling that the War Committee, though much of its work had been promptly and capably carried through, had not succeeded in fulfilling the purpose of its creation—that of a quite small body of selected Ministers advised by a few picked naval and military experts and enabled by almost daily sittings to effect rapid decisions on all matters directly concerned with the war. Much of its time and energy had been consumed by discussions on subjects of domestic importance, all claiming a bearing on the conduct of the war, but demanding the presence, and the inclusion in discussion, of a number of other Ministers not themselves members of the Committee. Nor did the creation of the Man Power Board seem to afford much relief to the supreme body. Its examination of the facts was thorough and valuable, but its conclusions were *ad referendum*, and differences of opinion had to be dealt with. The general result was that the meetings of the War Committee tended to become far too large, and to produce general discussions similar to those that had clogged the action of the earlier War Council; while the Cabinet remained in the background as the final court of appeal, furnished with the records of proceedings and with many of the Memoranda—though not all—with which the War Committee worked, and from time to time engaged in general discussions on war policy, with which its size and its composition alike unfitted it to cope.

[1] See note 2 on previous page.

It was in these circumstances that a suggestion was made at the Cabinet of the 29th of November for the formation of a Committee to deal with the domestic aspects of war policy— labour, food supply, and the like—covering the ground administered by the Boards of Trade and Agriculture and some other departments, and advised by suitable experts, as with the War Committee. The idea was generally favoured, and the principle was agreed, but it was not then attempted to enter on any details. Towards the end of the same week I wrote to the Prime Minister pressing the adoption of this suggestion, pointing out that its complete acceptance in a practical shape involved the abolition of the Cabinet as a consultative body, though with no actual change in the position of Ministers; and I believe that other of our colleagues were also engaged in working out a scheme. But either the movement came too late, or it precipitated an intended crisis; for, on Friday the 1st of December, Mr. Lloyd George wrote to the Prime Minister suggesting the formation of a new War Committee entrusted with practically absolute powers for the conduct of the war; and on Sunday the Unionist members of the Cabinet, except Lord Lansdowne, who was at Bowood, and Mr. Balfour, who was unwell, met in a conference which proved to be decisive. I have no means of knowing the true relation of these two events; but I am clear that Mr. Bonar Law and Mr. Lloyd George were acting in close concert throughout, but that several other Unionist Ministers were not. As it happened, I was less favourably placed than usual for following the events of these memorable days, being greatly occupied by the important deputation of Scientific Societies, which I received on Friday the 1st of December, and by other public engagements. I remained in London over Sunday the 3rd, and was surprised by receiving at luncheon that day, from the Prime Minister, whom I believed to be at Walmer, a request to come to Downing Street at once. I found Mr. Asquith sitting on after luncheon, and with him Mr. Edwin Montagu. For the first time I then heard of the correspondence with Mr. Lloyd George, and saw the letters that had passed up to that date. The Prime Minister pointed out that there were two quite distinct points at issue. The first was his own relation to the War Committee from which Mr. Lloyd George had suggested he should be entirely dissociated, merely retaining as Prime Minister a general power of veto, presumably in concert with the Cabinet. He did not see how he could be anything but Chairman of the War Committee, even though he might not always be able to attend, and Mr. Lloyd George acted in his absence. He was confident that an arrangement could be come to on this point, and that it would work well in practice. But on the second point he was far less hopeful, that of the composition of the Committee. As proposed, this included Mr. Bonar Law, Sir E. Carson, and a representative of Labour, probably Mr. Henderson. Mr. Asquith's objection to this body was its absolute inefficiency for the purpose of carrying on the war; but he questioned whether Mr. Lloyd George would agree to modify it. We entirely agreed with the Prime Minister that this would be a hopelessly bad War Committee; and that in the matter of powers he ought to retain the Chairmanship, while coming to any terms he could with the Secretary of State for War on the conduct of business.

I then heard the startling news that at the Unionist meeting of that morning it was agreed that the Prime Minister ought to resign his office, and that Mr. Bonar Law had just been at Downing Street with this message, it being added that in the event of a refusal the Unionist Ministers must themselves hand in their resignations. The intimation was curtly delivered, it appeared; but in further conversation it was implied that the demand was not made in Mr. Lloyd George's interests, but in order that the Government might be reconstructed. Assuming this to be the fact, the action of the Unionist Ministers seemed disproportionate to the need, for reconstruction could quite well have proceeded as it did last year by the resignation of all the Prime Minister's colleagues, he himself retaining his place and the commission to form a new Government. Still, whatever might be the motive there the fact was, and it had been arranged that the Prime Minister would again see both Messrs. Lloyd George and Bonar Law later in the day. He would be dining at Mr. Montagu's house, and I arranged to call there after dinner to hear what had passed.

Accordingly I proceeded to Queen Anne's Gate at about 10 p.m., and found the Prime Minister with Mr. Montagu and Lord Reading. The interviews with the two discontented colleagues had produced no positive change in the situation, but seemed to have confirmed Mr. Asquith in the belief that an accommodation with Mr. Lloyd George would ultimately be achieved, without sacrifice of his own position as chief of the War Committee; while it appeared that a large measure of reconstruction would satisfy the Unionist Ministers. After some conversation, in which Mr. Asquith was strongly supported in his opinion that no compromise of principle could be admitted regarding the War Committee, he decided to inform the King at once that the Government must be reconstituted; and a notice was drafted for the Press to that effect. We separated with the hope, though with no assurance, that the resignation of all Ministers, as in the summer of 1915, might lead to the formation of a stable Administration on a new principle.

On Monday the 4th of December appeared *The Times* article of which the effect was explained by Mr. Asquith at the Liberal Meeting held at the Reform Club on the 8th of December, when he also described the gist of his ensuing correspondence with Mr. Lloyd George: and that afternoon the Prime Minister briefly informed the House of Commons of the intended organic reconstruction of the Government, moving the adjournment till Thursday the 7th. It was abundantly clear by this time that Mr. Lloyd George was determined to develop to the utmost the possibilities of the situation, and that the chances of continued union were fast diminishing.

At the same time it appeared to some of the Unionist Ministers that the action taken at their meeting of the 3rd of December was open to possible misconstruction, and that it had probably been so misconstrued by the Prime Minister after Mr. Bonar Law's delivery of his message. Accordingly Lord Curzon, Lord Robert Cecil, and Mr. Chamberlain went to 10 Downing Street to explain on their own behalf and on that of Mr. Walter Long that their consent to the demand that Mr. Asquith should be asked to resign in no way indicated a wish that he should retire. On the contrary, they did not believe that anybody else could form a Government, certainly not Mr. Lloyd George; so that the result would be the return of the present Prime Minister with a stronger Government and a greatly enhanced position. There can be no reason to doubt the complete sincerity of these declarations, as the situation appeared to their authors at the moment.

On the morning of Tuesday the 5th of December I attended the Privy Council at Buckingham Palace and found the King anxious about the crisis, but confident that a way out would be found without a complete change of Government. I explained to His Majesty the plan for instituting two small committees, one for the actual conduct of the war, the other for business necessary to the war; but I did not touch nearly on the personal questions.

Later in the morning I received a summons to 10 Downing Street to talk over the situation with the Prime Minister before a meeting of Liberal members of the Cabinet summoned for 1 o'clock. He showed me the text of Mr. Lloyd George's letter of the previous day, announcing his resignation in the absence of agreement with his War Committee proposals. It seemed as though the gravity of this step depended on the extent of support to be anticipated from the Unionist Ministers: if they refused reconstruction and insisted on Mr. Asquith's resignation, whether in order to substitute Mr. Lloyd George or not, the Government could not continue in any form. Such was also the opinion of Mr. Asquith's Liberal colleagues, who unanimously agreed that the terms imposed by the Secretary of State for War could not be accepted. Since the Unionist Ministers for their part refused to agree to even the most drastic reconstruction without the resignation of the Prime Minister, only one course was open to him. He therefore wrote declining Mr. Lloyd George's plan, and the same evening placed his resignation in the King's hands, with the suggestion that Mr. Bonar Law should be sent for.

This was done the same night, when it is understood that Mr. Bonar Law explained his inability to undertake the duty, at any rate unless Mr. Asquith would serve under him. As it happened, we were dining at 10 Downing Street, and our host was called away from a game of bridge to see Mr. Bonar Law, who had come on from the Palace in order to enquire whether he could look for Mr. Asquith's help as a colleague if he proceeded to form an Administration. The reply was altogether discouraging, if not definitely in the negative.

On the morning of Wednesday the 6th, Mr. Lloyd George

was in turn received at the Palace and apparently declared that he also could not expect the necessary support, but I am not aware whether any stipulation regarding Mr. Asquith's support was made by him. Thus a deadlock was produced, but a suggestion was conveyed to Lord Stamfordham, at the particular instance it is believed of Lord Derby and Mr. Montagu, that it might be ended if the King would confer with the principal personages concerned, as in the attempt to settle the Irish question in 1914. This proposal naturally appealed to His Majesty; and Mr. Asquith, Mr. Bonar Law, Mr. Lloyd George, Mr. Balfour, and Mr. Henderson attended at Buckingham Palace accordingly the same afternoon. The general course of the discussion there was described by Mr. Asquith to his late Liberal colleagues at 10 Downing Street immediately after the meeting. It appears that at the opening there was some expression of opinion by the two alternative Prime Ministers that Mr. Asquith should endeavour to continue; but both, when asked by him if he could claim their assistance in any capacity, declared that this was impossible. Mr. Lloyd George, however, urged Mr. Asquith to attempt to form a Government from among his own supporters. It was next discussed whether, if Mr. Bonar Law or Mr. Lloyd George became Prime Minister, Mr. Asquith would serve under either. Both Mr. Balfour and Mr. Henderson hoped that he would do so, and the King may also have favoured this course: Mr. Asquith, however, neither declined nor accepted, but decided to consult his friends before replying.

Another meeting of Liberal ex-Ministers was therefore called at Downing Street that evening, Mr. Henderson also attending. In the first place it was unanimously agreed that it was not possible to proceed with a Government including no Unionist representation and without Mr. Lloyd George, more especially if the latter carried out the intention frankly stated in his letter of resignation, of conducting a campaign throughout the country against the methods hitherto pursued in carrying on the war. The next subject of discussion, for which the meeting was indeed principally called, was the possibility of Mr. Asquith's joining an Administration formed by Mr. Bonar Law or Mr. Lloyd George. No mention was made on this occasion of any other alternative premiership, so that the issue was in some degree simplified. Mr. Henderson began by strongly urging the adhesion of Mr. Asquith, in order that a truly national Government might be formed. The only other Minister sharing this opinion was Mr. Montagu, who held that the prestige of Mr. Asquith ought not to be lost to the country. All the rest took the view that the combination would be mistaken and futile; and it was strongly expressed by Mr. McKinnon Wood, Lord Buckmaster, Mr. McKenna, Mr. Runciman, Lord Grey and myself. Mr. Asquith entirely concurred with our statements, which were to the effect that no sentiments of personal dignity or of *amour propre* ought to prevent him from accepting a lower position, but that two fatal objections barred the way. The first was that, given the personalities involved, the scheme would not in fact work. Mr. Asquith had declined to become a Merovingian ruler as Prime Minister, and as a subordinate member of the new Government he would not submit to the autocracy of the War Committee, of which there was no assurance that he would even be a member. A collision was therefore probable, perhaps before very long; and it was felt that though the present break-up might be a national misfortune, it would amount to a serious disaster if later on Mr. Asquith and those Liberals who might join with him felt compelled to bring about another crisis. Mr. Lloyd George would in all probability find no difficulty in getting the requisite support; and if a new system was to be tried it had best be entrusted to colleagues of the same school of thought as the new Prime Minister.

In the second place it was felt that Mr. Asquith's influence, though now so powerful and pervading, would melt away if he were thus to accept office. There would be no little resentment among many of his supporters both in Parliament and in the country. This was all the more significant because the advent of a new Administration under a headstrong Minister mistrusted by many might of itself quicken extreme and reckless opposition, and perhaps drive not a few recruits in the direction of peace-making. The creation therefore of a sober and responsible opposition (if that be the proper term) steadily supporting the Government in the conduct of the war, criticising when necessary, and in the last resort offering an alternative Administration, was the best outcome of the crisis in the national interest. Mr. Asquith therefore stood out, and the present Ministry was formed by Mr. Lloyd George. It should be observed that concurrently with this gathering at Downing Street the Unionist members of the late Government were meeting in Mr. Bonar Law's room at the Colonial Office, whence Lord Curzon came over to 'Number Ten' to hear the result of our conference, and was told of Mr. Asquith's refusal.

A survey of these quickly succeeding events compels the conclusion that the issue depended more upon a clash of personalities than upon any basic contradiction of principles. Victory was the goal of both; but Mr. Lloyd George undoubtedly held that Mr. Asquith was unfitted to achieve it, from temperament not less than through the strain imposed by a long term of office, and by advancing years. He was confident, on the other hand, that his own activity and resource could inspire the country and hasten a glorious end to the war. At the same time he was by no means blind to Mr. Asquith's unrivalled Parliamentary capacity, or to his hold over the solid forces of Liberalism. He therefore, it may be asserted, contemplated two distinct policies, by either of which his purpose might be attained. Mr. Asquith might continue as Prime Minister, leaving the conduct of the war to Mr. Lloyd George and two or three weaker lieutenants: the veto of whatever Cabinet was left would not be seriously hampering, because it could not in fact be exercised against a War Committee with all the knowledge, and with their resignations in their pockets. In some respects this would be the preferable system, because the Prime Minister's mastery of the House of Commons would be at the service of the practically independent War Committee. Mr. Lloyd George therefore pressed for this solution, and induced others to do the same. If it was declined, as in fact it was, Mr. Asquith must be forced to resign. In the words of Gambetta—of whom Mr. Lloyd George may regard himself as in some respects the reincarnation—'*il faut se soumettre, ou se démettre.*' For this purpose the aid of Mr. Bonar Law was indispensable, and it was no doubt easily secured. To prevent any rift in the Unionist party was the first object of its leader; and he perceived that a concentration under a new chief whose watchword was 'action' was more likely to secure this than any possible reconstruction of the old Government. He doubtless foresaw that some of his Unionist colleagues who had small taste for a Lloyd George Administration, and who disliked the methods by which Mr. Asquith was forced to resign, could be shepherded into the new Government by appeals to their public spirit. After this had occurred, Lord Curzon explained to me the reasons which actuated himself and others of the same way of thinking; and I was able to tell him that in my judgement, having regard to the action of others for which they were in no way responsible, he and his friends had taken the correct course.

20 December 1916.   CREWE.

Index

Index

Index

House of Lords—*cont.*
125–35; Edward VII's scheme for giving peerages to eldest sons of Liberal peers, 115; public opinion and crisis, 123; Crewe's recollections of, 135; Prime-ministership and, 168

Houses of Parliament, Opposition restored after war, 152–153

Howe, Julia Ward, 12

Hurlbert, William Henry, 12

Imperial College of Science and Technology, 151, 154

India, Houghton unable to pay projected visit (1887), 26–7; Kitchener favoured for Vice-royalty; Hardinge appointed (1910), 85; Crewe as Secretary of State (1910–15), ix, 58, 83, 125; Liberal policy, 83–9; questions of special boons (1911), 93, 99; Queen as 'Empress' problem, 96; Secretary of State's visit to India sets precedent, 97–8; Government of India Bill (1912), 99–102; transfer of capital to Delhi, 99, 155; dangerous proximity of Russian power to, 142–3; dispatch of troops to Europe (1914), 145–6; Crewe succeeded by Chamberlain as Secretary of State (1915), 149; Curzon's personal resentment over policy, 155

Bengal, re-unification of, 93, 99–101, 155, 174

Curzon's Durbar (1903), Crewes attend, 58, 84; criticism of, 100; cost, 101–2

Delhi Durbar (1911), 87–8, 93–98, 155; special Crown 94–5; Crewe attends George V at, 83, 98; cost, 101–2; honours, 103

Morley-Minto reforms (1909), 84, 87

India Office, Crewe's room re-decorated, 103–4

Insurance Act, National, 116

Ireland (*see also* Home Rule), Crewe's visit to (1875), 17; land question, 23, 25, 26, 46; Phoenix Park murders (1882) recalled, 16, 37; relative powers of Lord-Lieutenant and Chief Secretary, 35, 36; Lord Aberdeen's Vice-royalty (1886), 35, 36; Crewe as Lord-Lieutenant (1892–5), xiii, 34–7, 139, 161; conditions in 1892, 37–8; life at Dublin Castle, 36–7, 38, 40–2; repeal of Crimes Act, 37; Coercion Act, 37; Special Commission on evicted tenants, 37; Crewe's state entry into Dublin, 39; Crewe reports to the Queen, 39–44; Dublin season boycotted by landed gentry and Unionists, 40–2, 46, 47; wood-cock pie sent to the Queen, 42; Royal family's neglect of, 43; dynamite explosions at Dublin Castle, 44; witch-burning, 44–5; Crewe on future of Ireland, 46–7; Crewe succeeded by Lord Cadogan (1895), 46; Crewe's impressions of, 46–8; Protestants and Royal Accession Declaration (1910), 89; Lloyd George and Irish Revolution, 118; fear of civil war (1913–14), 136; Crewe recalls debates on the Irish Church in 1869, 135

Isaacs, Rufus: *see* Reading, Lord

Italy, Crewe's visit (1889), 29; Corfu incident (1923), 166–7; protest against MacDonald's letter to Poincaré, 170

Iveagh, Lord, 138

Jamaica, 68
James, Mrs., 162
James, Sir Henry, 52
Japan, 167
Jekyll, Colonel H., 44
Jenkins, Roy, 111
Jockey Club, 55, 179, 180
Joicey, Lord, 138

Keats, Lord Houghton and, 1, 6
Kensington, Bill, 16

Index

Longfellow, H. W., 12, 13
Lord President of the Council, 61-2, 66, 81
Lord Privy Seal, 64-5, 86
Loreburn, Lord, 125
Lotos Club, New York, 10
Lutyens, Sir Edwin, 102-3
Lytton, Lord, 161

McCook, General, 11
MacDonald, Ramsay, 169, 170, 173
Machell, Captain, 180
McKenna, Reginald, 188
Macpherson, Isobel, 10
Madeley, Lord (son), birth (1911), 92-3; death (1922), xv, 153, 154
Madeley Manor, 51, 176, 178
Malta, 68
Man Power Board, 182
Manchester Guardian, 60, 174
Mary, Queen, as Princess May: and Crewe's verses, 32; as Duchess of York: proposed visit to Ireland (1893), 43; as Queen: Coronation (1911), 82-3; visits India and attends Delhi Durbar, 95-8, 104; stays at Crewe Hall, 141
Maurice, Frederick, 5
Mecklenburg-Schwerin, Grand-Duke and Grand-Duchess of, 98
Medina, 96-7, 98, 103
Melgund, Lord, 15
Mentmore, 54, 178
Meshed, 142-3
Midleton, Lord (earlier St. John Brodrick), 153, 164
Midshipman, accused, Crewe's generosity to, x-xi
Mill, John Stuart, 137
Millais, Sir John, 56
Millerand, President, 163
Milner, Lord, 67, 69
Milnes, Amicia (sister): see Fitzgerald, Lady Amicia
Milnes, Florence (sister): see Henniker-Major, Florence
Milnes, Richard (son), 24; death (1890), xiii, 32, 153

Milnes, Richard Monckton (father): see Houghton, first Lord
Milnes, Robert Offley Ashburton: see Crewe, Marquess of
Milnes, Robert Pemberton (grandfather), 2
Minto, Lord, ix, 15, 84, 87, 95
Montagu, Mrs., 43-4
Montagu, Edwin, 183, 184, 187, 188
Montrose, Duchess of, 18
Montrose, Duke of, 32
Morison, Sir Theodore, 160
Morley, Lord (earlier John Morley), joins Cabinet (1886), 25; policy as Chief Secretary for Ireland, 35-6, 39, 44, 47-8; resigns Liberal leadership, 59-60; and Campbell-Bannerman, 62; Secretary of State for India (1905-10), 84-8; acting Secretary of State after Crewe's accident (1911), 91-2, 101, 125; mentioned, ix, 46, 52, 53, 54, 64, 90, 156
Morning Post, 123, 124
Munitions supply (1915), 148
Murat, Prince, 162
Murray, Alastair, 14-15
Mussolini, Benito, 166-7

Nash, Vaughan, 62, 63, 131-2
National Government (1931), 173
Navy, Crewe's criticism of Admiralty (1914), 145-6, 148
Nesfield, William, 49
New York, Crewe's visit to (1875), 12, 13
New York World, 12
Newton, Lord, 36
Nicholas of Russia, Emperor, 143
Nicolson, Sir Arthur, 142, 143
Nicolson, Sir Harold, quoted, 77, 111, 139
Nigeria, Southern, 68
Nightingale, Florence, 18-19, 144
Nonconformists, 106, 107, 119
Norfolk, Duke of, 65, 103, 150
Normanby, Lord, 42, 161
North American Review, 46
Northcliffe, Lord, 148
Norton, Caroline, 18

Index

Offley (family), 51
Offley, Mrs. Cunliffe, 4
O'Neill, Lady (Annabel Crewe-Milnes) (daughter), xiii, 20, 56, 147
O'Neill, Lord, 147
Ottawa Conference (1932), 173
Oxenbridge, Lord, 27, 28
Oxford, Lord: *see* Asquith, H. H.

Pall Mall Gazette, 20
Palmerston, Lord, xi
Pankhurst, Mrs., 136, 137
Paris, Crewe Ambassador in: *see under* France
Parliament Bill, 79, 99, 111–16, 121–135, 155; passed by House of Lords (1911), 134–5; proposed creation of peers to ensure passing: *see under* House of Lords
Parnell, C. S., 37
Paul, Herbert, 61, 150
Peace terms, Lord Lansdowne's memorandum (1916), 181–2
Peers, creation to ensure passing of Parliament Bill: *see under* House of Lords
Pendleton (family), 11
Persia, Shahzada visits London (1895), 52; Russian bombardment of Meshed, 142–3
Pless, Prince Henry of, 38
Pless, Princess of, 76, 77
Poincaré, Raymond, 157, 163–5, 168, 170
Ponsonby, A., 169
Ponsonby, Sir Frederick, 75
Ponsonby, Sir Henry, 33–44, 71, 113
Porter, John, 179
Primrose, Lady Margaret (Peggy): *see* Crewe, Marchioness of
Primrose, Neil, 147
Privy Council, Edward VII suggests Paris meeting, 63
Probasco (family), 11
Proctor, Mrs., 23, 27
Protectionist creed, 53, 60
Pugin the younger, 49
Punch, 151

Quarterly, 174

Raby Castle, 175
Racing, Crewe's love of, xi, 37, 55, 72, 179–80
Railway rates, Committee on, 33
Raleigh, Sir Walter, 152
Rayleigh, Lord, 124
Reading, Lord (earlier Rufus Isaacs), 85, 173, 184
Reform Bill (1832), 120, 137
Reform Club meeting (1916), 185
Regalia, special Indian Crown, 94–5
Reid, Sir Thomas Wemyss, 32–3
Revelstoke, Lord, 151
Reynolds, Sir Joshua, 50
Rhodesia, 68
Ripon, Lord, 55, 64–5, 110–1, 174
Roberts, Lord, 95
Roman Catholics, 89, 90
Rosay, Madame, xiv–xv
Rosebery, Lady, death, 54, 55
Rosebery, fifth Lord, and Sudan crisis (1884), 21, 22; on Lord Houghton, 24; Foreign Secretary (1886), 25; rivalry with Harcourt, 59; Prime Minister (1894), 43, 45, 52, 55, 59; resigns (1895), 45–6, 59–60; and House of Lords, 53, 113, 123; Crewe's friendship with, 54–6; on poetry, 54–5; resignation as Liberal leader (1896), 55; daughter's marriage to Crewe (1899), 55–7; forms Liberal League (1902), 55; and woman's suffrage, 138; Crewe's 'Life,' 175–6: mentioned, 51, 78, 91, 92, 106, 150, 178
Rosebery, sixth Lord, note on Crewe and racing, xi, 179–80
Rothermere Press, 160
Rothschild, Hannah, 175
Rothschild, Leopold de, 180
Rothschild, Baron Mayer de, 56, 178
Rothschilds, 138, 175
Roumania, 146, 182
Royal Accession Declaration, new formula, 89
Royal Agricultural College, Cirencester, 27–9

203

·

Date Due

PRINTED IN U. S. A.   CAT. NO. 23233

Lightning Source UK Ltd.
Milton Keynes UK
UKHW022140060223
416587UK00005B/135